Regulating the Health Professions

In recent years the health professions have been subject to unprecedented regulatory changes. Exposure of poor practice has provoked widespread criticism of self-regulation and calls for a system in which the interests of healthcare consumers and employers are more fully recognised. Examining the historical and contemporary context, this topical book provides an in-depth analysis of professional self-regulation and the implications of regulatory change for the future of healthcare.

- **Part One** sets out general regulatory issues in the healthcare arena, with chapters covering the impact of globalization on the professions; the purpose of professional regulation; the legal context of regulation; and the significance of professional codes of ethics.
- **Part Two** explores issues specific to the different professions through chapters on medicine, nursing, dentistry, the professions allied to medicine, clinical psychology and alternative medicine.

Regulating the Health Professions will be of interest to students, educators and researchers in a wide range of disciplines including sociology, social policy, politics and health studies, and to healthcare professionals and their managers.

Judith Allsop is Professor of Health Policy of De Montfort Universtiy. **Mike Saks** is Professor and Pro Vice Chancellor at the University of Lincoln.

Regulating the Health Professions

Edited by

Judith Allsop and Mike Saks

SAGE Publications
London • Thousand Oaks • New Delhi

First published 2002

 SAGE Publications Ltd
6 Bonhill Street
London EC2A 4PU

SAGE Publications Inc
2455 Teller Road
Thousand Oaks, California 91320

SAGE Publications India Pvt Ltd
32, M-Block Market
Greater Kailash - I
New Delhi 110 048

British Library Cataloguing in Publication data

A catalogue record for this book is available from
the British Library

ISBN 0 7619 6740 0

Library of Congress Control Number: 2002104872

Typeset by C&M Digital (P) Ltd., Chennai, India
Printed in India at Gopsons Papers Ltd, Noida

Contents

Contents

Acknowledgements

The editors would like to thank all of the contributors for the very positive and responsive way in which they have engaged with us in the construction of this volume. Thanks also go to a number of other colleagues for their advice – not least Anthony Hazzard on the ethical aspects of professional regulation and Louis Orzack on the international regulatory framework. Finally, we would like to express our sincere appreciation to our families, without whose support this book would not exist.

Contributors

Professor Judith Allsop is Professor of Health Policy at De Montfort University. She has written widely on health policy, complaints and the health professions. Her recent books include *Health Policy and the NHS* and *Regulating Medical Work* (with Linda Mulcahy). She is currently researching health consumer groups and the national policy process. She was a member of the Cabinet Office Complaints Task Force and a special adviser to the House of Commons Health Committee on adverse events.

Professor Rob Baggott is Professor of Public Policy and Director of the Health Policy Research Unit at De Montfort University. His main research interests are health service reform, public health policy, pressure group politics and public participation. His publications include *Health and Health Care in Britain*, *Pressure Groups Today* and *Public Health: Policy and Politics*.

Professor Celia Davies is Professor of Health Care at the Open University and writes on health and social care policy and organization. She has recently completed a history of the regulation of nursing in the UK, entitled *Interpreting Professional Self-Regulation* (with Abigail Beach). She is currently researching lay participation in the regulatory bodies across the health field.

Professor Gerry Larkin is Professor of Sociology in the School of Social Science and Law at Sheffield Hallam University. He has written extensively on both historical and contemporary issues related to health professions. His books include *Occupational Monopoly and Modern Medicine* and *Health Professions and the State Europe* (with Terry Johnson and Mike Saks).

Professor Michael Moran is Professor of Government at the University of Manchester and editor of *Government and Opposition*. His most recent publications include *Governing the Health Care State: A Comparative Study of the United Kingdom, the United States and Germany*. From 2000 to 2002 he held a Leverhulme Major Research Fellowship to conduct a study of the British regulatory state.

Professor David Pilgrim is Head of Adult and Forensic NHS Psychology Services in Preston, Lancashire, and Professor of Mental Health in the Department of Sociology, Social Policy and Social Work at the University of Liverpool. His books include *Clinical Psychology Observed* (with Andy Treacher) and *A Sociology of Mental Health and Illness* (with Anne Rogers).

Professor David Price is Professor of Medical Law at De Montfort University. He researches and teaches medical law. His main research areas include organ and tissue transplantation, euthanasia and abortion. He is the author of *Legal and Ethical Aspects of Organ Transplantation* and has been a member/chair of various national and international committees. Most recently he was a member of the Steering Committee for the Health Support Workers Project funded by the Department of Health.

Professor Mike Saks is Pro Vice-Chancellor (Research) at the University of Lincoln. He has written widely on professional regulation, particularly in the health field and been a member/chair of a variety of NHS committees at national, regional and local level. His most recent books include, amongst others, *Professions and the Public Interest, Health Professions and the State in Europe* (with Terry Johnson and Gerry Larkin), and *Complementary Medicine: Challenge and Change* (with Merrijoy Kelner, Beverly Wellman and Bernice Pescosolido).

Julie Stone is Senior Lecturer in Ethics and Law Applied to Medicine at St Bartholemews and the London Hospital. A lawyer by background, she has just completed a period as Visiting Scholar in the Department of Political Science at the University of Hawaii. Her main longstanding research interest is in the regulation of complementary and alternative therapies, a field in which she is the author of *Complementary Medicine and the Law* (with Joan Mathews) and *An Ethical Framework for Complementary and Alternative Therapists*.

Dr Nicki Thorogood is Senior Lecturer in Sociology in the Health Promotion Research Unit of the London School of Hygiene and Tropical Medicine. She has published in a number of areas, including the sociology of the body and public health and health promotion. She is author of *Analysing Health Policy: Sociological Approaches* (with Judy Green). She has a longstanding interest in the profession of dentistry and is currently researching the relationship between gender and dentistry.

Introduction: The Regulation of Health Professions

Judith Allsop and Mike Saks

The focus of the volume

This book examines general changes in the regulation of the health professions in the United Kingdom from a social scientific perspective. It also considers the historical and contemporary development of regulation for a selection of key occupational groups in this context, with reference to wider debates about the health professions. Interest in new approaches to regulation was prompted by the fact that, by the late 1990s, a number of important shifts were taking place in relation to such groups in this country. These included the following trends. First, public trust in some traditional professions had declined, although there was still no sign of any significant fall in the demand for professional services. Second, the government had moved to change the regulatory structures of nursing and the professions supplementary to medicine, and put pressure on other mainstream professions such as medicine and dentistry to reform themselves, while at the same time encouraging the licensing of new professional groups. Third, the government's growing emphasis on multi-professional education for all health workers and flexible career structures in the health service raised questions about traditional hierarchies in the health care division of labour. Fourth, there had been increasing pressure for regulation within the nation state to reflect trends towards a global economy and a cross-border European legal framework, to encourage the mobility of labour within the European Union. These trends were partly linked to a concern – common to governments throughout the developed world – to rationalize health care and obtain enhanced value for money.

Awareness of these trends led to the compilation of this volume, which appropriately, emerged from discussions between the two editors following an International Sociological Association conference in Gothenburg in Sweden in May 1998 on Professional Identities in Transition. Of course, such challenges to the health professions, and other professional groups, did not arise only in the 1990s. With the development of the strong counter-culture which swept Western societies from the mid-1960s onwards, the health professions in the United Kingdom had already come under growing pressure from the public and organizations representing the consumer, as well as from the government (Saks 2000). These professions, and especially the dominant profession of medicine, were increasingly seen as paternalistic, insufficiently accountable, and self-interested – assessments that were sustained by the many academic critiques that were conducted of the professions at this time (see, for example, Johnson 1972; Kennedy 1983; Klein 1989). This came to be most fully expressed in public policy following the election of the Conservative government in 1979.

From the viewpoint of the New Right, health and other professions represented self-interested monopolies that hindered the operation of the market. A number of measures were taken by the Conservatives to bring them to heel, which culminated in the radical health care reforms that ensued from the late 1980s onwards in Margaret Thatcher's third term of office. These were intended to increase control of the health professions within a more competitive internal market based on the purchaser/provider split (Alaszewski 1995). However, despite minor internal adjustments, the health professions appeared remarkably resistant to organizational change. This was clear from the limitations of the Griffiths' reform of the early 1980s that had endeavoured to strengthen general management in the National Health Service in relation to medical and other health professional groups (Harrison et al. 1992). This is not to say that no shifts in position occurred as a result of later policies more explicitly based on enhancing market control. Ophthalmic and dispensing opticians, for example, were privatized and deregulated in 1984, losing their monopoly over the sale of spectacles (Higgins 1988). The views of the public were given greater prominence in health care too as *The Patient's Charter* (1991) was implemented, as part of a wider drive to articulate citizens' rights. This period also marked the restratification of the medical profession – as the status of general practitioners rose compared to hospital specialists with the development of 'fundholding' practices in primary care in the early 1990s (Allsop 1995b).

The position shifted again in the latter half of the 1990s as the Labour government took office. At this time there were heightened concerns over public safety in the wake of a number of cases that highlighted the continuing existence of poor practice in the health professions, coupled with ever-rising bills for litigation. In this context, the new government had a political commitment to improving the quality of public services through direct state intervention rather than market forces (see, for instance, Department of Health 1997). The effect of this was to place greater emphasis on quality control through the introduction of the concept of clinical governance, at the same time as elevating further the voice of the public. However, the general powers of the health professions – including that of medicine – still remained relatively untouched by the end of the 1990s (Saks 1998). The 'hands-off' approach of the government, however, became less and less tenable with the scandals that hit medicine as the new millennium began. These included such cases as those of Shipman, the prolific serial killer whose crimes as a general practitioner for long went undetected; Alder Hey, where human body parts were removed from deceased patients without consent; and Bristol, where surgery performed on children led to unacceptably high mortality rates.

In its second term of office, therefore, the Labour government pushed forward a modernizing agenda that involved an even more direct attempt to reform the professions to protect the public. A number of measures, including the reform of the General Medical Council, are designed to provide greater assurance of quality for patients (Department of Health 2001a). There is also a new Nursing and Midwifery Council (Department of Health 2001b) and a new Health Professions Council to replace the Council for the Professions Supplementary to Medicine (Department of Health 2001e), following reports commissioned by government from JM Consulting (1996; 1998). The health professions involved have a smaller governing body, but this includes a larger proportion of lay members to represent the public interest. Currently the government is in the process of establishing a United Kingdom Council for the Regulation of Healthcare Professionals, an independent regulatory body for the health professions, to increase accountability to Parliament (Department of Health 2001d). The Council will include a range of professions from doctors, nurses and midwives to dentists, opticians and pharmacists, as well as representatives from the health service and the public. These developments highlight the timeliness of this volume.

The structure of the book

A major aim of the book is to analyse the changing social and economic environment for the practice of professional work in the health sector in the United Kingdom and to gauge the impact of these changes for both the professions concerned and health care more generally. Part One on Professional Regulation in Context sets the scene through four general chapters on key issues. Part Two on Professional Case Studies traces the response of selected occupational groups in the health arena to the challenge of regulation. The volume has been deliberately restricted to health care. The collection does not attempt to consider in any detail social work and other related areas, notwithstanding the desire of the present government for a more joined-up approach across health and social care (see Department of Health 2000b). This limits the territory covered by the volume and increases its coherence, given the very different historical roots of these two fields (for a recent overview of the interface between health and social care see Brechin et al. 2000). The chapters in the two Parts have been written by established academics whose expertise ranges from sociology and social policy to law and politics. Each contributor was asked to set out the theoretical framework within which they were operating and to address common defined themes, to enhance integration.

Part One begins with an overview chapter by Michael Moran, who draws on his research on international economic trends shaping the work of the health professions to examine the implications of globalization and Europeanization. This is considered not only at a macro-theoretical level, but also comparatively in relation to the effect on health professions in specific national settings, including the United Kingdom. Rob Baggott, another political scientist, then discusses the purpose and problems of regulation and political theories about the various interests that influence the process of regulatory change. As such, he sheds light on how, and why, particular patterns of health professional regulation were established. The third chapter by David Price, whose background is in law, provides a general account of the legal framework within which the wide range of health professions in this country operate, as well as their unique characteristics. Finally, Julie Stone gives a critical review of the employment of ethical codes by professional groups, which she sees as having only a limited impact on the day-to-day work of the health professions. She argues that, without training in ethical reasoning and effective grievance procedures, such codes may not be applied in practice – to the detriment of the public.

Part Two is comprised of chapters contributed by social scientists with expert knowledge of the history and development of particular occupational groups in the health sector in the United Kingdom. These are based on their view of regulatory issues in each specific field and the relationship of these groups to government. While not all the health professions could be covered in the available space, the illustrative selection ranges from longer established professional groups to those that are at present professionalizing. Thus, Judith Allsop writes on medicine, Celia Davies on nursing, Nicki Thorogood on dentistry, Gerry Larkin on the professions allied to medicine, David Pilgrim on clinical psychology and Mike Saks on alternative medicine. The latter field covers a variety of occupational groups from herbalists and homoeopaths to acupuncturists and aromatherapists. Some are professionalized, while others may soon win their professional spurs. Many, though, still have a long way to go if they are to become professions. This highlights the dynamic nature of the process of regulation in the health field. It is also a reminder that, while groups such as nurses and doctors are the largest professionalized groups in the health service in the United Kingdom, their numbers are still collectively dwarfed by health workers who are not yet professionalized. These include not only alternative practitioners, but also the wide spectrum of health support workers from generic health care assistants to more specialized groups such as pharmacy technicians and physiotherapy aides (Levitt et al. 1995). This leads neatly on to a discussion of the formal meaning of the concept of a profession in the health context.

The nature of a health profession

The approach that has been taken to defining the professions in this volume is that these are special kinds of knowledge-based occupations. The type of knowledge, the social and cultural value attributed to it and the way in which each occupation handles that knowledge are seen as central to both the process of professionalization and maintaining/extending professional positions. Of course, knowledge is not unique to professional groups and only those occupations that have been successful in obtaining a licence to practise from the state are regarded here as professions. Larson (1977), following Weber, sees this as the achievement of 'social closure' by the occupational groups concerned. This involves drawing a boundary around their knowledge and creating a monopoly through certification and credentialism, which excludes outsiders. Such a regulatory bargain is not struck automatically or without a struggle. Rather, it is won through political engagement. The regulation on which it is based is legally underwritten and brings market control. It is associated with enhanced income, status and power, as well as self-regulation – in which the professional body has the responsibility to police itself, not least through the adoption of ethical and disciplinary codes. That statutory recognition is not easily achieved is well illustrated by the case of medicine. Even this elite occupational group took many years before it finally gained legislation in the mid-nineteenth century supporting its professional standing (Saks 1998).

Much the same was true of other groups of health workers that professionalized at a later stage. In this respect, the form of the licensure underpinning professionalization – based on the Anglo-American model of professions – varies considerably. An important typology in this context has been set out by Turner (1995) who distinguishes the autonomous and dominant profession of medicine from professions based on occupational subordination, such as nursing and the professions supplementary to medicine, and those centred on occupational limitation, such as dentistry and pharmacy. It is important to emphasize that the neo-Weberian definition of a profession adopted here is not uncontentious. Contributors from the functionalist camp, for example, would regard this as unsatisfactory as they infer that a key characteristic of the professions is that they also meet the needs of society, which is seen as integral to explaining their professional privileges (see, for example, Goode 1962). Some Marxist writers, moreover, assume that, as part of their very nature, professions serve the sectional interests of capital and argue that their position in the social structure cannot be understood without reference to the class-based relations of production under capitalism (see, for instance, Navarro 1978). The advantage of the definition advanced here is that it avoids the straitjacket of assumptions imposed by functionalist and Marxist theorists.

Neo-Weberians themselves do not stand above criticism. They have in the past perhaps rather too readily stressed the role of professional self-interests in creating and sustaining the monopolistic privileges of a profession (Saks 1999). The concept of professional self-interests, though, is a powerful explanatory tool. It also pervades the interactionist perspective on professional groups, which shares common Weberian roots – even though it is predominantly focused at a micro-level. Interactionists, as exemplified by the currently much neglected work of Hughes (1963), regard a profession as an ascribed symbolic, socially negotiated status based on day-to-day interaction rather than a legally underwritten monopoly. While this approach can be seen to have limitations because it abstracts professions from their historical and structural moorings (Saks 1998), the two conceptions nonetheless come together in providing a crucial key to understanding the origins of the regulatory authority of professions. In this respect, the value of the interactionist perspective is that it underlines the interest-based negotiation surrounding the achievement of professional standing – and avoids seeing it simply as an inevitable outcrop of a distinctive knowledge base.

Finally, it is worth highlighting the Foucauldian perspective, particularly since it is a further strand that underpins the contributions to this volume. This shares with the neo-Weberian perspective a generally critical view of the role of professions. It draws on the work of Foucault (1977: 162) on the archaeology of knowledge that aims 'to reveal relations between discursive formations and non-discursive domains (institutions, political events, economic practices and processes)'. The main benefit of the approach is that it has enabled challenge of the notion of rational scientific progress – which has so often been assumed to underpin the professionalization process. As a result, those operating within this framework have been able to expose the disciplinary focus of the apparently emancipatory work of the medical and other health professions in areas as diverse as obstetrics (Arney 1982) and dentistry (Nettleton 1992). While the approach can extend the boundaries of our thinking about professional regulation, it has frequently been criticized. The main weaknesses are its cavalier attitude to evidence and its failure to create the conditions under which the claims of its proponents can be tested (Macdonald 1995).

The proponents of the now dominant neo-Weberian perspective typically argue that the knowledge base of professions in general, and health professions in particular, is theoretically open to all, in that it is generalized and self-expanding. However, access is through courses of education and training that are typically overseen by the leaders of the occupational group in question, who act as gatekeepers. They provide experiential and practical knowledge, as well as an abstract understanding of the field, to a limited group of socially defined eligibles who have been carefully selected (Parkin 1979). In the professions, the education and training that is delivered is considered to be part of the socialization process that creates ways of organizing thoughts and actions and a particular set of dispositions (Sinclair 1998). For neo-Weberian contributors, access to such formally accredited education and training is also a critical portal on which exclusionary closure is based, that generates definitions of 'insiders' and 'outsiders' (Saks 1998).

What is common to knowledge-based, exclusionary professional groups in the health arena in the United Kingdom is that their main work site is usually the biomedically conceived human body (Cantor 2000). In the orthodox health professions the abstract, generalized knowledge has tended to be centred on subjects such as physiology, anatomy and the biological sciences, although the social sciences are now becoming more significant. As will be seen in this book, there are exceptions – clinical psychology, for example, is focused on the functioning of the mind, while some forms of alternative medicine have more holistic mind–body orientations. Nonetheless, the orthodox health professions have a largely common knowledge base, even though they differ in the nature and scope of specialization; the diagnostic model applied to determine the presence or absence of illness and disease; and the treatments that may be offered. The development of a social relationship between the practitioner and the patient/client is also vital to them all, given their general need to gain access to the body. Consequently, trust is of crucial importance. This may derive in part from the fact that the health professional is defined as the expert and the person seeking help is not, as well as the formal existence of professional ethical and disciplinary codes – however poorly or otherwise these may be implemented in practice.

Professional self-regulation in health care

As a number of contributors to this book observe, while professions have diverse histories of professionalization, the form of state licensing in this country has been based on the model of the medical profession in the mid-nineteenth century. It can be seen as representing a form of self-regulation centred on private interest government. In this respect, all the health professions are licensed by statute, and the terms of the licence may be modified by Parliament. The governing body is typically made up of members appointed either by the Privy Council or the Department of Health, as well as members elected by the rank and file of the association. The governing body is accountable to Parliament and carries out a number of core functions. It sets the qualifications necessary for entry to the register and oversees education and training, along with other more specialized bodies. In most developed countries there are strong links between institutions of higher education and the professional bodies concerned. In the United Kingdom, the state provides the resources and the institutional framework of higher education, with the professional bodies generally defining the curriculum. The profession establishes and maintains standards of practice, both technical and ethical, and has procedures for disciplining those who do not meet these standards. Interestingly, as Mike Saks notes in his contribution to this volume, this model now also applies to osteopaths and chiropractors – the most recently professionalized groups in the health arena.

Although there are similarities in the form of regulation of the health professions, there are also differences in the level and form of autonomy that they enjoy (Turner 1995). This is partly because of longstanding relationships of medical dominance and partly because, as Gerry Larkin argues in this book, the nature of the state has changed since the nineteenth century. Whatever position a profession occupies in the health care division of labour, functionalist writers usually claim that there is an implicit bargain that underlies its state licensing. The profession fulfils various important knowledge-based functions for society, which is assured of a certain standard if patients or clients seek treatment from an accredited health practitioner. In return the profession is allowed to engage in self-government, with all the attendant economic, political and status rewards. As has been seen, though, neo-Weberian contributors argue that the concept of professionalism is based more on professional self-interests than the collective interest (Saks 1998). In this regard, Stacey (1992), who was a lay member of the General Medical Council, has remarked that there is an inherent tension in self-regulation between protecting the good name of the profession and acting in the public interest by exposing poor practice. However, as Saks (1995) points out, the pursuit of private interests is not necessarily incompatible with the public interest, as the two can work in the same direction and are not necessarily counterposed. This is illustrated by the campaign of the British Medical Association against rivals who purveyed potentially harmful secret remedies early in the twentieth century, which can be seen to have served both the public interest and the self-interest of the medical profession.

Several contributors to this book focus on the relationships between the public, the state and the professions in the health field and how these have changed. While the theoretical interpretation of these changes may differ, all agree that the historical period in which a profession emerges shapes its subsequent form of regulation. This is exemplified by differences in disciplinary procedures between nursing and medicine. In nursing, which became a profession more than half a century after medicine, the United Kingdom Central Council for Nursing, Midwifery and Health Visiting has generally worked on the balance of probabilities in determining the outcome of cases, while the General Medical Council has traditionally used the criminal standard test (Allsop and Mulcahy 1996). Another historically based difference between these two health professions is that specialist education is carried out by the Royal Colleges in partnership with the General Medical Council in the case of medicine. There is not an equivalent to these bodies in the case of nursing, so the span of the regulatory task for the United Kingdom Central Council for Nursing, Midwifery and Health Visiting has been much greater (Davies and Beach 2000).

The chapters in Part Two of the volume also show that the size of the professions to be regulated varies widely – from the largest group, the nurses discussed by Celia Davies, to the smallest, the clinical psychologists covered by David Pilgrim. Davies observes that the variety of backgrounds and specialties within the nursing profession has complicated the regulatory task considerably. Simply maintaining a register in a profession where many members take career breaks is a challenge. In addition, different health professions have variable degrees of exposure to market forces. As Nicki Thorogood notes in her contribution, dentistry is now more exposed to market factors and less protected by its niche within the National Health Service, although it remains tightly focused in terms of the boundaries of its work and the qualifications required on registration. From the account by Pilgrim, it is evident that clinical psychologists have generally benefited from their state shelter within the National Health Service, although, as with medicine, there is a mixed economy between those who work in public and private practice. As Mike Saks indicates, alternative practitioners probably have the strongest concentration in the private sector of any of the health occupations considered here. As will be seen, such variation has considerable implications for the way that such occupations are regulated.

The professional regulatory body, however, is only one aspect of a profession – albeit a key symbol of self-governance. For all the health professions discussed in this book, the regulatory body is part of a network of institutions that make up the wider profession. These include, at a minimum, the education and training institutions and the organizations that deal with the lobbying and the associational activities of the professional group in question. Their distinctive scale and spread constitute a further variation between health professions, linked to their structure and history. In the United Kingdom, medicine continues to maintain a dominant position in the division of labour in health care – despite competition from other groups both inside and outside of the ranks of orthodox practitioners. This can variously be attributed to such factors as the early establishment of medicine as a self-regulating profession; tight restrictions over entry; the ability of elites to maintain some control over the actions of the rank and file; and the continuing high social utility accorded to medicine. In addition, the entrenched power relationship with government in a nationally funded health service should not be forgotten. Although this can no longer be described in terms of the medical–Ministry alliance that existed in the period before the Second World War, the relationship between the two is still strong (Larkin 1995).

In this regard, another major thread running through the contributions is the regulatory relationship between the state and the professions, which Michael Moran refers to as a 'symbiotic relationship'. Using the example of medicine, Gerry Larkin also sees the nature of the professions changing as the state has developed. For him, a minimalist state gives rise to an autonomous profession, a welfare state spawns a corporate relationship, while a regulatory state leads to a breakdown of the alliance and an uncertain future. Both of these contributors draw on the interesting application by Johnson (1995) of Foucault's notion of governmentality to the health professions. Johnson sees the establishment of the health professions as part of state formation and the process of governing. There is no duality between the state and the professions as they are both part of the same project of generating and controlling expert knowledge. Abstract and codified knowledge is itself viewed as a product of modern society, to which the growth in the nineteenth century of a number of self-governing professional groups testifies. He therefore argues that professionalism became part of the state – with expert technologies, the practical activities of professions, and the social authority associated with professionalism helping to render the complexities of modern social and economic life knowable, practical and amenable to governing.

In this light, Johnson (1995: 16) says:

> we are forced to conclude not only that the independence of the professions depends on the interventions of the state, but that the state is dependent on the independence of the professions in securing the capacity to govern as well as legitimating its governance. The obvious implication of all this is to suggest that we must develop ways of talking about the state and profession that conceive of the relationship not as a struggle for autonomy and control but as the interplay of integrally related structures, evolving as the combined product of occupational strategies, governmental policies and shifts in public opinion.

The value of this position can, of course, be debated, as the fusion of the professions and the state raises conceptual difficulties in empirically analysing the links between the two. It does, however, dilute the frequent claim that the state is a necessary challenge to the health professions. The theme of contemporary challenges to the health professions will now be pursued further in relation to the United Kingdom.

Contemporary challenges to the health professions

One challenge to the health professions is the possible demise of the nation state. Although Michael Moran may be correct that the nation state still primarily defines the jurisdiction of the health professions, the process of globalization seems to have had an effect on professional bodies and those who practise professional work. Moran sees the global economy, particularly as manifested by the pharmaceutical and medical technology industries, as creating continuing pressure on health care spending. He argues that this will constrain governments in the budgetary allocations that they make to health, as well as to health care professionals who work with the National Health Service. However, a counter argument is that these changes are simply exogenous factors that affect the internal politics of regulation between government and the health professions and between health professions themselves. On this interpretation, the expertise of health professionals remains crucial to decision making on a range of issues within both old and new institutional arrangements.

Moran also draws attention to the changing nature of the nation state through Europeanization. One of the major objectives of the European Union has been the harmonization of national regulations affecting the provision of goods and services. Liaison committees have been in existence since the 1970s, linking national professional associations in Europe (Orzack 1998). In the health field, professional services and sectoral directives were set up for six professions (doctors, dentists, nurses, midwives, pharmacists and veterinary surgeons). Agreements were reached on the minimum level of experience necessary for registration to practise within a member country, with the proviso that the host country could determine specific requirements to either complete a further two years of supervised practice or sit a special examination. However, Lovecy (1999) argues that, whereas in the past the structure of European Union institutions enabled professionals themselves to reach agreements, with a restructuring of institutions their role has diminished in favour of the civil service. Furthermore, the legal regulator in the form of the European Court of Justice has upheld the rights of individual migrants. Moran in this volume notes that there are divergent views about how these trends should be interpreted. Some see European Union directives as emanating from a supranational state, while others interpret them as re-enforcing regulations through the nation state. In either case, the professional associations will have to find ways of accommodating and influencing such changes in a more challenging environment.

Contrary to the interpretation of Johnson (1995), a further challenge to the health professions may be posed by the growth of the regulatory state at a national level. In his chapter, Rob Baggott discusses regulation as a form of control and the different styles and forms of regulation. He argues that self-regulation had traditionally been favoured in the United Kingdom, but has a number of advantages and disadvantages. The main disadvantages are a lack of transparency and accountability – which mean that it can be a way of protecting private interests. Baggott notes that both recent Conservative and Labour governments have increased the pressure on the health professions to reform their structures. The Thatcher project was to break professional monopolies that were resistant to market forces. The Blair project, on the other hand, is to modernize professional regulation by increasing accountability, transparency and consistency across the health professions in the interests of public protection and safety – and to reduce demarcations between professional groups in the interests of efficiency. Indeed, it is envisaged that the new United Kingdom Council for the Regulation of Healthcare Professionals will have more powers for scrutiny and review than the Privy Council, with direct accountability to the Secretary of State (Department of Health 2001d).

As David Price comments in his chapter, the 1999 Health Act also gave residual powers to government to change the form of professional regulation without recourse to primary legislation. The Department of Health too has been gradually increasing its ability to ensure that relevant information is collected; standards set and monitored; and clinical reviews undertaken. The assessment of grass roots professional practice is now pervasive. This is being undertaken by both managers and professionals within health organizations and by professional bodies. In addition to the National Institute of Clinical Excellence and the Commission for Health Improvement established early in the first Blair administration (Department of Health 1997), *The NHS Plan* (Department of Health 2000b) outlines a number of changes to increase accountability and obtain more consistent quality in the National Health Service. The National Clinical Assessment Authority, for example, will oversee clinical standards in medicine and the National Patient Safety Agency will collect data to monitor adverse or 'sentinel' events and issue guidance as appropriate. It is possible too that an organization like the new national patients' body, established through the National Health Service Reform and Health Professions Act, 2002, the Commission for Patient and Public involvement, will have a role in relation to complaints (Department of Health 2001c).

In the interests of a safer health service and the protection of the public, the links between the Department of Health as an employer and the professional bodies have been strengthened and made more transparent. The emphasis is on promoting a learning culture based on a systems approach. The aim is not to blame the individual for poor service or errors of judgement, but to analyze the events that have led to this and take managerial responsibility for preventing a recurrence. This approach is contrary to the traditional disciplinary procedures of professional bodies, which involve disciplining individuals who are held responsible for acts of omission and commission in relation to what are held to be reasonable professional standards. In this vein, as Judith Allsop shows in this volume, the General Medical Council has introduced supportive measures to deal with poorly performing doctors and a system for reaccreditation, as well as reforms to its own structure. This has followed government pressure to either reform themselves or face imposed changes – a policy designed to ensure that health professional bodies follow the new approach.

The regulatory bodies of other health professions have introduced similar measures. These bodies have greater oversight over day-to-day practice, while at the same time they, and their professional members, are more accountable to employers and the Department of Health (Department of Health 2001d). Gerry Larkin, in his contribution, refers to such developments as a form of 'co-regulation' as health authorities now have the power to discipline and suspend any employee, representing a shift from the previously more professionally protectionist structures (Allsop and Mulcahy 1996). There are also plans to introduce radical changes in professional training so that there is a greater common foundation of clinical studies for all the health professions (see, for example, Department of

Health 1999). These developments highlight the fact that a closer and more interactive relationship is emerging between leading figures at the Department of Health, the health professions and institutions of higher education.

A further challenge to the health professions has come from the public and the media. Both expect greater responsiveness and accountability when things go wrong. While there is still a high demand for curative and caring services – particularly where they meet the perceived needs of consumers – there has been a change in public attitudes. In addition, the myth of delivering health care according to need has been replaced by a widespread recognition that health professionals within the National Health Service act as mediators for the state in providing access to health care services. Changes within the National Health Service that introduced the purchaser/provider split have made geographical differences in service availability more visible too (Allsop 1995a). Against this background, while public polls suggest that trust remains relatively high for doctors and especially nurses (*British Medical Journal* 2001), public confidence in health professionals has been shaken. The major recent catalyst has been the high-profile cases where they have been shown to exploit their privileged access to the patient to do physical or psychological harm, or to undertake procedures without the consent of the patient or relatives. Poor standards of care and a neglect of the duty of care, as well as adverse events due to avoidable errors, have also been widely reported.

Slow, cumbersome and restrictive redress mechanisms have added to the sense of betrayal of trust by those affected. The rise in the numbers of complaints and litigation, as well as difficulties in recruitment for clinical trials, provide harder indicators of a change in public attitudes (Allsop and Mulcahy 2001). The inquiries into the Royal Liverpool Hospital (Royal Liverpool Children's Inquiry 2001) and the Bristol Royal Infirmary (Bristol Inquiry 2001) indicate a mismatch of attitudes in relation to what people want to be told and what doctors tell them. More particularly, they highlight the disjuncture between some parents' and relatives' views of bodily parts, and routine practices within the National Health Service for disposing of tissue. As Julie Stone points out in her contribution to this book, the diversity in belief systems, generalized ethical codes and lack of training in law and ethics leave many health professionals ill equipped to identify ethical dilemmas, let alone to work through their implications in terms of the patient. In addition, the collective representation of health consumers through the formation of alliances of patient and carer groups has increased (Allsop et al. 2002). This strengthens the power of patients and carers who are heavy users of the National Health Service.

The future of professional regulation in health care

These challenges have combined to bring into the political arena regulatory issues that were hitherto the preserve of professionals. As Starr and Immergut (1987) have argued, the scope of the political has the capacity to expand and contract. In the politics of regulation, areas of decision making that were once considered neutral or technical can become politically contentious. For instance, public–professional relationships were for many decades largely invisible. It was assumed that professions in general served the public interest and that, by and large, professionals once trained, remained competent. However, since the 1960s and 1970s the public and politicians alike have been more critical of the behaviour of health professionals at both a macro and a micro level (Saks 2000). They have served to make life as a health professional rather less straightforward than hitherto in the United Kingdom.

These challenges also highlight the inherent tension within the traditional model of self-regulation observed by Stacey (1992). The governing councils of the health professions are elected as well as appointed and their functions are carried out, and paid for, by their membership. Self-regulation, therefore, means that professional associations have to handle three main constituencies. The first is their own rank-and-file membership, whose fees pay for regulation and whose interests are represented by other institutions within the professional world. The second is the public, which sees the regulatory body as responsible for setting appropriate standards. The final constituency is that of the government and Parliament with whom ultimate responsibility lies.

In response to these challenges, a number of regulatory bodies have attempted to reform their structures from within. Although arcane structures and internal politics have hampered their efforts, changes are now under way. The new structures aim to be more cost effective, involve greater numbers of lay members to represent the public interest, and meet the contemporary criteria of accountability and transparency. What is emerging is a new partnership between the public, professionals, employers and government, albeit with a self-regulatory base – the extent of which varies from profession to profession. This model extends beyond health professions to social care, as illustrated by the emergence of the new General Social Care Council (Davies 1999). As a result of the government's 'joined-up' agenda it also allows greater collaboration to occur between governing bodies of the different health professions.

Wherein, though, lies the future for the regulation of health professions in the United Kingdom? If current government health policy is followed through, then some of the boundaries of the work tasks carried out by particular health care practitioners may well shift. Greater possibilities for practitioners to transfer between professions are developing and task boundaries continue to be fluid (Department of Health 2000a). Practising health professionals may also become more heterogeneous, cross-cutting some of the status hierarchies within, and between, professions. However, for all the pressures to enhance the flexibility and accountability of health professional groups, the editors believe that the future for the professions from a regulatory standpoint remains relatively bright. Expert knowledge is still highly valued in the United Kingdom and there are advantages to governments in keeping expertise out of politics. If there are problems requiring expert advice, governments may wish to distance themselves from the consequences of applying knowledge that is contingent and uncertain in its outcomes. As Johnson (1995) argues, governments depend on the neutrality of expertise to make social realities governable.

In the future, though, professional self-regulation seems certain be more heavily based on 'stakeholder' regulation – as it will need to embrace a larger number of members of other constituencies to ensure both legitimacy and instrumentality. In this respect, an increased lay element on regulatory bodies helps to counter the · charge that professional self-interests are being pursued unscrupulously, at the expense of the public welfare. Against this, the Council for the Regulation of Healthcare Professionals sets a precedent in that health professions – alongside other stakeholders – will also in effect be able to regulate each other. However, rather than seeing this as an opportunity to settle past competitive scores, it may help them to join forces to protect their own self-regulatory powers. This is because the Council could be seen as a body that is waiting in the wings should self-regulation fail to deliver high-quality health care. In this respect, new approaches to regulation in the United Kingdom are likely to stop short of subverting the concept of legally underwritten, self-regulating, professions based on exclusionary closure. This is underlined by the unattractiveness of other more bureaucratic arrangements for dealing with complex bodies of health knowledge (Carrier and Kendall 1995) – as well as the high cost to the public purse of an entirely state-based regulatory system.

References

Alaszewski, A. (1995) 'Restructuring health and welfare professions in the United Kingdom: The impact of internal markets on the medical, nursing and social work professions', in T. Johnson, G. Larkin and M. Saks (eds) *Health Professions and the State in Europe*. London: Routledge.

Allsop, J. (1995a) *Health Policy and the NHS*. London: Longman, 2nd edn.

Allsop, J. (1995b) 'Shifting spheres of opportunity: The professional powers of general practitioners within the British National Health Service', in T. Johnson, G. Larkin and M. Saks (eds) *Health Professions and the State in Europe*. London: Routledge.

Allsop, J. and Mulcahy, L. (1996) *Regulating Medical Work: Formal and Informal Controls*. Buckingham: Open University Press.

Allsop J. and Mulcahy, L. (2001) 'Dealing with clinical complaints', in C. Vincent (ed.) *Clinical Risk Management*. London: British Medical Journal Books, 2nd edn.

Allsop, J., Baggott, R. and Jones, K. (2002) 'Health consumer groups and the national policy process', in A. Petersen and S. Henderson (eds) *Consuming Health: The Commodification of Health Care*. London: Routledge.

Arney, W. (1982) *Power and the Profession of Obstetrics*. London: University of Chicago Press.

Brechin, A., Brown, H. and Eby, M. (eds) (2000) *Critical Practice in Health and Social Care*. London: Sage.

Bristol Inquiry (2001) *Learning from Bristol*, Public Inquiry into Children's Heart Surgery at the Bristol Royal Infirmary 1984–1995. London: Stationery Office.

British Medical Journal (2001) 'MORI poll', *British Medical Journal*, 222: 694.

Cantor, D. (2000) 'The diseased body', in R. Cooter and J. Pickstone (eds) *Medicine in the Twentieth Century*. Amsterdam: Harwood Academic Publishers.

Carrier, J. and Kendall, I. (1995) 'Professionalism and interprofessionalism in health and community care: Some theoretical issues', in P. Owens, J. Carrier and J. Horder (eds) *Interprofessional Issues in Community and Primary Health Care*. London: Macmillan.

Davies, C. (1999) 'Rethinking regulation in the health professions in the UK: Institutions, ideals and identities', in I. Hellberg, M. Saks and C. Benoit (eds) *Professional Identities in Transition: Cross-Cultural Dimensions.* Södertälje: Almqvist & Wiksell International.

Davies, C. and Beach, A. (2000) *Interpreting Professional Self-Regulation: A History of the United Kingdom Central Council for Nursing, Midwifery and Health Visiting.* London: Routledge.

Department of Health (1997) *The New NHS: Modern, Dependable.* London: HMSO.

Department of Health (1999) *Making a Difference.* London: Department of Health.

Department of Health (2000a) *A Health Service of All the Talents: Developing the NHS Workforce.* London: Department of Health.

Department of Health (2000b) *The NHS Plan,* London: The Stationery Office.

Department of Health (2001a) *Assuring the Quality of Medical Practice: Implementing Supporting Doctors, Protecting Patients.* London: The Stationery Office.

Department of Health (2001b) *Establishing the New Nursing and Midwifery Council.* London: Department of Health.

Department of Health (2001c) *Involving Patients and the Public in Healthcare.* London: Department of Health.

Department of Health (2001d) *Modernising Regulation in the Health Professions.* London: Department of Health.

Department of Health (2001e) *Modernising Regulation: The New Health Professions Council.* London: Department of Health.

Foucault, M. (1977) *The Archaeology of Knowledge.* London: Tavistock.

Goode, W. (1962) 'Encroachment, charlatanism and the emerging profession: Psychology, sociology and medicine', *American Sociological Review,* 25: 902–14.

Harrison, S., Hunter, D., Marnoch, G. and Pollitt, C. (1992) *Just Managing: Power and Culture in the NHS.* London: Macmillan.

Higgins, J. (1988) *The Business of Medicine: Private Health Care in Britain.* London: Macmillan.

Hughes, E. (1963) 'Professions', *Daedalus,* 92: 655–68.

JM Consulting (1996) *The Regulation of Health Professions: Report of a Review of the Professions Supplementary to Medicine Act (1960) with Recommendations for New Legislation.* Bristol: JM Consulting Ltd.

JM Consulting (1998) *The Regulation of Nurses, Midwives and Health Visitors: Report on a Review of the Nurses, Midwives and Health Visitors Act 1997.* Bristol: JM Consulting Ltd.

Johnson, T. (1972) *Professions and Power.* London: Macmillan.

Johnson, T. (1995) 'Governmentality and the institutionalization of expertise', in T. Johnson, G. Larkin and M. Saks (eds) *Health Professions and the State in Europe.* London: Routledge.

Kennedy, I. (1983) *The Unmasking of Medicine.* London: Granada Publishing.

Klein, R. (1989) *The Politics of the National Health Service.* London: Longman, 2nd edn.

Larkin, G. (1995) 'State control and the health professions in the United Kingdom: Historical perspectives', in T. Johnson, G. Larkin and M. Saks (eds) *Health Professions and the State in Europe.* London: Routledge.

Larson, M. (1977) *The Rise of Professionalism: A Sociological Analysis.* London: University of California Press.

Levitt, R., Wall, A. and Appleby, J. (1995) *The Reorganized National Health Service.* London: Chapman & Hall, 5th edn.

Lovecy, J. (1999) 'Governance transformation in the professional services sector', in B. Kohler-Koch and R. Eising (eds) *The Transformation of Governance in the European Union.* London: Routledge.

Macdonald, K. (1995) *The Sociology of the Professions.* London: Sage.

Navarro, V. (1978) *Class Struggle, the State and Medicine: An Historical and Contemporary Analysis of the Medical Sector in Great Britain.* London: Martin Robertson.

Nettleton, S. (1992) *Power, Pain and Dentistry.* Buckingham: Open University Press.

Orzack, L. (1998) 'Professions and world trade diplomacy: National systems and international authority', in V. Olgiati, L. Orzack and M. Saks (eds) *Professions, Identity, and Order in Comparative Perspective*. Onati: Onati International Institute for the Sociology of Law.

Parkin, F. (1979) *Marxism and Class Theory: A Bourgeois Critique*. London: Tavistock.

The Patient's Charter (1991) London: HMSO.

Royal Liverpool Children's Inquiry (2001) *Summary and Recommendations*. London: House of Commons.

Saks, M. (1995) *Professions and the Public Interest: Medical Power, Altruism and Alternative Medicine*. London: Routledge.

Saks, M. (1998) 'Professionalism and health care', in D. Field and S. Taylor (eds) *Sociological Perspectives on Health, Illness and Health Care*. Oxford: Blackwell Science.

Saks, M. (1999) 'Professions, markets and public responsibility', in M. Dent, M. O'Neill, and C. Bagley (eds) *Professions, New Public Management and the European Welfare State*. Stafford: Staffordshire University Press.

Saks, M. (2000) 'Medicine and the counter culture', in R. Cooter and J. Pickstone (eds) *Medicine in the Twentieth Century*. Amsterdam: Harwood Academic Publishers.

Sinclair, S. (1998) *Making Doctors: An Institutional Apprenticeship*. Oxford: Berg.

Stacey, M. (1992) *Regulating British Medicine: The General Medical Council*. Chichester: John Wiley & Sons.

Starr, P. and Immergut, E. (1987) 'Health care and the boundaries of politics', in C.S. Maier (ed.) *Changing Boundaries of the Political*. Cambridge: Cambridge University Press.

Turner, R. (1995) *Medical Power and Social Knowledge*. London: Sage, 2nd edn.

PART ONE

PROFESSIONAL REGULATION IN CONTEXT

1 The Health Professions in International Perspective

Michael Moran

The health professions and regulation

'Regulation' virtually defines a profession. Attempts in the literature to adopt an 'essentialist' approach to the definition of a profession have long been discredited: the variety of occupational practices and market locations that distinguish jobs claiming the professional label are too diverse to allow the identification of some definitive core of professional practice. Likewise, attempts to adopt a normative approach to the definition of professionalism – by, for instance, identifying the professional project with some distinctive moral commitment to the care of clients – founder because they conflate a profession's public philosophy with the tactics adopted by occupations in the struggle for markets. These tactics are, among other things, designed to foster trust among clients and to delimit the boundaries of competition between members of an occupation (Freidson 1970).

These limitations on traditional approaches to the study of professionalism explain why, increasingly, professionalization is identified as a regulatory strategy employed by, and on behalf of, occupations to exercise control over labour markets (Johnson 1972). This regulatory strategy involves three key elements, each of which is central to the discussion of the international dimension of professionalism in health care. These can be set out as follows.

The first of these is that the regulatory strategy is largely the product of the era before the movement towards globalization, which will shortly be discussed further. In the case of the United Kingdom, which is central to this volume, the regulatory strategy was fundamentally a nineteenth-century creation. The most important institutional pattern, notably the idea of regulation as a system of 'franchising' by the state of control over a labour market to a particular occupation, dates back at least to the Medical Act of 1858. This established such a pattern for doctors, but may originally stem from the passage of the Apothecaries Act of 1815 which stipulated that a course of training was a legal requirement for entering the examinations to obtain a licence to practice as an apothecary (Reader 1966). All subsequent professionalizing projects in health care have had to respond to this early institutional pattern. It is, moreover, only a small simplification to say that they have all been shaped by the effort to emulate it.

The second central element of the regulatory structure associated with professionalization is the fact that the initial contours of the professionalizing project were established on a national basis in the period prior to advanced globalization. This means that professional regulation has historically been a national matter, or, to be more precise, has been confined to the boundaries of the nation state. It is true that some elements of professional regulation occasionally transcended the nation state – as, for instance, the licensing of medical education by the British General Medical Council in some foreign jurisdictions (Stacey 1992). This, however, was largely an echo of imperial power from the past.

The third feature is connected to this observation, and is vital to any discussion of the international dimension. Professionalism was fundamentally a project of nation states. One reason is obvious – namely, that professional regulation itself involves the state as a central partner. As Wilding (1982: 12) puts it: 'What produces the privileges of professional status is a profession–state alliance.' The explanation for state involvement is plain. Viewed as a strategy of self-regulation, professionalism faces the familiar problem of all self-regulatory systems: from where is to come the authority to discipline those who decline to obey the disciplines of self-regulation? The solution is to position the state as a guardian, standing as a power of last resort behind the institutions of self-regulation. From this flow a number of consequences, all of which are important for professionalism in the age of globalization. In particular, as we shall see later, the partnership with the state deeply implicates professions in nation state power, and the distinctive state traditions mean that the institutions, the political cultures and historical experiences of different national professions, vary greatly.

The health professions and globalization

'Globalization' is one of the most seductive, and also one of the most difficult, concepts in contemporary social science. It is best conceived as a process rather than as an end state – something that is happening rather than a destination at which we have arrived. In this sense, as Braithwaite and Drahos (2000) show, it is a process that has ancient historical roots, at least going back to the Romans. In the most everyday sense, it is not at all difficult to find striking examples, even from the ancient world, of health professionals who operated across wide geographical areas (Moran and Wood 1996). But four aspects of globalization are especially important for health care systems, and therefore have particularly significant implications for health care professions. They all reflect the intensification of the process of globalization that has occurred during the last three decades.

The first of these is that globalization has involved great changes in productive processes. Health care is a personal social service delivered by, among others, health care professionals, but it is a service whose delivery, in the age of scientific medicine, involves an elaborate industrial infrastructure. That infrastructure in turn involves not only physical capital – most notably the hospital, which is at the centre of medicine in the advanced industrial nations – but also the infrastructure of medical technology. The most obvious feature of the medical technology industries is that they are at the frontier of innovation in modern economies, and are therefore at the frontier of the global organization of production too.

The second important aspect of globalization is that it involves great changes in the organization of product and service marketing – most obviously in the creation of global brands. It is plain, again, that these developments have deeply penetrated health care systems. This hardly needs to be emphasized to anyone writing in the United Kingdom, which has a health care system that is increasingly designed with the export of both services and products in mind.

The third key aspect of globalization is that it has a cultural face. In part this is symbolic, as in the creation of 'world brands'. In part, it reflects fundamental developments in discourse: the rise of English as an increasingly universal language, especially as the universal language of scientific communication; and the rise of a particular scientific discourse itself which corresponds exactly to the culture of scientific medicine, a culture which has shaped the dominant model of medical practice now for over a century.

These three features of globalization all imply an increasingly open, integrated and homogeneous world economic order, but the fourth and final feature complicates the picture, in a way which has profound implications for our understanding of the international environment of health care professionalism. At its heart, globalization is a process by which a single world economy is being created. And the essence of the creation of a single economy – whether at national or global level – is the development of an increasingly refined division of labour. The fourth feature of globalization is, therefore, precisely this refined international division of labour. It involves specialization through the allocation of different roles in the division of labour to different social groups and, at the global level, to different national jurisdictions. It also entails growing divergence in the resources of different territories. Thus, globalization as the refinement of the division of labour involves, not the creation of an increasingly homogeneous world economy, but an increase in diversity as specialization, and inequality in the distribution of resources, grows.

This increasingly segmented economy is developing in a world of nation states. Indeed, the intensification of globalization over the last generation has been accompanied by a sharp growth in the number of nation states. The most obvious consequence as far as health professionals are concerned is that it leads to increasing attempts to regulate the flow of labour in the world economy. This is highlighted in those parts of the world advantaged by the global division of labour – principally in the Northern Hemisphere, and especially in Western Europe and North America. These seek simultaneously to recruit labour to meet particular market shortages and to restrict the flow of immigrants from the poorest parts of the globe.

Globalization is therefore a critical part of the environment of health care professionals. However, as this brief sketch shows, it has complex, and often contradictory, implications for the regulation of professional labour markets. It simultaneously creates a more integrated and more differentiated world system. This is, again, something to which I return below.

Health professions in comparative perspective

Globalization is taking place in a world of nation states, and these nation states have deeply shaped the character of professional regulation. Three examples – the United Kingdom, the United States and Germany – serve to make this point. They all represent large and distinctive health care systems and they show that, while the strategies of professional regulation have commonalties, there are also strikingly different national variations. The United Kingdom is chosen both because of its relatively small size and because much of this volume is written from a British perspective. The United States is chosen because it is both the largest health care system in the world and the dominant actor in the global system. Germany is chosen because it is the biggest health care system in Europe and because it exemplifies a particular, mainland European, approach to professionalism.

The system of professional regulation in the United Kingdom is marked by the distinctive imprint of the country's historical development. Britain's early industrialization created both opportunities and problems in the markets for health care as a personal service. It created opportunities because the new industrial society opened up vast and lucrative markets for health care. It created problems because, for existing professional groups, which principally meant branches of medicine as an ancient profession, it created the threat that these markets would be colonized by upstart occupations. Regulation was therefore designed to govern access to these lucrative markets; to create trust among potential clients in the probity and competence of providers of professional services; and to create an ordered hierarchy within the world of health care providers. As is well known, that hierarchy, especially after the 1858 Medical Act, involved placing doctors at the head of the pyramid of health workers. Regulation was therefore inevitable because of irresistible structural forces, but it had to be developed within a particular political environment. Although the state claimed the power of *imperium*, it had scant bureaucratic resources to enforce its will. Moreover, it was a pre-democratic, oligarchic political structure. The system of professional regulation that developed, therefore, kept that state power firmly in the background, although it invoked it as the guardian of the authority of professional institutions. The modern history of professional regulation in the United Kingdom can be read as an attempt to cope with this legacy: in particular, to reconcile a professional pattern created in a pre-democratic, non-interventionist world with a world of democratic politics and state intervention (Stacey 1992).

The United States exhibited a different pattern. There, too, the system of regulation has nineteenth-century origins, but these origins had distinctively American features. Any medical authority was uncertain in a populist political culture where there periodically occurred great waves of revolt against authority. For much of the nineteenth century health care was therefore the domain of the charismatic and the charlatan. The central (federal) state was weak and internally divided, and the locus of authority favoured the individual, separate, states of the Union. These problems of professional authority were only finally solved in the early decades of the twentieth century, and their solution gave a particular 'cast' to health professionalism in the United States. The solution involved creating a close alliance with the laboratory sciences and endowing health care professionals with the new authority of science. The result was to ally health care professionalism uniquely closely with a scientific, curative model of medicine – an alliance that still deeply colours the culture of medical professionalism in the United States (Brown 1979; Starr 1982).

If one feature linking the United States and British professionalism was the weakness of state structures, a distinctive feature of the German system of regulation was the historical importance of state institutions. This was partly reflected in the history of professional organization, which had deep, pre-industrial roots in state sponsorship even in pre-unification Germany. It is also reflected in the contemporary character of professional organization, where the institutions of self-regulation take a particular form. Legally, the professions in Germany are organized around public law organizations, self-regulatory professional institutions that are deeply embedded in the legal structure of the state. The particular form of this embeddedness has magnified a feature already present in a marked form in the United States and the United Kingdom – the dominance of the medical profession in the professional structure. This is partly a matter of cultural understandings, especially in the hospital system. But it is also a consequence of the system of health administration and the system of policy formulation, which has given the networks dominated by doctors' organizations a uniquely powerful place (Moran 1999).

These thumbnail sketches of different systems of professional regulation in three uniquely important national systems are intended to reinforce one vital point: the globalizing environment of health care professionalism, important though it is, occurs in a world of great national diversity. National cultural traditions, and national state structures, remain particularly important because of the way health care professionalism as a project has been linked to the history of the modern nation state.

The Europeanization and globalization of health care professionalism

Health care professionalism has a highly complex relationship with the twin phenomena of Europeanization and globalization. On the one hand, the historical dominance of the scientific-curative model of medical care produces exactly that kind of standardization in medical-scientific reasoning, technologies and medical procedures, which encourages the crossing of cultural and national boundaries. On the other hand, the fact that at root most health care professions are delivering a personal service in highly sensitive, individual circumstances, considerably complicates this process of standardization. We only have to think of the sensitive role of language in personal relations between professionals and clients to get a sense of some of the complexities involved.

The impact of Europeanization on health care professionalism has been particularly complex. Even after the renewal and revival of the integration project following the passage of the Single European Act in 1986, the impact of integration on professional markets generally has been more limited than the impact on product markets. The reasons for this are complex, but undoubtedly take us back to some of the factors noted above – especially the extent to which health care professionalism is entwined with particular state structures and different senses of national identity. It is well known that, while free movement of labour was one of the central parts of the Single Market Project, a truly integrated labour market has been far less completely achieved than has integration in other markets. The reasons for this state of affairs in general are plain. Language, cultural diversity, and the inability of the Union to construct an integrated social welfare regime to underpin labour markets are all at work (see, *inter alia*, Ferrera and Rhodes 2000).

The integration of health professional services has involved a mixture of attempts at harmonization and at adaptation of the very different principles of the *Cassis de Dijon* judgment.[1] Since the essence of trust in medical professionalism involves trust in training and in continuing clinical competence, much detailed work has gone into attempts to harmonize training syllabuses as a basis for mutual recognition on the *Cassis de Dijon* principles. This is the basic principle around which European Union directives designed to facilitate the mobility of health labour generally (and not just the medical profession) have been designed. The United Kingdom is in a potentially strong position to exploit labour mobility, and indeed already shows signs of doing so – as, for instance, in the market for doctors. A heavily controlled system of professional recruitment has led to periodic shortages which can be alleviated by recruitment from other jurisdictions – most notably from among the southern European members of the European Union – where the absence of any effective system of tight manpower planning has produced a surplus of physicians.

In some respects, this short-term exploitation only builds on an established British policy of exploiting the globalized character of professional markets. However, recent developments show the complex relations between different parts of international labour markets. As is well known, in the early history of the National Health Service labour market planning depended heavily on the legacy of an earlier episode in the process of globalization – namely, that involving the creation of an empire. Imperial and post-imperial possessions were important sources of labour recruitment at all levels of the service, from the very apex of professional status, the consultant, downward (Stacey 1992). In some instances this was reinforced by the historical tutelage of domestic professional authorities over training institutions, like medical schools, in the colonies and former colonies. The institutional reconfiguration of regulation to encourage the creation of an integrated European labour market has considerably modified this process, raising the barriers to labour mobility from outside the European Union at the same time as the barriers to labour mobility within the Union have been lowered. The interaction of Europeanization and globalization in this context is therefore much more complex than a simple increase in international labour mobility.

Theoretical perspectives

Do the twin phenomena of Europeanization and globalization oblige us fundamentally to recast our theoretical understanding of the nature of professionalism in health care? In favour of the view that they do indeed demand such a fundamental shift is our whole historical understanding of the character of the professional project. I have argued in this chapter that health care professionalism as a regulatory strategy depended historically on developing close relations with the nation state: no nation state, no health care professionalism as we understand it. And, as the sketches of different national regulatory systems outlined above show, this close connection produced highly distinctive relations both between professions and the state and in the character of professionalism itself. At a more obvious level, professional markets were largely nationally delimited, and the internal hierarchies between different occupational groups depended heavily on the different relations of sponsorship that various groups formed with the state.

However, it is natural to expect that the reshaping of the geographical boundaries of labour markets, and the reshaping also in the European context of the national boundaries of regulatory institutions and procedures, will oblige us to rethink the professional project as primarily one born and raised within the nation state. Regulatory compacts – such as those covering professional curricula – are already being renegotiated at the European level, and it is likely that this will require some corresponding political realignment. Indeed, as can already be observed, professions have begun to mobilize for lobbying purposes at European Union level. Strengthening these tendencies are the contextual developments in Europeanization and globalization. These include not only the increasingly international character of medical product markets referred to earlier in this chapter. They also concern the increasing penetration of systems of health care delivery by large, often United States controlled, multinational corporations, such as those owning hospital chains (Mohan 1995).

On the other hand, there are some powerful arguments for retaining the theoretical perspective that professionalism is fundamentally a national strategy for regulating labour markets. In part these arguments derive from the present limited impact of the internationalizing tendencies outlined above. Even if they represent the wave of the future, at the moment they do not represent a very large wave. There is therefore plenty of life left in national structures yet. But there is a more fundamental reason for continuing to see professionalism primarily as a national strategy, connected in particular to how we understand the character of the Europeanizing project. In this respect, what we think the European Union does to the process of regulation generally – not only to the process of regulating health care professions – depends heavily on our view of the European Union as a state formation.

Two views can be contrasted, both of which see the European Union as a new kind of state, but both of which picture the state that is emerging in very different terms. On the one hand, the European Union can be seen as a new kind of supranational entity that is moving in the direction of dissolving national boundaries and differences. On that understanding, we should start to think of health care professionalism in European, not nation state, terms. A second view, associated with the work of the Italian social scientist Giandomenico Majone (1996), sees the distinctive nature of the European Union as a 'regulatory state': a state concerned primarily to pass regulations, and to hand responsibility for implementing those regulations down to national institutions. The effect of the regulatory state is actually to strengthen, not weaken, the national structures of professional regulatory bodies. This is precisely what seems to have been happening in health care, where national regulatory bodies have had extra responsibilities and powers conferred on them, notably in the implementation of European Union directives. On our view of the European Union – as a supranational state denuding national institutions of power and resources, or as a regulatory state operating through strengthened national regulatory institutions – therefore rests our expectations about the future theoretical character of the study of health care professionalism.

Policy challenges

It will be obvious that there is a connection between theoretical developments in the study of health care professionalism and the final issue sketched here – that of likely policy developments. The policy challenges connected with globalization and Europeanization may for convenience be divided into three types. First, there is a set of challenges produced by wider contextual developments, most notably in the evolution of the international economy. This reinforces a point that lies behind much of this chapter – namely, that the character of international influences on health care professionalism is not just, or even mainly, a matter of what is happening to the professions themselves. Second, there is a further set of contextual changes that are being produced within health care systems. And, finally, there are the most direct influences of all – those that are taking place within the world of health care professionalism.

The peculiar significance of the wider economic context is shown by the recent history of professionalism. The golden age of health care professionalism, especially of the medical profession, coincided with a particular episode in the international history of the global economy. It followed the 'long boom' in the advanced capitalist nations that stretched from the beginnings of the Korean conflict to the recession produced by the oil price rises of 1973–4. The end of the long boom created a 'cold climate' for the wider welfare state, for health care systems, and for those employed in health care. Three distinct forces were at work.

First, although some countries recovered relatively quickly from the worst effects of the recession of the early 1970s, it nevertheless brought to an end the period of historically high, across-the-board economic growth in the advanced industrial world. Second, the end of the long boom coincided with a sharp acceleration in the process of globalization, and thus in the severity of international competitive pressures, forcing most states to operate austerity policies in health and welfare. Third, there were particularly severe effects in the weaker economies of the advanced capitalist world, of which Britain in the 1970s was a particularly striking case. Britain's weakness had been masked by the general buoyancy of the international economy in the 1950s and 1960s. The 1970s were a decade of deepening economic crisis, a crisis that led in turn to the radical economic and social reforms of the 1980s and 1990s. This helps explain why in health care, as in so many other areas, Britain was a policy pioneer, but the British case only magnified tendencies observable in other countries. It magnified them because of the special weakness of Britain's position and the correspondingly drastic solutions that were needed.

Faced with recession, growing global competition and economic turbulence, states responded by trying to squeeze more efficiency out of their institutions, including their health care institutions. This put health care professions in the front line, for two reasons. First, health care is a labour-intensive activity and current costs are dominated by pay. Second, the tradition of professional discretion and autonomy meant that, beyond the resources they consumed in pay, health care professionals were also central to the wider process of resource commitment and allocation. The decades since the end of the long boom have therefore seen a persistent tendency, across a wide range of jurisdictions, for states to try to restrict the independence of professional judgement; to manage in a more interventionist way the demarcation lines between different professional groups; and to control more precisely the rewards of professionalism (see for instance, Freeman and Moran 2000).

The economic recovery from the mid-1990s, led by the greatest boom in the United States for a generation, has eased some of the more immediate pressures on states to pursue austerity policies. However, it is difficult to see any change in the fundamental structural forces that have produced the long-term pressures to curb professional autonomy. On the contrary, if anything, the pressures of global competitiveness are intensifying. In addition, there are convergent pressures on health care systems that are also at work. The convergent contextual developments in health care systems are well known and need only be briefly summarized here. They amount to inexorable pressure on resources that are forcing policy makers to continue to squeeze professionals in the search for more efficiency in service delivery. The most obvious force is a direct outgrowth of globalization, and it relates to the character of innovation in the medical technology industries.

The global organization of the medical technology industries has three particularly important consequences. First, these are industries where an important key to securing competitive advantage in markets lies in product innovation and in the successful marketing of those products. Typically, for instance, the budget of a large pharmaceutical multinational will be dominated by its budgets for research and development and for its large marketing teams. As a result, the technology industries are a powerful pressure for cost escalation in health care, because they have a powerful interest in widening the range of therapy options available, and marketing that wider range as aggressively as possible. In short, market strategies in the industries are a powerful independent force pushing policy makers into squeezing efficiencies out of workers in health service delivery.

The second mainstream consequence of the global organization of the medical technology industries is that, precisely because these are industries operating on a global scale, it is very difficult for individual national governments to do much about cost escalation pressures in medical technology. They must therefore look elsewhere for solutions, and the nationally delimited health care professions are an obvious place.

Finally, the global nature of medical technology nevertheless has a particular national bias. It is dominated as far as both production and sales are concerned by the United States. And it is in the United States that the scale of health care spending, and of health care inflation, is most extravagantly developed. This American domination, coupled with the global organization of markets and production in the medical technology industries, makes the task of containing the cost pressures produced by technological innovation uniquely difficult for other nation states. In these circumstances, it is hardly surprising that they turn to constraints on health care professionals as an alternative means of containing costs. These pressures are inexorable. It is impossible to see, short of some presently inconceivable revolution in the dominant paradigm of modern medicine, a future in which large-scale technological innovation by big multinational corporations is not a fundamental feature of health care systems across the advanced industrial world (Moran 2000).

The wider economic context of globalization, and the particular impact of globalized medical technology industries, have thus been powerful sources of policy challenge for several decades, and are likely to remain so for the foreseeable future. But the changes within health care professions that are directly due to international pressures must also be borne in mind. Three are particularly worth highlighting. The first takes us back to medical technology, whose innovations constantly have the capacity to destabilize professional interests in hierarchies. Innovations in the technology of surgery deskill some traditional sources of professional power. Other innovations, such as those making possible a wider range of day surgical procedures in outpatient clinics, destabilize the boundaries between institutions – notably between the hospital and the institutions of primary care (Curtis and Taket 1996). The critical point is that technological innovation is a destabilizing force. It creates new professional specialisms, deskills others, and blurs the boundaries between still more areas of professional expertise.

A second set of changes is the product of social processes which exist in more or less pronounced fashion across the advanced industrial world, and which are deeply impacting on professional labour markets. There are many complex and contradictory changes here. Some involve changes in the gendered division of labour. Traditionally, professional hierarchies were gender hierarchies by another name, represented in particular by the almost universal domination across the advanced world of a male-led medical profession, and the subordination of the largest occupational group in health care, nursing, which was traditionally overwhelmingly female (Riska and Wegar 1993). Wider social changes – notably in female participation in the labour market and in the education system – are considerably complicating these traditional gendered hierarchies. They involve, for instance, the growing 'feminization' of the medical profession, at least in its lower reaches, and the renegotiation of traditional skill boundaries between medicine and other professions. These changes are so complex that they are not easily summed up in the traditional language of professional hierarchies. In some respects they may indeed be leading to reinforcement, through a reconfiguration, of male domination in the hierarchical system. For a United Kingdom readership, however, the important point to bear in mind is that these forces, evident in the United Kingdom, are not uniquely British. They represent wider international processes. Just as complex are changes in the ethnic mix of medical professions. The exploitation of former imperial connections to fill labour market shortages has long given the British medical profession, for instance, an ethnic composition that has been twisted around professional hierarchies (Stacey 1992). One possible future, given the gradual creation of a more integrated European labour market, is a 'fortress European Union' policy in professional medical services.

A third and final pressure comes from changes in the relations between health care professions and their clients. The 'golden age' of the professional in the decades after the Second World War was also a golden age of professional domination over patients who, dazzled by the achievements of scientific medicine, were in the main prepared to defer to professional judgement. Long-term cultural and structural changes across the advanced industrial world have eroded this professional authority. The general decline of deference to traditional institutions, rising levels of formal education that put many patients on at least a formal educational parity with professionals, and an increasingly sceptical and investigative system of mass media are all creating a crisis of professional authority over patients in the health care systems of the advanced industrial world.

In short, the future for professionalism in health care, viewed from an international perspective, looks bleak – pressured by the imperatives of globalization, technological developments and cultural change. Nation states and national regulatory institutions will mediate all these forces, but mediation will not blunt their uncomfortable edge. Of course bleakness is in the eye of the beholder. Globalization is subjecting traditional professional hierarchies to immense stress. From the point of view of the consumers of health care – above all, from the point of view of individual patients – the decline of the traditional national world of medical hierarchies may not be bad news at all.

Note

1 The judgement of the European Court of Justice, dates from 1979. The substance of the judgment laid down the principle that a good or service properly authorized in one state of the Union should be allowed freely to circulate in the other member states. The principle is an alternative to the more difficult-to-achieve standard of harmonization, implying the negotiation of single common standards across the whole Union.

References

Braithwaite, J. and Drahos, P. (2000) *Global Business Regulation*. Cambridge: Cambridge University Press.

Brown, E. (1979) *Rockefeller Medicine Men: Medicine and Capitalism in America*. Berkeley: University of California Press.

Curtis, S. and Taket, A. (1996) *Health and Societies*. London: Arnold.

Ferrera, M. and Rhodes, M. (eds) (2000) *Recasting European Welfare States*. London: Frank Cass.

Freeman, R. and Moran, M. (2000) 'Reforming health care in Europe', in M. Ferrera and M. Rhodes (eds) *Recasting European Welfare States*. London: Frank Cass.

Freidson, E. (1970) *Profession of Medicine: A Study in the Sociology of Applied Knowledge*. New York: Dodd, Mead & Co.

Johnson, T. (1972) *Professions and Power*. London: Macmillan.

Majone, G. (1996) *Regulating Europe*. London: Routledge.

Mohan, J. (1995) *A National Health Service? The Restructuring of Health Care in Britain since 1979*. Basingstoke: Macmillan.

Moran, M. (1999) *Governing the Health Care State: A Comparative Study of the United Kingdom, the United States and Germany*. Manchester: Manchester University Press.

Moran, M. (2000) 'Understanding the welfare state: the case of health care', *British Journal of Politics and International Relations*, 2: 135–51.

Moran, M. and Wood, B. (1996) 'The globalization of health care policy', in P. Gummett (ed.) *Globalization and Public Policy*. Cheltenham: Edward Elgar.

Reader, W.J. (1966) *Professional Men*. London: Weidenfeld & Nicolson.

Riska, E. and Wegar, K. (1993) (eds) *Gender, Work and Medicine: Women and the Medical Division of Labour*. London: Sage.

Stacey, M. (1992) *Regulating British Medicine: The General Medical Council*. Chichester: John Wiley & Sons.

Starr, P. (1982) *The Social Transformation of American Medicine*. New York: Basic Books.

Wilding, P. (1982) *Professional Power and Social Welfare*. London: Routledge.

2 Regulatory Politics, Health Professionals, and the Public Interest

Rob Baggott

> The regulation of doctors obviously has its own special features. But to treat the regulation of the medical profession as simply something special to medicine is to miss a key feature: doctors are regulated in societies where numerous other occupations and markets are also regulated. (Moran and Wood 1993: 16)

The regulation of doctors and other health professionals in the United Kingdom and elsewhere must not be studied in isolation. To do so closes off important avenues of inquiry arising from studies of the regulatory process that employ a range of social science perspectives, including those of sociologists and economists. Political scientists, too, have a long-established interest in regulation. Their contribution, on which this chapter focuses, lies in the analysis of the processes of state intervention – in particular about how and why regulation occurs, and why regulatory systems change. They can help us to understand the barriers to effective regulation by studying how certain groups can resist regulation or, failing this, exert influence over the type of regulation adopted by the state. Furthermore, the study of regulation from a political science perspective can tell us much about how the state and other actors judge the public interest and how they manage democratic and populist pressures.

This chapter explores the politics of regulation and sets out a number of relevant analytical frameworks primarily with reference to the United Kingdom. It begins by seeking to clarify the concept of regulation and examines the controversy surrounding the term, before going on to examine theories and concepts pertaining to different styles and types of regulation. Finally, it considers various models that seek to explain the dynamics of regulatory change.

What is regulation?

Regulation has been defined as 'the activity by which the rules governing the exchange of goods and services are made and implemented' (Moran and Wood 1993: 17). Despite the appeal of such definitions, disagreement often occurs over the multi-faceted nature of regulation (see Mitnick 1980). As Baldwin and Cave (1999) point out, regulation has several different meanings. Narrowly, it is viewed as a specific set of commands in the form of rules applied by a body devoted to this purpose. In a wider sense it can be seen as deliberate state influence to control behaviour using a variety of instruments. Even more broadly, it can cover all forms of social control or influence, even those operating outside the boundaries of state institutions, such as markets and private organizations. Regulation is multi-faceted in another sense. It can apply to different dimensions of activity. For example, in their study of the medical profession, Moran and Wood (1993) identify four regulatory tasks covering different aspects of activity: market entry, competitive practices, market structures, and remuneration. Other dimensions of activity may also be addressed by regulation – for example, ethical standards and the quality of a product or service. Indeed, what constitutes a legitimate area of activity for regulation is open to dispute.

There is also much disagreement over what constitutes 'good regulation'. Although the standards by which regulation can be judged are widely acknowledged, there is conflict over the meaning of these principles, and over the priority that should be accorded to each, particularly when they conflict in practice. Baldwin and Cave (1999) identify several principles of regulation. First, regulatory systems should have a clear and legitimate purpose. Second, they should have an appropriate scheme of accountability, both to the public in general and to those who are regulated. Third, they should be fair, consistent, accessible and open. Fourth, they should operate with sufficient expertise. The fifth and final principle is that they should be efficient.

Although it is difficult to disagree with these principles, others have identified alternative benchmarks, which, although not radically different from those identified by Baldwin and Cave, emphasize different priorities. For example, the Better Regulation Taskforce (1999; 2000) has identified five principles against which regulation can be judged. First, transparency: a clear definition of powers and rules, clear guidance to those affected by regulation, consultation over regulatory proposals, and openness about any regulatory failure that may occur. Second, accountability: a clear mechanism of accountability to government, Parliament, the public and those who are being regulated, including an effective appeals systems for the latter. Third, targeting: a clear definition of goals, the targeting of regulatory efforts, the avoidance of universal approaches, flexibility of enforcement, and modification or elimination of regulations shown to be ineffective or outdated. Fourth, consistency: compatibility of written rules with the activities of other regulators and existing regulations, consistency with European Union and international trade policy, and consistency in enforcement by relevant authorities at local level. Fifth, proportionality: penalties for breaking rules should be appropriate, with measurement of the impact of regulation to establish the balance between risk and cost and the consideration of alternatives to state regulation.

Different priorities with regard to benchmarks reflect contrasting views about the aims and purposes of regulation. This makes it difficult to assess the impact of regulation because there are different value judgments about the criteria that should be used. Such conflicting viewpoints are also evident when concepts and theoretical positions relating to different styles and types of regulation are analysed.

Types of regulation

Much of the literature on regulation seeks to identify various types or 'styles' of regulation. There seem to be two main aims behind this line of inquiry. The first is to explain why particular regulatory approaches emerge in certain situations. Explanations may be historical: why did certain periods encourage specific types of regulation? They may be political: why do certain political systems appear to encourage certain types of regulation? Or they may be sectoral: why do regulatory styles vary according to the characteristics of economy and society? The second aim is to set out the advantages and disadvantages of the various types of regulation. Thus, the advantages and disadvantages of formal regulatory systems are often compared with informal styles of regulation in order to produce theoretical arguments in favour of one system over another.

Even so, this analysis is often much more complex than it at first appears. Self-regulation, which is often highlighted as a key feature of informal styles of regulation, can be highly formalized and may even be underpinned by statute. The regulation of health professionals exemplifies this. Most of the professions covered in this book were established by statute and carry out their self-regulatory functions within a legal framework. Moreover, as Baldwin and Cave (1999) have observed, the process of self-regulation may be constrained by government in the form of statutory rules; supervision by government agencies; government approval of rules; procedures for the public enforcement of self-regulatory rules; and the threat of direct intervention by the government (Baggott 1989). By the same token even formalized systems of direct regulation can involve a degree of self-regulation. There are many possible reasons for this, including the need to build consensus among those whose activities are being regulated in order to establish a higher degree of compliance and more generally to improve implementation and enforcement. In practice, then, self-regulation can and does operate within a broader framework of regulation. This is certainly evident in relation to health professions where other regulatory procedures – such as National Health Service complaints and disciplinary procedures, clinical audit and clinical governance – operate alongside professional self-regulatory systems (Allsop and Mulcahy 1996).

There has been considerable academic criticism of existing self-regulatory systems, which has also related to professions outside the health sector – including the legal profession (see, for example, Ogus 1997). The United Kingdom is seen as traditionally favouring self-regulation over more formalized systems (Baggott 1989), but, like many other institutional arrangements in this country, it has been criticized because of a perceived lack of openness and accountability, and doubts about its effectiveness. In contrast, academics from countries which have more formalized systems of regulation, such as the United States, have shown an interest in self-regulation because of its potential for improving the cost-effectiveness of regulation in certain areas. Indeed, in recent years self-regulation has been advocated in a North American context, with environmental protection being identified as one field where it might promote better regulatory outcomes (see, for instance, Vogel 1986). It is argued that self-regulation using codes of conduct, internal controls and negotiated agreements, harnesses the expertise and resources of those whose activities are being regulated in order to reduce pollution and associated problems such as global warming. Even so, the jury is still out on the relative effectiveness of self-regulation in this field (as illustrated by Segerson and Miceli 1998; Wu and Babcock 1999).

Similar debates about self-regulation have taken place on other public policy issues in recent years. Efforts have been made to test the theoretical claims discussed above, although there is continued disagreement on the significance of the findings. For example, on the subject of industrial health and safety, an academic debate rages on – with some arguing that self-regulation by firms has played an important role as a supplement to existing regulatory systems and should be encouraged to promote better health and safety outcomes. Thus, Kharbanda and Stallworthy (1991) suggest that regulatory systems should encourage greater self-regulation in their analysis of the chemical industry. Others are not so convinced and cast a more baleful eye over the evidence. Smith and Tombs (1995), for instance, claim that self-regulation has not improved the health and safety record in the most hazardous industries, and that in some respects – multiple fatality accidents, serious injuries and major disasters – outcomes have worsened. They highlight key failings of self-regulation – notably that it induces complacency – and call for a more punitive system of regulation in this field.

Another topical issue is the regulation of the internet. Concerns about the use of the internet for purposes connected with crime and pornography have generated demands in some quarters that this be subjected to direct regulation by government. But others argue that direct regulation represents an infringement of civil liberties. The fear of direct regulation, coupled with the difficulties of imposing an effective system in this field, has produced initiatives to promote self-regulation by the industry (Internet Law Policy Forum 2001). This debate again highlights the different arguments for and against self-regulation.

Arguments for and against self-regulation

Regimes which emphasize self-regulation and tend to have less formalized regulatory procedures are believed to have certain theoretical advantages and disadvantages compared with those which emphasize formal and direct regulation (see, for instance, Baldwin and Cave 1999; Baldwin et al. 2001). On the positive side, it is argued, first, that self-regulation is more effective because it enables 'insider knowledge' to be brought to bear on the problem. Those in the sector are held to be in the best position to decide on and enforce standards because of their superior technical knowledge. Second, self-regulation is felt to improve compliance because the regime is seen as more reasonable and acceptable to those being regulated. This is supposed to produce higher levels of trust between the regulated and the regulatory bodies than is the case with direct regulation. Third, self-regulation is relatively 'low cost', largely because of lower monitoring costs and greater flexibility and targeting in the application of rules. It is also believed to reduce the costs to government of maintaining systems of direct regulation, although in practice it is expected that some monitoring costs will fall on the state. Fourth, it is argued that self-regulation is flexible and responsive to new problems. It is assumed that self-regulatory bodies can act more quickly, partly because they do not have to pass additional legislation.

However, it has also been pointed out that self-regulatory systems have a number of disadvantages. First, they are seen as lacking legitimacy in a number of ways. The public may be cynical about their effectiveness and it is easy for the media to accuse them of bias and 'protecting their own'. Second, self-regulation may not be able to succeed in protecting the public particularly when the issues relate to the economic well-being or status of those being regulated. There are concerns too about the lack of public accountability of self-regulatory bodies, although, as will become clear later, there are ways in which this can be improved within a self-regulatory framework. Furthermore, self-regulation has to be acceptable to members of any self-regulatory regime. If it is not fully endorsed, they may not comply with it in practice. Finally, as noted earlier, even with self-regulation some costs will fall on the public purse, such as in approving and monitoring these arrangements.

These advantages and disadvantages have been presented from a standard 'public interest' or 'consumer' perspective. The balance of advantages and disadvantages may well be different when viewed from the perspective of those being regulated. Self-regulation may well be advantageous for those who wish to establish a 'light-touch' system, especially if this places a low-cost burden on them. However, if the loss of public confidence, trust and esteem follows, this may produce a more intrusive and costly system of regulation.

Recognizing that in practice systems of direct regulation and self-regulation operate alongside each other, another approach has been to reject a comparison of theoretical advantages and disadvantages and to focus instead on how self-regulation might contribute to improved outcomes. An important consideration here is the notion of 'compliance'. This can be measured by various indicators such as commitment to regulatory objectives, attitudes, work record, quality of management, organizational ability to comply, and the treatment of staff (Baldwin et al. 2001). The lesson appears to be to design systems of regulation that are appropriate, which promote compliance, while avoiding 'creative' compliance where those who are regulated are able to frustrate policy objectives while operating within the rules.

This illustrates a more general point. When it comes to regulation, as in politics generally, there is much pragmatism. Self-regulation tends to be seen as an appropriate intervention in sectors where knowledge is highly specialized and technical; where markets are fragmented (that is, there are a large number of small operators making it difficult for external bodies to regulate); where the environment is fast-moving; and where there is a broad range of stakeholders with varying interests (Better Regulation Task Force 2000). Another factor affecting regulation is the political influence of the industry or profession being regulated. In the past self-regulation has undoubtedly been a privilege granted to powerful interests by the state and has favoured elite groups and those that are well organized. Even in countries that have generally adopted more formalized regulatory systems, there will tend to be an element of self-regulation in sectors where these conditions hold. Moreover, in such sectors, pressures will tend to promote reform rather than the abolition of self-regulatory systems.

Self-regulation and the professions

The above conditions are found in the field of health professional regulation, where the pace of technological change and the levels of technical knowledge are particularly relevant factors. As Baldwin et al. (2001: 5) have observed, 'areas of professional judgement present special problems of risk management and special problems for "command" or rule based, regimes of control'. They add that 'professionals often make decisions that are of high importance, low visibility and high discretion' and that professionals are protective of their domains of judgement and resist efforts to control by the imposition of rules. They go on to argue that professional regulation should emphasize openness, peer review, incentives, training, self-appraisal and collective approaches to improve standards in the context of an understanding of the cultural context.

Nonetheless, there is a strong current of opinion that the traditionally closed world of self-regulation is no longer tenable for professions operating in the health and other fields. In this context, a report from the National Consumer Council (1999a) argued that self-regulation must be able to command public confidence and should operate within a public law framework. This report also set out several principles of fairness as a means of judging self-regulatory systems. These included the following. First, there should be a strong external element built in to the design and operation of self-regulatory schemes. Second, there should be full representation of consumers and outsiders in the self-regulatory body. Third, self-regulatory schemes should be separated from the institutions of the industry as far as practicable. Fourth, there should be a clear statement of principles and standards – normally a Code of Practice. Fifth, there should be clear, accessible, well-publicized complaints procedures to deal with breaches of the Code. Sixth, there should be adequate sanctions for breaching the Code. Seventh, provision should be made for maintaining and updating the self-regulatory system and for reporting annually on the operation of the scheme.

Notably, a subsequent report from the National Consumer Council (1999b) specifically relating to the regulation of health professions made similar points, arguing for greater transparency and openness in the regulatory procedures. It also argued for more co-ordination to produce a more integrated system of regulation. In particular, it claimed that this would involve clarifying and improving the links between statutory professional self-regulation and other procedures such as discipline, complaints and clinical governance. The report also called for improved lay representation, leading in the medium term to up to a minimum of 50 per cent lay and consumer membership of the Councils of each regulatory body. Furthermore, it recommended that each Council should have a lay or consumer chair.

On the one hand, therefore, while there are strong arguments for retaining self-regulation for health professionals, these systems will have to be reformed and perhaps subjected to a greater degree of external regulation than has been the case in the past. Certainly this is reflected in the current Labour government's policy, which in the health field combines a raft of new monitoring, standard-setting, assessment and regulatory bodies with a commitment to strengthen existing systems of self-regulation. But what factors lie behind these trends in regulation? This brings the chapter neatly on to a discussion of the emergence of regulatory systems and their subsequent reform, particularly in the context of the United Kingdom.

Theories of regulatory origin and change

As Baldwin and Cave (1999) have observed, the origin and development of regulation can be explained with reference to five conceptual frameworks: private interest theories, public interest theories, interest group theories, ideas and ideologies, and institutional theories. This is used as a basis for the following discussion, focusing particularly on explanations of regulatory origin and development in the health professions.

Private interest theories

According to Stigler (1971), industries and occupations have a clear incentive to seek regulation in order to raise barriers to entry and reduce competition. As he stated, 'every industry or occupation that has enough political power to utilise the state will seek to control entry' (Stigler 1971: 5). At first sight, the logic seems unassailable. It appears to explain why pressure for regulation often comes from those who wish to see off potential competitors through protection of product definitions or title, or through the prohibition of unlicensed providers. This is not confined to 'big business'. With specific regard to the regulation of health care, it has been argued that regulation has placed a higher value on the protection of professional privileges, status and incomes, than the protection of the public. For example, the 1858 Medical Act, which gave birth to the General Medical Council, was initiated in an effort to protect the professional claims of medical practitioners and protected their use of this title. Stacey (1992: 20) observes that 'it seems clear that the impetus came from medicine – it was a desire to create circumstances in which their income and status could be improved that led medical men to press for reform of medical regulation'. However, it should be noted that such sentiments are rarely articulated explicitly. Professionals and businesses generally argue that regulation will protect the consumer or client by keeping out the 'charlatans', 'cowboys' or 'rogue traders'. Indeed, public protection was frequently cited in the debates for medical regulation during the nineteenth century, and is still the main argument overtly employed for regulatory reform in contemporary debates.

The self-interest perspective is rooted in a fundamentally cynical view of the professions as reflected in the often-quoted aphorism of George Bernard Shaw that 'all professions are conspiracies against the laity' (Shaw 1932: 106). This had earlier echoes in Adam Smith's equally famous observation that 'people of the same trade seldom meet together, even for merriment and diversion, but the conversation ends in a conspiracy against the public or in some contrivance to raise prices' (Smith 1970: 232). This perspective is also relevant to notions of 'regulatory capture', which recognize that there is an economic incentive for private interests not only to seek regulation but to ensure that its practice is consistent with their priorities (see Bernstein 1955). Some have applied this specifically to health care, arguing that medicine in particular – and, by implication, other health professions too – have sought to control education, training and expertise in an attempt to limit the supply of doctors and raise incomes (see Green 1985; Gladstone 1992). As far as the dangers of regulatory capture are concerned, the fact that health professional regulation has been predominantly self-regulatory is offered as *prima facie* evidence that regulation has been conducted primarily for the benefit of these professions.

Certainly there is much in the sociology of the professions to support this notion of control. A major theme in the sociological study of the health professions has been a desire of such groups to secure control over the substance of their own work (see Freidson 1970). Similarly, the current efforts of complementary and alternative therapists to promote statutory regulatory bodies in Britain, described by Saks later in this volume, could be interpreted in the same way (see also Saks 1999). But to seek to secure control over the substance of one's work is not necessarily rooted wholly in self-interest. As will be seen, the health professions have viewed themselves, and to some extent have been given the right to view themselves, as the legitimate judges of the public interest in relation to standards of care. It is far too crude to equate this purely with the self-interested pursuit of economic gains. To do so neglects important ethical values. Sir Donald Irvine (1997), the President of the General Medical Council, has talked of 'a vocational commitment to put patients first'. The Code of Practice for nurses, health visitors and midwives also states that practitioners 'shall act, at all times, in such a manner as to ... safeguard and promote the interests of individual patients and clients' (UKCC 1992). Authors such as Stone in her later chapter in this book may argue that such vocational commitments are no more than ideals or aspirations. Nonetheless, the ethical dimension of the health care professions is an important consideration that cannot be easily disregarded when examining regulatory processes in this field.

Public interest theories

From this perspective, regulation is introduced and developed as a result of the pursuit of the public interest. This, however, begs another set of questions surrounding the concept of the public interest itself. While there is no agreed definition, a number of different approaches can be identified (see, for example, Saks 1995). From a populist perspective, the public interest can be seen as the view of the majority, expressed through mechanisms that clearly reflect public preferences at a variety of levels and stages in the decision-making process. In contrast, from a paternalist perspective, the public interest is interpreted by elites that believe they can legitimately gauge the public interest. In reality this may not be a single elite; there may be competition between various 'interpreters' of the public interest.

Certainly, as far as the United Kingdom is concerned, the paternalist rather than the democratic model has undoubtedly predominated in the field of professional regulation, although populist pressures have become more evident in recent decades. Decisions about the regulation of health professions have tended to be issued by the government of the day, but were in practice determined largely by the self-regulatory bodies themselves. That the professions were the best judge of the public interest continued through to the Committee of Inquiry into Medical Regulation, chaired by Sir Alec Merrison (Merrison Committee 1975). This endorsed self-regulation on two grounds: that it provided a contract between the public and the profession guaranteeing satisfactory treatment; and that only doctors were capable of judging the standards of professional conduct. It should be noted that other professions in health care have also been granted a certain amount of autonomy by the state on similar grounds in regulating professional conduct, training and registration, including nursing (Davies and Beach 2000).

The paternalistic nature of professional regulation therefore has a long history. The point has been made that self-regulation, particularly in the United Kingdom, was closely associated with an elite approach to regulatory matters based on the 'gentlemen's agreements' and self-discipline that emerged in the Victorian period, associated with the rise of the professions (Perkin 1989). The relative decline in the political influence of the traditional professions, along with the fragmentation of the informal elite networks that supported this regulatory approach, could partly explain the declining appeal of informal self-regulation as an instrument of government in the United Kingdom today (Paxman 1991). Furthermore, as Moran notes in this volume, this form of self-regulation was vulnerable partly because of the movement away from the oligarchic political system that created it. In recent times, there has been an increasing level of public concern about the effectiveness of these regulatory systems, a view articulated by elite groups, particularly the media. The media has played a crucial role in airing concerns about seriously deficient practice in both medicine and nursing – alerting the public to cases of poor, and in some cases dangerous, practice. In the 1970s and 1980s this prompted Parliament to seek to widen the scope for General Medical Council investigations (see Stacey 1992).

Although new measures to deal with seriously deficient practice were eventually introduced, the media and Parliamentary interest in professional regulation in the health field has continued unabated in the light of further scandals. This added to pressure on government and the regulatory bodies to initiate further reform, as highlighted in this book by Allsop. It should be noted that other professional groups were not insulated from this heightened media interest. As Davies and Beach (2000) have observed, there was a definite growth in media interest in nurse regulation from the late 1980s. A number of controversial cases where nurses were restored to the register despite having earlier committed serious criminal acts led to public criticism, as well as to criticism from within the nursing profession itself. Growing media interest was not the only factor that added to the pressures for reform. Parliament was also taking a greater interest in these matters, and the closer scrutiny of quality of care issues in turn forced ministers and civil servants to take a more careful look at the performance of the self-regulatory system. The rise of organized health consumer groups representing the interests of patients and the general public was a further factor too, as we shall see shortly.

As a result, the traditional view of the public interest, which was largely based on the judgement of professional elites, has been challenged. Nowadays, even though the level of trust in doctors and other health professionals by the public remains high relative to other professions and trades, it has been accepted that professionals should not be the sole judges of what is in the public interest (Davies 1999). But even with greater lay involvement, the health professional elites are still in a very powerful position to judge standards and interpret the public interest.

Interest group theories

Regulation can be seen as emerging from concerns about the public interest. However, a third approach views regulation as resulting from the interaction of various stakeholders within a pluralist framework. In today's health care context it is recognized that these stakeholders should include service users and the public as well as the health professions. But this is a fairly recent development. As many commentators have noted, professional regulation in health care in the past was primarily the product of forces within and between professional groups. The dynamics of the regulation of nursing (Abel-Smith 1960) and midwifery (Donnison 1988), for example, were shaped by the political battles within these professions and by their relationship with the medical profession which sought to control and restrict their area of practice (Salter 1995). Davies and Beach (2000) describe the 'intense professional disunity' which accompanied the introduction of the United Kingdom Central Council for Nursing, Midwifery and Health Visiting in 1979 and the associated intra-professional compromises. The chapter on nursing by Davies in this volume also exposes the more recent internal tensions involved in the latest review of the profession.

Similarly, the regulation of doctors was the product of pressures within the profession which arose from tensions between different factions (such as hospital consultants, general practitioners, public health doctors, junior doctors, and overseas doctors) and different institutions (such as the British Medical Association, the Royal Colleges, the Medical Schools, and the General Medical Council itself). This was reflected in not only the legal regulatory framework, but also the practice of regulation. As Moran (1999: 103) notes, 'it sometimes seemed that the General Medical Council's conception of misconduct was concerned more with how doctors treated each other than with how they treated their patients'. Moreover, according to Stacey (1992), the pressure to reform the Council during the 1970s was largely the result of intra-professional tensions within medicine. There were several issues, including the irritation felt by general practitioners by their under-representation on the General Medical Council and the discontent felt by junior doctors and consultants located outside London. A 'professional revolt' was then triggered by a decision to introduce an annual retention fee for doctors to remain on the medical register. This culminated in an inquiry into the regulation of the medical profession by the Merrison Committee (1975) which, as earlier noted, reaffirmed the principle of self-regulation.

The regulatory politics of the 1980s, however, was different from the previous decade, being strongly influenced by consumer pressures. In this context, Salter (1995) notes that the privileges of the medical profession, which gave it a key role in the allocation of health care resources and the maintenance of service standards, came under challenge. This arose mainly as a result of its unique access to medical knowledge and the growing assertiveness of patients. Moran (1999: 107) agrees, arguing that the form of regulation adopted by doctors, which marginalized clinical treatment issues, was 'not sustainable in a democracy, especially in a democracy where patients were becoming daily more informed, better educated and more self confident'. This growing assertiveness operated on a collective, as well as an individual, level. As Stacey (1992) observes, the rise of patients' groups was a key factor in effecting change, alongside the ascendancy of radical right ideology. Watkins (1987), too, notes the importance of the emerging patients' movement in putting the health professions on the defensive.

Certainly the reform of regulatory systems in the past two decades has emphasized the protection of the public, rather than the protection of professional interests. This has been illustrated by the fact that, for much of the 1980s and 1990s, the General Medical Council has been under siege. The General Medical Council survived, although it had to make major concessions. As Moran (1999: 109) has noted, the net effect was that the last two decades of the twentieth century saw 'an acceleration in the pace at which the enclosed regulatory world of medical government was invaded by agencies of the state'. Nursing, midwifery and health visiting experienced similar pressures and their regulatory bodies have also had to react to a changing environment. Although the disciplinary processes of the United Kingdom Central Council for Nursing, Midwifery and Health Visiting were regarded more highly by consumer representatives than the General Medical Council, the low level of lay representation was criticized. The Central Council responded by establishing a panel of consumers – and from 1994 consumer representatives were engaged in professional conduct work (Davies and Beach 2000).

One way forward in dealing with the conflicts between professional and other interests, including those of consumers, is to incorporate all those with a stake in the outcome and to create an effective dialogue between the different parties. This makes explicit the various interests and perspectives that exist in the field of health care regulation and places a premium on resolving tensions and conflicts through deliberative practices. Davies (2000) has expounded this idea of stakeholder regulation and has discussed various organizational arrangements that can facilitate such dialogue – including citizens' juries, forums, consensus conferences, standing panels, mediation, conflict resolution, and changes to education and training. Notions of stakeholder empowerment are undoubtedly exerting a strong influence on the direction of regulatory reform at present. This is exemplified by plans to increase lay representation on professional regulatory bodies, although the impact of these ideas on dialogue and decision making remains to be seen. This brings us to a broader discussion of the influence of ideas and ideologies on regulatory reform.

Ideas and ideologies

Several ideas have exerted an influence on regulation in recent years. During the 1980s New Right ideology was a crucial factor. This ideology, espoused by the Conservative governments of the 1980s and 1990s, emphasized the role of markets; valued the private sector over the public sector; called for competition and deregulation; endorsed stronger performance management within the public sector; and championed consumerism over producer power (Alaszewski 1995). However, the tensions inherent in this ideology, not to mention the practical and political difficulties of redrawing the boundaries of the modern state meant that pragmatic choices often had to be made. Where elite, populist and ideological factors conjoined, political initiatives tended to emerge. So media and Parliamentary pressures, coupled with public concern and government hostility to the public sector professions, produced a powerful drive towards a policy that heralded a much more serious assault on the privileges of self-regulation than had hitherto been thought possible.

This assault continued under New Labour. The Blair government has sought to strengthen the management and monitoring of the professions, emphasizing the importance of transparency of professional regulatory arrangements; improving professional accountability to the public and the health service; and involving lay people as stakeholders in the regulatory process. Up to a point these policies are a product of similar pressures from the media, public and Parliament faced by the Thatcher and Major governments. But their ideological underpinnings are different in several respects. The Third Way approach, espoused by the current government, emphasizes user empowerment, democratic renewal, social inclusion, stakeholding, and communitarian notions of active citizenship (see Hutton 1996; Giddens 1998). In many respects these ideas pose a far more serious challenge to existing systems of professional regulation because of the justification they provide for genuine user involvement and greater professional accountability. Further ideological impetus is provided by the Blair government's commitment to 'modernization'. This principle, which reflects a desire to sweep away traditional ways of doing things, is clearly a further threat to longstanding regulatory systems such as those operated by the professions.

Another idea influencing the field of professional regulation is the notion of the risk society. According to writers such as Beck (1992) and Giddens (1991), we live in a society that increasingly appreciates the scale of risk and seeks to control it. This general idea has permeated many areas of regulation and is reflected in principles of public policy. It has also penetrated the specific area of professional regulation (see Baldwin et al. 2001). Increasingly too, proposed reforms are discussed in terms of protecting patients or reducing risks, thus adding further impetus to efforts to strengthen regulatory systems and provide reassurance to the public.

Institutional politics

This brings us to the fifth and final approach to the analysis of regulatory origin and development, which focuses on institutional politics. At one level this concerns the operation of individual regulatory institutions, including health professions themselves. At another level it relates to the relationship between regulatory institutions. Important too in analyzing this area from the viewpoint of institutional politics is the relationship between regulators and the public on the one hand, and the regulators and the regulated, on the other.

The study of the internal politics of regulatory bodies can produce great insights into the dynamics of regulation. The chapters in Part Two of this book clearly document some of the tensions between elite bodies within professional groups in the United Kingdom. Other regulatory authorities have also had an impact. Membership of the European Union, for example, has exposed some of the United Kingdom's professional regulatory practices to criticism. The system of specialist medical training and accreditation was reformed, for example, following a decision that it discriminated against doctors qualifying in Europe and was therefore in breach of European law. It was once argued with some justification that the United Kingdom's involvement in Europe would lead to more direct regulation, and in particular less self-regulation (Baggott 1989). However, as Baldwin and Cave (1999: 162) note, self-regulation – albeit of a more formalized variety – has actually been encouraged as a means of implementing European Union directives.

In this context, it should be stressed that the international dimension of regulation is becoming ever more important. States often look abroad for solutions to their own regulatory problems. Thus the decision to introduce a form of reaccreditation for doctors in the United Kingdom raised interest in how other countries handled this. In regulation, as in other areas of public policy, there is a capacity for learning from the experiences of others.

A final point regarding institutional politics concerns the accountability of health professional regulators. There have long been concerns about the regulatory bodies' lack of public accountability (Pollitt 1984). Over the last two decades this has been turned against these institutions. As Baeza (1999: 115) puts it: 'It has been the regulatory bodies' apparent inertia, lack of transparency and effectiveness in the field of managing poor performance that has in general led to the media vilification of health professionals.' In this regard, as has already been noted, much of the present agenda of reform in this field has centred upon accountability and transparency of regulatory processes.

Conclusion

The main intention of this chapter has been to relate particular issues concerning the regulation of health care professions to broader concepts of the regulatory process identified by political scientists. This has provided a useful framework for discussing key regulatory issues in the field of health professional regulation and shed some light on the dynamics of regulatory change. It has also provided a background to controversial debates about the nature of 'good regulation' and the choices between different regulatory regimes.

The lessons to be drawn are, first, that because of the different meanings of regulation, one must be clear what is meant by the term when using it. Second, when analyzing the impact of regulation one must be aware of the different priorities accorded to the various benchmarks for assessing its effectiveness. Third, one must appreciate that, despite the theoretical 'polarization' of self-regulation and direct regulation, most regulatory regimes are in practice a mixture of both. Fourth, although there is no single explanation of regulatory change, the five approaches outlined here help to identify key factors for further detailed analysis. In the case of the health professions, a range of factors has shaped regulation. These include contemporary political ideas, demands for greater accountability and openness articulated by the media, MPs, consumer pressure groups, tensions between and within professional groups, and finally relationships between the various regulatory institutions themselves.

References

Abel-Smith, B. (1960) *A History of the Nursing Profession*. London: Heinemann.

Alaszewski, A. (1995) 'Restructuring health and welfare professions in the United Kingdom: The impact of internal markets on the medical, nursing and social work professions', in T. Johnson, G. Larkin and M. Saks (eds) *Health Professions and the State in Europe*. London: Routledge.

Allsop, J. and Mulcahy, L. (1996) *Regulating Medical Work: Formal and Informal Controls*. Buckingham: Open University Press.

Baeza, J. (1999) 'Self-regulation of health professions: the need for a coherent framework', in J. Appleby and A. Harrison (eds) *Health Care UK 1999/2000*. London: King's Fund.

Baggott, R. (1989) 'Regulatory reform in Britain: The changing face of self-regulation', *Public Administration*, 67: 435–54.

Baldwin R. and Cave, M. (1999) *Understanding Regulation: Theory, Strategy and Practice*. Oxford: Oxford University Press.

Baldwin, R., Hutter, B. and Rothstein, H. (2001) *Risk Regulation, Management and Compliance: A Report to the BRI Inquiry* (unpublished report).

Beck ,U. (1992) *The Risk Society*. London: Sage.

Bernstein, M. (1955) *Regulating Business by Independent Commission*. Princeton, New Jersey: Princeton University Press.

Better Regulation Task Force (1999) *Self Regulation: Interim Report*. London: Cabinet Office.

Better Regulation Task Force (2000) *Alternatives to State Regulation*. London: Cabinet Office.

Davies, C. (1999) 'Rethinking regulation in the health professions in the UK: Institutions, ideals and identities', in I. Hellberg, M. Saks and C. Benoit (eds) *Professional Identities in Transition: Cross-Cultural Dimensions*. Södertälje: Almqvist & Wiksell International.

Davies, C. (2000) 'Professional self-regulation: Is there an alternative?', *Stakeholder Regulation: A Discussion Paper*. London: Royal College of Nursing.

Davies, C. and Beach, A. (2000) *Interpreting Professional Self-Regulation: A History of the United Kingdom Central Council for Nursing, Midwifery and Health Visiting.* London: Routledge.

Donnison, J. (1988) *Midwives and Medical Men.* London: Historical Publications.

Freidson, E. (1970) *Profession of Medicine: A Study in the Sociology of Applied Knowledge.* New York: Dodd, Mead & Co.

Giddens, A. (1991) *Modernity and Self-Identity: Self and Society in the Late Modern Age.* Cambridge: Polity Press.

Giddens, A. (1998) *The Third Way: The Renewal of Social Democracy.* Cambridge: Polity Press.

Gladstone, D. (1992) *Opening up the Medical Monopoly.* London: Adam Smith Institute.

Green, D. (1985) *Which Doctor? A Critical Analysis of the Professional Barriers to Competition in Health Care.* London: Institute for Economic Affairs.

Hutton, W. (1996) *The State We're In.* London: Verso.

Internet Law Policy Forum (2001) 'ILPF announces self regulation initiative', www.ilpr.org/selfreg/announce.htm.

Irvine, D. (1997) 'The performance of doctors I: Professionalism and self-regulation in a changing world', *British Medical Journal*, 314: 1540–2.

Kharbanda, O. and Stallworthy, E. (1991) 'Industrial disasters: Will self-regulation work?', *Long Range Planning*, 24: 84–9.

Merrison Committee (1975) *Report of the Committee of Inquiry into Regulation of the Medical Profession.* London: HMSO.

Mitnick, B. (1980) *The Political Economy of Regulation: Creating, Designing and Dismantling Regulatory Forms.* New York: Columbia University Press.

Moran, M. (1999) *Governing the Health Care State.* Manchester: Manchester University Press.

Moran, M. and Wood, B. (1993) *States, Regulation and the Medical Profession.* Buckingham: Open University Press.

National Consumer Council (1999a) *Models of Self-Regulation: An Overview of Models in Business and the Professionss.* London: NCC.

National Consumer Council (1999b) *Self-Regulation of Professionals in Health Care: Consumer Issues.* London: NCC.

Ogus, A. (1997) 'Self-regulation', in B. Bouckaert and G. De Geest (eds) *Encyclopaedia of Law and Economics*, vol. 5. Aldershot: Edward Elgar.

Paxman, J. (1991) *Friends in High Places: Who Runs Britain?* Harmondsworth: Penguin.

Perkin, H. (1989) *The Rise of Professional Society.* London: Routledge.

Pollitt, C. (1984) 'Professionals and public policy', *Public Administration Bulletin*, 44: 29–46.

Saks, M. (1995) *Professions and the Public Interest: Medical Power, Altruism and Alternative Medicine.* London: Routledge.

Saks, M. (1999) 'The wheel turns? Professionalization and alternative medicine in Britain', *Journal of Interprofessional Care*, 13: 129–38.

Salter, B. (1995) *The Politics of Change in the Health Service.* Basingstoke: Macmillan.

Segerson, K. and Miceli, T. (1998) 'Voluntary environmental agreements: Good or bad news for environmental protection?', *Journal of Environmental Economics and Management*, 36: 109–30.

Shaw, G.B. (1932) *The Doctor's Dilemma.* London: Constable & Co.

Smith, A. (1970) *The Wealth of Nations.* Harmondsworth: Penguin.

Smith, D. and Tombs, S. (1995) 'Beyond self-regulation: towards a critique for self-regulation as a control strategy for hazardous activities', *Journal of Management Studies*, 32: 619–37.

Stacey, M. (1992) *Regulating British Medicine: The General Medical Council.* Chichester: John Wiley & Sons.

Stigler, G. (1971) 'The theory of economic regulation', *Bell Journal of Economics and Management Science*, 2 (Spring): 3–21.

UKCC (1992) *Code of Professional Conduct.* London: United Kingdom Central Council for Nursing, Midwifery and Health Visiting.

Vogel, D. (1986) *National Styles of Regulation: Environmental Policy in Great Britain and the United States.* London: Cornell University Press.

Watkins, S. (1987) *Medicine and Labour: The Politics of a Profession.* London: Lawrence & Wishart.

Wu, J. and Babcock, B. (1999) 'The relative efficiency of voluntary versus mandatory environmental regulations', *Journal of Environmental Economics and Management*, 38: 158–75.

3 Legal Aspects of the Regulation of the Health Professions

David Price

To 'regulate' incorporates the notion of being controlled by means of rules, and consequently implies the potential for regulation from many quarters. Stone and Matthews (1996: 37) comment that:

> If regulation can be defined in simple terms as the means by which control is exercised over the exchange of goods and services in society, then the practice of medicine has been regulated for centuries. Today, medicine is one of the most highly regulated of all economic and social activities in Britain.

Indeed, it is increasingly necessary to have regard to the bigger picture and the interacting and interlocking facets of regulation in analysing the health professions. In so doing, the inquirer needs to look beyond the boundaries of particular professional organizational frameworks – to external as opposed merely to internal processes of regulation.

Self-regulation has traditionally been pervasive among the health professions in the United Kingdom. It has been defined by the Better Regulation Task Force (1999: 3) as:

> the means by which members of a profession, trade or commercial activity are bound by a mutually agreed set of rules which govern their relationship with the citizen, client or customer. Such rules may be accepted voluntarily or may be compulsory.

In Chapter 2 in this volume, Baggott rightly emphasizes that self-regulation operates within a wider framework of regulation. Artificial boundaries with regard to the delivery of health care, between health and social care, the public and private sector and primary and secondary care, and between different professional groupings, are progressively being seen as arbitrary. They may impede efficiency and quality of delivery and create the potential for risk to patient safety through variability between, and gaps in, regulatory structures. These issues will be examined in this chapter from a legal perspective.

Regulatory models and their meaning

Within the United Kingdom a very large measure of freedom has been accorded historically to health care professionals in terms of establishing themselves in a clinical setting, and practising autonomously. This is highlighted by the breadth of the Common Law right to practise in this country. In this regard, the Report of the House of Lords Select Committee on Science and Technology (2000: para. 5.9) on complementary and alternative medicine stated that:

> The Common Law right to practise medicine means that in the United Kingdom anyone can treat a sick person even if they have no training in any type of healthcare whatsoever, provided that the individual treated has given an informed consent [although] ... persons exercising this right must not identify themselves by any of the titles protected by statute and they cannot prescribe medicines that are regulated prescription-only drugs. ... The Common Law right to practise springs from the fundamental principle that everyone can choose the form of healthcare that they require.

However, if a person without any medical training conveys the impression, whether deliberately or not, that a procedure has a medical purpose when this is not the case, this will amount to a criminal and civil assault by virtue of the lack of such an adequate consent.[1]

By contrast, in many other jurisdictions, legal provisions are focused on specific spheres of practice. In Belgium, for instance, Article 38 of the Law on the Practice of Medicine stipulates that it is an offence to carry out in an habitual way an act or acts that belong to the field of medicine either without holding the required diploma, or without being legally exempted from it. This approach also applies to nursing and paramedical professional activity. In Ontario in Canada, too, legislation defines specific clinical activities that can only be undertaken by specified professions or persons authorized by the relevant professional bodies. These prescriptions display varying levels of specificity, and in turn dictate the amount of autonomy for practitioners to define task boundaries. There is only a handful of examples of such 'exclusivity' embedded in United Kingdom law. One example is that under the 1984 Dentists Act dentists alone are permitted to practise or hold themselves out as practising, or being prepared to practise, 'dentistry'. It is also an offence under the 1997 Nurses, Midwives and Health Visitors Act for anyone other than a qualified midwife or a registered medical practitioner (with some exceptions for trainees) to attend a woman in childbirth other than in emergency circumstances.

In sum, there has been a general reluctance in the United Kingdom to regulate specific areas of activity, as opposed to professional groupings that award titles and maintain a professional register. It is crucial to understanding the basis of the legal regulation of the health professions to note the distinction between these two alternative strategies. This can again be illustrated with reference to complementary and alternative medicine. In giving evidence to the House of Lords Select Committee on Science and Technology (2000: para. 5.31), the General Osteopathic Council stated that there is:

a difference between a restriction of title and a functional closure. We have, under the Osteopaths Act, a protection of title only, so it is possible for members of the medical profession or physiotherapists to use osteopathic techniques provided they do not hold themselves to be an osteopathic practitioner. ... it was felt at the time of the Act going through parliament that it would be inappropriate and, indeed, impossible to produce a functional closure.

A functional closure will tend to 'freeze' in time activities that are the province of relevant professional groups, such as the 'field of medicine', and consequently is not necessarily a favourable state of affairs. JM Consulting (1998: 45), in reporting on the regulation of nurses, midwives and health visitors, considered that:

protection of function is necessarily restrictive and inflexible, and is only appropriate where functions can be defined in an unambiguous way; are unlikely to change; and it is accepted by all interests that the functions are not likely to become appropriate for others to undertake.

It is certainly not conducive to fluidity in terms of the allocation of tasks and roles, and may emphasize professional boundaries that inhibit multidisciplinary team working. Indeed, it runs counter to the recent declaration of the government that it is 'committed to expanding the roles which allied health professions play in health and social care, ensuring that they can use their skills flexibly, and creatively to the benefit of the patient' (Department of Health 2000a: 5).

This flexibility in the division of labour is also set out in *The NHS Plan* (Department of Health 2000b) and is designed to improve cost-effectiveness and enhance patient safety. Indeed, it is in this spirit that the government has fostered the growth of primary care and integrated home care teams to help people live independently and avoid hospitalization. The philosophy also underpins the encouragement given to staff in the National Health Service to develop competency-based frameworks, rather than work plans organized around traditional professional roles. There is already substantial fluidity in professional roles and functions in practice and a growing range of health care professionals have been given new powers to prescribe through the Health and Social Care Act 2001. These go beyond the powers currently conferred upon doctors, dentists, midwives, health visitors and certain specified nurses. There will be a shift in the role of pharmacists from simply dispensing medicines to planning individual drug therapies, as well as the delegation of a number of traditional nursing functions to nursing auxiliaries and other health support workers.

In the United Kingdom there is an emphasis on the professional register and the protection of title. This has limitations in terms of patient protection, which are accentuated by the move towards flexible working. The House of Lords Select Committee on Science and Technology (2000: para. 5.31) comments that:

one of the main advantages of statutory regulation, protection of title, is not as clear-cut as it may seem. Although statutory regulation does provide protection of title, the common law right to practise medicine means that anyone can use the techniques of a therapy, even if it is statutorily regulated, as long as they do not identify themselves by using the title which is protected.

To illustrate this, the Select Committee noted that some former osteopathic practitioners, refused registration under the Act, now practise as osteomyologists or cranio-sacral practitioners without impediment. Nurses removed from the register have also been known to reappear as health support workers. Moreover, while National Health Service employers are obliged in relation to most statutorily regulated professional groups to employ only registered professionals, this does not apply to private sector employers.

The 'privilege' of professional self-regulation

The concept of professional self-regulation in the United Kingdom warrants exploration. During the debates on the Health Bill in the House of Commons Standing Committee, Philip Hammond asserted that: 'One of the great foundations on which our liberal democracy is built is the existence of self-regulating professions that have, by and large, served the country well over the years.' However, as other chapters in this volume highlight, in the last few years this concept has increasingly been viewed as self-serving and designed to promote the interests of professionals rather than the public. Self-regulation has also been called to account as a result of a significant loss of public confidence arising from the Ledward, Shipman and other affairs described more fully later in this volume. Indeed, the number of complaints to the General Medical Council regarding doctors rose threefold between 1993 and 1998, while the number of complaints to both the General Medical Council and the United Kingdom Central Council for Nursing, Midwifery and Health Visiting rose by 50 per cent between 1999 and 2000 (GMC 2001a; GMC 2001b).

The government's response has been to promote change within the self-regulatory framework, but not to abandon its belief in the appropriateness of the traditional regulatory model. The Health Minister Lord Hunt recently asserted that: 'Modernising and strengthening professional regulation is central to our overall strategy to modernise the NHS.'[2] Attention has focused instead on the piecemeal nature of the regulatory canvas as a whole and deficiencies of individual regulatory regimes. In this regard, the National Consumer Council (1999) was scathing about the diversity of self-regulatory schemes. It stated that:

> In our examination of the current regulatory system, we found a patchwork of varying arrangements for different professions, differences in regulation between public and independent sectors and legislation governing many regulatory bodies which has not caught up with changes in public demand or with current health care practices. (National Consumer Council 1999: 1)

There are various glaring anomalies, inconsistencies and gaps. Whereas, for instance, maxillo-facial surgeons may be subject to the regimes of two regulatory frameworks – that of the General Medical Council and the General Dental Council – emerging professions such as operating department practitioners with responsibility for direct patient care, and health support workers, may have no regulatory framework whatsoever.

Such self-regulatory frameworks that do exist may be either voluntary or statutorily underpinned, with the historical trend being evolution from the former to the latter on a more or less gradual basis. Indeed, the House of Lords Select Committee on Science and Technology (2000), reporting on complementary and alternative medicine, regarded robust voluntary self-regulation as a prerequisite for statutory self-regulation. It saw the main purpose of regulation of any health care profession as being to protect the public from unqualified or inadequately trained practitioners. In these terms, statutory self-regulation of certain occupational groups, such as medical photographers, has sometimes been resisted on the basis of an absence of a significant potential for harm to patients. But where patient protection is a significant concern, is voluntary rather than statutory regulation sufficient?

JM Consulting (1998: 42) observes in its report on nurses, midwives and health visitors that:

> Statutory self-regulation is a strong mechanism in protecting the public, but it is also heavy-handed and cumbersome. History has generally found it to be inflexible, and it can limit development. It is restrictive to individuals, employers and public. It provides a barrier to individuals' choice of work, and restricted choice also places burdens on employers. It is costly (especially in terms of members' time). It should only be used when other provisions are not adequate.

This perception is largely a product of the fact that historically self-interest has resulted in anti-competitive policies and practices, and hindrances to necessary changes in statutory regulation. The House of Lords Select Committee on Science and Technology (2000) ultimately considers the type of regulation to be less important than whether the regulation is delivered effectively by a single regulatory body. However, it argues that there are various advantages of statutory regulation, including that it has the force of law to ensure that its aims are fulfilled. The Committee concludes that it is desirable for therapies that have high inherent risk.

This viewpoint is supported by the Working Party on Chiropractic (1993: 19) which observed that:

> voluntary registering organisations have no effective sanction against unlicensed, untrained practitioners, or against a practitioner who is adjudged to be guilty of unacceptable professional conduct. A voluntary registering body cannot prevent an unlicensed or professionally negligent practitioner from continuing to practice even though it is against the interests of patients for him or her to do so.

The National Consumer Council (1999) has also vigorously asserted that voluntary regulatory arrangements are inadequate for the health professions to enforce standards and protect patients. The benefits of statutory regulation are further reinforced by the fact that the statutory foundation of a regulatory scheme signals that a direct democratic mandate has been extended to the professional body concerned. This provides a proper basis for the 'contract with society' concept espoused by the Merrison Report (1975) on the regulation of the medical profession.

Statutory self-regulation models can be traced back quite some way, from the 1815 Apothecaries Act and the 1852 Pharmacy Act to the first comprehensive regulation of the medical profession under the 1858 Medical Act (Levitt et al. 1995). Towards the end of the millennium the pace of statutory regulation picked up considerably, however. The first complementary therapies were given a statutory basis for regulation under the 1993 Osteopaths Act and the 1994 Chiropractors Act. In 1999, there were also three additions to the professions allied to medicine under the 1960 Professions Supplementary to Medicine Act – speech and language therapists, paramedics, and arts therapists. Furthermore, the House of Lords Select Committee on Science and Technology (2000) recommended that statutory regulation be introduced for acupuncture and herbal medicine too, with the eventual prospect of a similar framework for non-medical homeopaths. In 2000 a Psychotherapy Bill with similar effect was also introduced into the House of Lords. Parallel phenomena can be witnessed outside the health sector. The 2000 Care Standards Act created the General Social Care Council, which is tasked with the registering of professionals providing social care, including social workers.

Not only have new professions lately been regulated for the first time by statute, but the government has also acted swiftly to reinforce the existing fitness-to-practise procedures and powers where necessary for the protection of the public. This is illustrated by the General Medical Council's new powers to deal with unfit doctors through the establishment of the new statutory Interim Orders Committee. This has the power to suspend a doctor's registration or render it conditional on compliance with certain specified conditions, where this is necessary for the protection of the public pending consideration of an allegation of misconduct or unfitness to practise, and to take into account criminal offences committed abroad. The precise character and quality of the relevant regulatory framework established is inevitably a function of the particular temporal, social and political context. Modern frameworks of regulation are much more comprehensive and sophisticated, partly because of enhanced expectations in terms of rights and entitlements generated by legal sources such as the European Convention on Human Rights, which was incorporated into United Kingdom law by means of the 1998 Human Rights Act. This helps to explain why, for instance, the osteopaths and chiropractors have particularly comprehensive regulatory regimes, including processes for dealing with such issues as poor performance and sick practitioners.

The process of change

An extremely important new provision has been enacted in Section 60 of the Health Act 1999. This relates to the possibility of modifying the existing statutory regulatory scheme of any profession, or regulating any other profession by statute, by means of an Order in Council as opposed to primary legislation.

However, no recommendation must be made to Her Majesty to make an Order in Council unless a draft has been laid before, and approved by resolution of, each House of Parliament. Where it is within the legislative competence of the Scottish Parliament the draft must additionally be laid before, and approved by, the Scottish Parliament. However, there is no power to abolish an existing regulatory body or to alter the composition of a regulatory body so as to impose a lay majority in this way. In the past, the need for primary legislation has proved to be a deterrent to action and has unduly protracted the creation and amendment process, as the legislative process leading to the statutory regulation of the osteopaths and chiropractors in the 1990s bears testimony.

John Denham, speaking for the Government, stated in Standing Committee that:

> The Order-making power provides a more streamlined way of legislating for the regulation of the healthcare professions. The professions will no longer be frustrated by the lack of parliamentary time for their Bills, which leaves the public without adequate protection from bogus and ill-qualified practitioners.[3]

This links the shift explicitly to public protection. However, the motives underpinning this change may run deeper. The Parliamentary Select Committee on Delegated Powers and Deregulation noted that considerable concern had been expressed about the breadth of this power, particularly in relation to its effect on the principle of professional self-regulation.[4] In this respect, it has commonly been seen as a mechanism whereby the government can exercise greater control over the professions, in bringing them into line with current policies in health and social care.

Against this, the large numbers of reforms in the pipeline suggest a need for a more efficient Parliamentary means for processing and implementing change. Dentists, opticians and pharmacists, amongst others, have important changes to bring into effect in the immediate future. The government has also recently declared plans to regulate counsellors and psychologists. In addition, the General Medical Council is currently conducting a thorough review of its constitution, structure and procedures. This will clearly generate new reform proposals, including the prospect of increased lay involvement, a more streamlined governing body and a common initial investigatory stage for all three types of procedures (GMC 2001a).

The Section 60 procedure is already in use. Draft orders have already been published and have been subject to comment prior to being laid before Parliament. The result of this is that a new Health Professions Council has replaced the Council for the Professions Supplementary to Medicine, and a Nursing and Midwifery Council has similarly replaced the United Kingdom Council for Nursing, Midwifery and Health Visitors (Department of Health 2001c; Department of Health 2001d). The Health Professions Council has been enabled to register new groups – and there are many queuing for the privilege – over and above the existing ceiling of 12 professions allowable under the 1960 Act, a number already reached. Although this 'umbrella' system of regulation is currently unique in the United Kingdom, there have been calls urging the establishment of an analogous regime for complementary and alternative medicine. The House of Lords Select Committee on Science and Technology (2000) nevertheless recommended against such a move. Whether any particular occupational group should seek uniprofessional statutory regulation or regulation linked to the Health Professions Council will be a strategic decision. There is little doubt, though, that the new Section 60 procedure will facilitate the growth and spread of statutory self-regulation in the United Kingdom.

The nature of change: structure, constitution and powers

Prime Minister Blair has stated that: 'The professions know they have to make professional regulation swifter, tougher and more open if it is to regain public support.'[5] The new orders relating to the Nursing and Midwifery Council and the Health Professions Council provide for offences of falsely representing being a registered practitioner, possessing professional qualifications, or using a title to which the practitioner is not entitled. This idea of protecting a general and recognizable (common) title, such as 'physiotherapist' or 'physical therapist', has much to recommend it, although there is debate as to whether more than one such title should be protected. For example, the Osteopaths Act 1993 protects the titles of 'osteopath', 'osteopathic practitioner', 'osteopathic physician', 'osteopathist', 'osteotherapist' and 'any kind of osteopath'. Clearly, the protection of title is not as straightforward as first meets the eye.

Both the Nursing and Midwifery Council and the Health Professions Council have 23 members, of which 12 are registered and 11 lay. They are therefore more streamlined and have greater lay involvement than in the past. The new Nursing and Midwifery Council, which replaced the United Kingdom Council for Nursing, Midwifery and Health Visiting, has four new statutory committees – the midwifery committee and the investigating, health, and conduct and competence committees. It is accountable to the Privy Council, whereas previously it was accountable to the Secretary of State – thus bringing it into line with other professional groups. The Health Professions Council also has four statutory committees – the education and training, investigating, conduct and competence, and health committees – and has the power to establish professional advisory committees. Under both of these orders, all registered members have 'alternate' counterparts and each country within the United Kingdom must be represented.

The limited nature and inflexibility of available sanctions for misconduct for some regulatory bodies was undoubtedly insufficient from the point of view of public protection. The Council for the Professions Supplementary to Medicine had extremely limited powers under the 1960 Act, which were restricted to removal from the register for 'infamous conduct'. The Health Professions Council has been given powers to suspend or attach conditions to continuing registration (JM Consulting 1996). The Nursing and Midwifery Council is also endowed with a power for the first time to impose conditions on practice as a sanction for misconduct. In addition, the government has suggested to the General Medical Council that it consider altering the burden of proof in misconduct cases to the civil (on the balance of probabilities) standard in law as opposed to the existing criminal (beyond reasonable doubt) standard used in practice.

While the National Consumer Council Report (1999: 45) speaks of 'variations in provisions ... gaps, loopholes and inconsistencies' between professional regulatory schemes, a more common framework of regulation is emerging in the new regulatory era. Thus, although the United Kingdom Central Council for Nursing, Midwifery and Health Visiting and the Council for the Professions Supplementary to Medicine had no powers to monitor individuals unfit to practise because of incompetence, the Nursing and Midwifery Council and Health Professions Council are now invested with such powers. This contrasts with the previous position in which only the General Medical Council, the General Osteopathic Council and the General Chiropractic Council had a Professional Performance Committee to investigate allegations relating to poor performance. Moreover, the existing regulatory bodies are all members of the new Council for the Regulation of Healthcare Professionals. There is a growing recognition that there are common threads across the professions in relation to ethical standards, health and discipline.

Regulation and the private sector

It is worth noting the contrasts between regulation in the state and private sectors. Indeed, the deficiencies in the regulation of the private and voluntary sectors have become increasingly apparent. The National Consumer Council (1999: 6) stated that: 'In the independent sector, self-regulation of professionals may be the only statutory form of protection for service users. Within the National Health Service there are further controls for protecting patients.' For example, the jurisdiction of the Commission for Health Improvement and the Health Service Commissioner is limited to the National Health Service sphere, and the new statutory 'duty of quality' introduced under Section 18 of the Health Act 1999 applies only to health authorities, primary care and NHS trusts.

Doctors and certain other practitioners disqualified from state employment can nonetheless work in the private sector. Moreover, while the National Health Service has been obliged to offer employment only to certain professionals who have registered status, the private and voluntary sector has had no such constraints. This has had the consequence that a person who has been removed from the relevant professional register may find employment in the private/voluntary sphere provided that he/she does not adopt and use a statutorily protected title. The National Consumer Council (1999) has recommended that health authorities, NHS Trusts, primary care groups/trusts, independent contractors and private sector providers should only be able to commission services from, and employ, accredited and registered professionals. This is an especially important safeguard in so far as certain professional groups, such as chiropodists, work primarily within the private sector.

In relation to private and voluntary sector residential care, the 1984 Registered Homes Act has been the primary legislative influence, requiring registration of various establishments such as residential care homes, and nursing and mental nursing homes. These were defined partly in terms of purpose, the services provided and the techniques they employed. The House of Commons Health Committee (1999) observed that there was almost universal agreement about the inadequacies of this regulatory regime and noted the inconsistency, and indeed arbitrariness, in terms of registration requirements between different premises and activities. Some premises were exempt even where dangerous activities were taking place. The system encouraged a search for loopholes in the legislative coverage and requirements. Furthermore, the health authorities responsible enforced the law inconsistently and erratically. The sanctions available were also described by the Secretary of State as being between a 'nuclear weapon and a feather duster' – as they were based either on the refusal or cancellation of registration, or a warning (Health Committee 1999).

The government has acted to address many of these concerns, including the protection of common title referred to above, through the enactment of the 2000 Care Standards Act, which creates a National Care Standards Commission for England (in Wales it is an arm of the National Assembly). This is responsible for the regulation of such areas as private and voluntary hospitals and clinics; care homes for elderly and disabled persons; and domiciliary care agencies. For the first time clear and comprehensive guidance will emanate from a central national agency. What impact this will have remains to be seen. The old regime was criticized for being preoccupied with the nature of the premises rather than the standard and quality of the care received, and early draft guidance on nursing homes has been accused of displaying the same bias. However, this statute marks an important step in breaking down the health and social care divide. Previously there was a distinction between 'personal' and 'nursing' care, with local authorities regulating residential homes and health authorities regulating nursing homes. They will now be subject to the same scheme. This allows for a more flexible approach whereby care homes will be enabled to provide a mix of personal and nursing care appropriate to the needs of the residents. The forging of partnerships between health and local authorities in providing integrated care packages will also be facilitated by the Health and Social Care Act which, in 2001, became law.

Regulation of clinical matters

In addition to the regulatory issues outlined above, there has been a progressive evolution of regulatory intervention into the sphere of clinical judgement and practice in the United Kingdom. Indeed, many of the recent incidents that have seriously eroded public trust have stemmed from failures of patient care, as opposed to flagrant misconduct. The unidimensional concept of 'serious professional misconduct' as a basis for removal from the professional register has generally excluded consideration of matters of alleged clinical misjudgement or performance.[6] Clinical judgement was rarely subject to censure in litigation and the Health Service Commissioner's jurisdiction was originally confined to non-clinical matters. However, the General Medical Council was given specific powers in relation to the performance of doctors separate from issues of misconduct, under the 1995 Medical (Professional Performance) Act – which were subsequently also applied to osteopaths and chiropractors. The introduction of the reaccreditation of doctors, linked to employer appraisal, and the acceptance of continuous professional development across the health care professions display the same trend. The Ombudsman's remit now also includes alleged clinical failings, since the passing of the 1996 Health Service Commissioner's (Amendment) Act.

The *laissez-faire* approach to regulation has historical roots. It was partially a function of the Hippocratic notion that the integrity and character of the physician were the principal ingredients of competent and appropriate patient care. However, increased litigation, the spread of medical audit, clinical governance, and the evolution of guidelines for certain types of treatment have shifted attention to the actual care delivered in specific circumstances. Moreover, concerns for patient rights have also focused attention on the professional/patient 'relationship'. Although all health care professionals owe duties of care to their patients enforceable in the civil law of tort through actions for negligence, Stacey (1992) has asserted that, in the medical negligence context, unlike elsewhere, medical evidence given in court has been taken as determinative, not advisory. It is not surprising, therefore, that Lord Chief Justice Woolf recently alluded to the 'excessively deferential' attitude on the part of the courts and judges towards medical practitioners.[7]

While Stone is correct in asserting later in this volume that the impact of professional codes of ethics in achieving high, consistent ethical standards is likely to be relatively minimal due to their level of generality, they are still extremely influential as a source of guidance in judicial adjudications. The General Medical Council's *Guidance on Confidentiality* has already significantly influenced outcomes in relation to actions for breach of confidence.[8] Since its recent guidance is even more patient-centred and progressive, it may well serve to drive standards up through litigation (GMC 1998). Indeed, there may be a shift in the nature of the legal regulation of clinical issues as a consequence.

Davies (2000: 444) remarks that doctors 'are already familiar with mechanisms of routine accountability for resource use, and for the non-clinical aspects of patient care. But accountability for clinical activity has traditionally been of a residual kind arising only when a mistake appears to have been made.' In this sense, the courts are increasingly faced with a 'tension' between traditional notions of clinical autonomy and centrally imposed constraints. However, the tendency is still to uphold clinical decisions, wherever feasible, because of the duty of professionals to act in the best interests of their patients in the circumstances.[9]

Nonetheless, clinical autonomy, such as in drug prescribing, is increasingly constrained not just by pressures to conform to peer-supported practices, but also by guidelines emanating from central agencies. The National Institute for Clinical Excellence was established in 1999 as a special health authority under the National Health Service Act 1977, with powers to produce and disseminate clinical guidelines. These will also increasingly come to be viewed as appropriate clinical standards to be adhered to, although in this instance such standards are formulated with regard to cost-effectiveness as well as safety and clinical efficacy. Of course, such constraints are not new. But Davies (2000: 444), among others, contends that: 'The 1999 [Health] Act heralds a new era of managerialist intervention by government, moving away from the traditional paradigm of professional autonomy and self-regulation.'

Such direct regulation has both social and economic imperatives, and is designed to avoid inequalities and inconsistencies in treatments across the National Health Service through the 'postcode lottery', a social justice function. It is also aimed at furthering economic efficiency by controlling and containing costs. Indeed, the drive towards greater patient protection is partially a function of cost containment, with the National Health Service facing an estimated medical negligence bill of £2.6 billion and 'adverse events' costing the National Health Service an estimated £2 billion in terms of additional inpatient stays. Indeed, support has rapidly grown for a move toward a fixed-tariff, no-fault, system of compensating victims of medical accidents – with both the Master of the Rolls, Lord Phillips, and the Secretary of State for Health, Alan Milburn, recently publicly advocating such a move.

Proper patient protection, which has been declared by government to be 'one of its highest priorities', is an ideal that requires an holistic approach. To date, it has been lacking. A recent editorial in the *British Medical Journal* observed that the current systems in the National Health Service for dealing with poor performance were ad hoc, fragmented, and procedurally tortuous (*British Medical Journal* 1999). The Department of Health, however, is developing new disciplinary procedures so that the same disciplinary processes and standards will be applied for the first time in both the primary and secondary sectors. Integration is also necessary between the different regulatory channels and processes. A further editorial in the *British Medical Journal* declared that:

> there is a need for clarity over how accountability for public protection should be shared across these complex professional and managerial systems. It is not the GMC but this wider system that really protects the public – though at present it is not doing so systematically. In any reform the GMC needs to be clear about its place in a wider system and establish consensus with other players in the regulatory game about how to work together. (*British Medical Journal* 2001: 690)

An instance of greater joined-up contemporary thinking in clinical areas can be seen in the obligation imposed in 2000 on the General Medical Council, through an amendment of the 1983 Medical Act. This requires it to report when proceedings have been instituted in respect of an allegation of fitness to practise, professional performance or misconduct, to the Secretary of State and to any person that the Council is aware has employed the individual to provide medical services.

Recent developments: towards a learning culture

The above account has provided an overview of patterns of legal regulation for the health care professions in the United Kingdom. As will be apparent, systems of regulation have traditionally been reactive rather than proactive in nature, and only preventive in seeking to ensure patient protection in a very loose, indirect sense. However, change is again afoot. The new National Clinical Assessment Authority established in April 2001 will have a significant impact, allowing employers to report doctors through a 'common pathway of referral' when doubts about clinical performance have arisen. The Department of Health (2001a: 6) has stated that the National Clinical Assessment Authority will see an end to 'lengthy, expensive suspensions, multiple investigations of the same problem, variable local approaches and delay in acting to protect patients'. This should have the desired effect, even though there are currently insufficiently clear criteria as to when a case should be referred to the Authority. When a doctor is referred, the Authority recommends a course of action for both doctor and employer, with reference to the Commission for Health Improvement when broader issues are raised. Only very serious cases of poor performance would be referred to the General Medical Council, as the professional regulatory body. The problem of the threshold for referral has also been recognized by the United Kingdom Central Council which believes that 'any allegations about a practitioner's deficient competence should have to reach a high threshold before they become the domain of the regulatory body' (UKCC 2000: 18). The symbiosis between the individual and institutional constraints is clearly an important dimension here. As JM Consulting (1998: 44) observes in its report on the regulation of nursing and midwifery: 'Professional self-regulation focuses on individuals, but there has to be an accompanying focus on the external influences on these individuals and the context in which they work.'

As well as the new National Clinical Assessment Authority, there is a new National Patient Safety Agency, which will collect data on 'adverse events' from staff and institutions, and patients and carers, so that lessons learnt from local events can be disseminated across the service as a whole. Both agencies are dependent for their success on the creation of a 'reporting culture' (Department of Health 2001b). A move towards a no-fault compensation system would encourage such a climatic shift. In order to facilitate the reporting of unsafe employees or practices speedily and effectively, extensive statutory protection for 'whistleblowers' has been introduced through the 1998 Public Interest Disclosure Act. This allows disclosures relating to, among other things, the health or safety of any individual to be protected in various ways. Any action taken against the employee with regard to the making of such a disclosure attracts sanctions under the Act.

In the past, there has been very broad discretion accorded to employers under the law in relation to recruitment, assuming there has been no discrimination on the basis of race, gender, disability or trade union membership or activities. The Rehabilitation of Offenders (Exception) Order 1975 exempts health care professionals from the provisions of the Rehabilitation of Offenders Act 1974, which permits applicants to ignore certain criminal convictions by virtue of their being 'spent', but this is not enough. Clearly, unsuitable individuals cannot be allowed to take up employment in critical positions in health care. The 2000 Care Standards Act and the 2001 Health and Social Care Act go further with regard to pre-employment checks. They facilitate the issuing of enhanced criminal record certificates to employers, such as trusts, who are seeking to employ persons to work with vulnerable adults or children, or to include them on general medical, dental, ophthalmic or pharmaceutical lists. Moreover, the 1999 Protection of Children Act and the 2000 Care Standards Act establish lists of persons who are unsuitable to work with children and vulnerable adults and require employers to report relevant incidents to the Secretary of State for inclusion on the list. Care providers will also be obliged to carry out checks of these lists before offering employment to persons in care positions. These are vital measures that supplement another proposed reform requiring employers to check the registration status of potential employees.

In conclusion, it can be argued that the sharing of information between agencies, including professional regulatory bodies, is an essential strategy for greater patient safety. It represents a proactive approach to risk and misconduct. The second Blair government is attempting to grasp the nettle, albeit at the price of the proliferation of new agencies, which may themselves be a potential source of confusion. There may also be some alteration of the relationship of government to the self-regulatory bodies at work in the health field. For example, the United Kingdom Central Council for Nursing, Midwifery and Health Visiting has commented on the apparently greater degree of intrusion on the Nursing and Midwifery Council (UKCC 2000: 18). The full extent of the changes to be introduced under Section 60 is still to unfurl. Whilst the potential for direct control by the state in the self-regulatory process is now present, this was already the case prior to 1999. However, the tightening of centralized control of professional practice through broader forms of regulation is a modern-day reality. Hopefully, it will not only serve to improve patient protection, but also ensure greater equity and cost-efficiency in health care.

Notes

1 See *R. v. Tabassum*, *The Times*, 26 May 2000.

2 See Department of Health Press Release: reference 2000/0465, 1 August 2000.

3 House of Commons Standing Committee A, *Hansard*, 20 May 1999, col. 915.

4 House of Lords Debates, *Hansard*, 4 March 1999, col. 1801.

5 Address on the National Health Service, 2 July 1998.

6 This is highlighted by changes in the content of the General Medical Council's Blue Book and the decision in *McCandless v. General Medical Council* [1995] 30 Butterworths Medico-Legal Reports 53.

7 This resulted principally from reliance on the principle established in *Bolam v. Friern Hospital Management Committee* [1957] 2 All ER 118, whereby adherence to a practice adopted or supported by a responsible, even a minority, body of opinion precluded a finding of negligence. However, this principle is now subject to the reworking by the House of Lords in *Bolitho v. City and Hackney Health Authority* [1997] 4 All ER 771 (HL). This requires that there is a logical basis and a proper assessment of risks and benefits underpinning such decision making – and thus a more discriminating judicial approach.

8 See, for example, *W. v. Egdell* [1990] 1 All ER 835.

9 See, for instance, R. v. *Secretary of State, ex parte Pfizer Ltd* [1999] Lloyd's Reports Medical 289.

References

Better Regulation Task Force (1999) *Self-Regulation: Interim Report*. London: Cabinet Office.
British Medical Journal (1999) 'Managing the clinical performance of doctors', *British Medical Journal*, 319: 1314–15.
British Medical Journal (2001) 'Reforming the GMC', *British Medical Journal*, 322: 689–90.
Davies, A. (2000) 'Don't trust me, I'm a doctor', *Oxford Journal of Legal Studies*, 20: 437–56.
Department of Health (2000a) *Meeting the Challenge: A Strategy for the Allied Health Professions*. London: The Stationery Office.
Department of Health (2000b) *The NHS Plan*. London: The Stationery Office.
Department of Health (2001a) *Assuring the Quality of Medical Practice: Implementing, Supporting Doctors, Protecting Patients*. London: The Stationery Office.
Department of Health (2001b) *Building a Safer NHS for Patients*. London: The Stationery Office.
Department of Health (2001c) *Establishing the New Health Professions Council*. London: Department of Health.
Department of Health (2001d) *Establishing the New Nursing and Midwifery Council*. London: Department of Health.
GMC (1998) *Seeking Patients' Consent: The Ethical Considerations*. London: General Medical Council.
GMC (2001a) *Acting Fairly to Protect Patients: Reform of the GMC's Fitness to Practise Procedures*. London: General Medical Council.
GMC (2001b) *Effective, Inclusive and Accountable: Reform of the GMC's Structure, Constitution and Governance*. London: General Medical Council.
Health Committee (1999) *The Regulation of Private and Other Independent Health Care*. Fifth Report, House of Commons Session 1998–9. London: The Stationery Office.
House of Lords Select Committee on Science and Technology (2000) *Report on Complementary and Alternative Medicine*. London: The Stationery Office.
JM Consulting (1996) *The Regulation of Health Professions. Report of a Review of the Professions Supplementary to Medicine Act*. Bristol: JM Consulting Ltd.
JM Consulting (1998) *The Regulation of Nurses, Midwives and Health Visitors. Report on a Review on the Nurses, Midwives and Health Visitors Act 1997*. Bristol: JM Consulting Ltd.
Levitt, R., Wall, A. and Appleby, J. (1995) *The Reorganized National Health Service*. London: Chapman & Hall, 5th edn.
Merrison Report (1975) *Report of the Committee of Inquiry into the Regulation of the Medical Profession*. London: HMSO.
National Consumer Council (1999) *Self-Regulation of Professionals in Health Care: Consumer Issues*. London: National Consumer Council.
Stacey, M. (1992) *Regulating British Medicine: The General Medical Council*. Chichester: John Wiley & Sons.
Stone, J. and Matthews, J. (1996) *Complementary Medicine and the Law*. Oxford: Oxford University Press.
UKCC (2000) *Ensuring Effective Public Protection*. London: United Kingdom Central Council for Nursing, Midwifery and Health Visiting.
Working Party on Chiropractic (1993) *Report of a Working Party on Chiropractic*. London: King's Fund.

4   Evaluating the Ethical and Legal Content of Professional Codes of Ethics

Julie Stone

All fully fledged professions in the United Kingdom have professional codes of ethics – not least in the health field (Harris 1989). Indeed, the dissemination of a professional code of ethics is seen as one of the core functions of a professional regulatory body. Although it is questionable how far such codes influence the ethical conduct of health care practitioners, their presence is held up as some sort of guarantee of propriety and a sign that the professional body takes its public protection role seriously. While the provisions contained in a code of ethics may be used as an ethical benchmark against which practitioners' standards of conduct may be judged in a professional disciplinary hearing, the substantive content of such codes, which is remarkably consistent from one health profession to the next, is rarely questioned. This may be unsurprising, given that the ethical and legal concepts that underpin codes of ethics are rarely made explicit. Rather, the legitimacy of the normative principles contained in codes of ethics is presumed to be self-evident. This chapter will challenge this proposition and recommend that codes of ethics must be seen as part of a broader regulatory framework if they are to achieve their intended aim of promoting the highest standards of conduct and protection for the public.

Individual accountability

Although there is an increasing tendency for health care practitioners to work within multidisciplinary teams, each professional is expected to be accountable for his or her individual practice. Health care practitioners are accountable to their patients/clients, to their employers, to their professional body and to the public at large. Attention to professional ethics, and the inclusion of ethics and law within the pre-registration curriculum, constitutes a tacit acceptance that many of the dilemmas faced by health care practitioners are of a moral, rather than a technical, nature. They include such questions as: whether to maintain the confidentiality of a patient whose behaviour places others at risk; whether to elicit consent to treatment from a psychotic patient who is acting irrationally; whether to accede to a patient's request to be helped to die; and whether to lie about the nature of treatment given, so that a patient's health insurer will reimburse the costs of care. These all involve complex ethical issues. Specialist technical knowledge, while central to safe and competent practice, will not provide the answers as to how a professional ought to act in any of the above situations. Nor are practitioners likely to find the answers to their day-to-day problems in a generalized code of ethics, since these give some guidance on minimal, legalistic requirements, but do not deal with specific situations.

The concept of professional autonomy means that individual practitioners generally have a wide degree of latitude in dealing with ethical, as well as technical, problems. The risk management, re-accreditation procedures and the government's new quality proposals referred to in other chapters in this volume may serve to make the decisions of health care practitioners more transparent (Department of Health 1997; Department of Health 2000). Nevertheless, for the main part, the majority of interactions between practitioners and patients go unsupervised, and professionals must draw on their individual sense of accountability in making decisions that fully respect the patient's rights and other ethical considerations. Ethics, one might say, is what practitioners do when no one else is looking. An appropriate professional training should equip a health care practitioner with the skills of practical reasoning and critical reflection to facilitate such decision making.

Practitioners faced with a seemingly identical dilemma may well respond in different ways. Ethically, there may be no such thing as 'the right thing to do' (Coope 1996). Rather, there may be a range of ethically acceptable responses that give differential weight to particular principles such as individual autonomy, justice or acting in the public interest. Individual decisions may also relate to particular moral imperatives or to a prediction of the probable consequences of decisions for one or more people likely to be affected by an action. Thus, a range of alternative actions might be considered justifiable in the event of the practitioner being called to account before his or her disciplinary body.

Provided practitioners have considered the patient's rights, the interests of other parties affected by the decision, the costs and benefits of all possible options, any relevant professional requirements and the implications of the law, their decision, if questioned, is likely to be found acceptable. What matters is that ethical decisions are arrived at through a process of informed, active deliberation and are not based merely on gut instinct. Unless the outcome is one that no reasonable practitioner could have arrived at, the precise weight given by the practitioner to the relative factors, or how the practitioner balances competing ethical theories, even if this could be articulated, is unlikely to be challenged.

What do codes of ethics contain?

Most codes combine vague aspirational statements with minimal legal requirements in key areas of practice. Based largely on duties requiring practitioners to be competent, to respect patient autonomy and to uphold the values of the given profession, codes tend to include the following provisions:

- a statement setting out the core values for the particular profession;
- recognition of the ethical basis of the relationship with the patient;
- recognition that the relationship is based on trust (that is, one of a fiduciary nature);
- a duty to respect the patient's values and cultural beliefs and to make sure that personal beliefs (and, increasingly, the practitioner's cultural values) do not prejudice patient care;
- a duty not to abuse the patient's trust;
- a reminder to work within the limits of competence and the need, where appropriate, to refer the patient;
- the duty to keep professional skills and attitudes up to date;
- a statement acknowledging the scope of professional practice;
- the practitioner's need to maintain accurate, comprehensive records;
- the practitioner's duty to work in an open and co-operative manner with other health care professionals for the benefit of the patient (including a duty to take appropriate steps if the actions of a colleague are placing patients at risk);
- provisions relating to the need to obtain consent;
- provisions relating to confidentiality and its limits;
- provisions concerning the treatment of minors and mentally incapacitated adults;
- a requirement that the practitioner be physically and psychologically fit;
- a requirement that the practitioner complies with relevant legal provisions;
- rules relating to advertising and publicity;
- the need to maintain appropriate professional indemnity and professional liability insurance.

It is important to remember that, in addition to their professional code of ethics, health care practitioners are subject to ethical guidance from a variety of sources. For example, doctors in the United Kingdom receive ethical advice not only from the General Medical Council, but also from the British Medical Association, the Royal College(s) appropriate to their specialty, their medical defence organization, and the Department of Health, as well as through their employer. Similarly, health care practitioners may be held to account through the National Health Service complaint mechanisms and employment disciplinary procedures, in addition to being accountable to their own professional body. This diminishes the centrality of their professional code of ethics, which will only be one of several overlapping sources of ethical and legal guidance.

The fiduciary nature of the health care relationship requires that health care practitioners do not exploit their relative power over patients, whose illness may render them potentially vulnerable. The United Kingdom lacks specific statutory provisions safeguarding patients' rights, but all health professionals already work within strict legal confines. Although within the National Health Service patients do not have a contractual relationship with their health carers, all health care professionals have a Common Law duty towards their patients. Broadly speaking, this places an obligation on practitioners to work with all due care and skill. A practitioner's legal duties mirror the ethical responsibilities owed by health carers to their patients to benefit them and not to cause them harm (the principles of beneficence and non-maleficence) and to respect their patients' autonomy (Gillon 1994). Accordingly, practitioners may be sued for negligence if any act or omission results in harm to the patient. Not all mistakes constitute negligence. A practitioner will only be held liable for failing to reach the standard of care expected of a reasonable practitioner.[1] Negligence may arise in any sphere of the practitioner's work, including diagnosis, treatment, or failure to provide adequate information.[2] The civil action of trespass to the person (otherwise known as battery) is also available to any patient who has been treated without consent, or where the practitioner has exceeded the limits of consent. Provided the practitioner has acted within the scope of his or her employment when the alleged mishap occurred, the employing institution will usually accept vicarious liability on the part of their employee.

Additionally, health professionals must take account of regulations specific to their sphere of practice. These may impose administrative burdens on health care practitioners, as well as technical requirements. They may be enshrined in primary legislation, as in the case of the Human Fertilisation and Embryology Act 1990, secondary legislation, for example notification regulations under the Abortion Act 1967 (as amended), or advice disseminated by governmental departments. In addition to their Common Law responsibilities, health professionals are also bound by their contract of employment, which may impose requirements on them over and above their Common Law duties, for example, in relation to confidentiality, or their statutory duties – for instance, in relation to patient records.

While the law provides an additional tier of regulatory control over health care practitioners, its usefulness in improving and maintaining professional standards is limited, even though it has been argued that legal judgments have a radiating effect (Allsop and Mulcahy 1996). Civil litigation is costly, both financially and emotionally, to the individual as well as to society. The overall expenditure on clinical negligence by 1998 has been estimated by Fenn et al. (2000) at £84 million. The overall financial liability has continued to rise. In 2001, the National Audit Office (2001) estimated that the likely cost of the rising numbers of new claims at March 2000 was £2.6 billion. Moreover, many adverse incidents are not reported, as there are numerous additional reasons why victims of professional abuse choose not to pursue their complaints through the courts (Mulcahy 2000). Although the criminal law may need to be invoked in the worst cases of professional abuse – such as those of the enrolled nurse, Beverly Allitt and the general practitioner, Harold Shipman[3] – this does not necessarily improve service provision unless remedial action is taken to avoid similar situations from recurring and recommendations from public inquiries following such tragedies are implemented in full (Dyer 1994). This has been recognized in a recent report from the Department of Health (2001) which aims to implement systems that ensure that there is organizational learning from adverse events, complaints and litigation.

The changing nature of professional ethics

The concept of what it means to act ethically is not static, and is historically and culturally determined. For example, the elevation to unparalleled heights of the principle of respect for autonomy is a recent product of Western individualism and is not shared by other cultures where notions of the extended self prevail – that is, the view that the individual patient cannot be regarded in isolation from their family or their wider community. Whereas medical paternalism is generally disapproved of in the United States and the United Kingdom, as Macer (1999) describes, in other cultures it is not only tolerated, but expected. For instance, doctors' representatives in Japan have only recently reversed their policy of generally withholding terminal diagnoses from patients.

In the United States in the early 1980s, the President's Commission for the Study of Ethical Problems in Medicine and Biomedical and Behavioral Research (1983) focused attention on the issue of individual patient autonomy. This has had a significant impact on professional ethics. As an example, the American Medical Association has proposed changes to its 1980 Code of Ethics to stress that a physician must recognize responsibility to patients first and foremost, and secondarily to society, to other health professionals and to the self. Further amendments include provisions about patient privacy and confidentiality.

The hi-tech nature of health care in the United States has increased patients' expectations about what treatment is possible. This, together with the medical profession's fear of legal action for failing to provide aggressive therapy, has resulted in a high level of defensive practice, and the patient being recast as a consumer. Defensive practice results in additional diagnostic testing, increased referrals by primary health physicians, and the avoidance of certain clinical areas (Andersen 1999).[4] Although health care practice within the National Health Service is less defensive – the resources are simply not available – the nature of professional guidance is nevertheless changing. The balance of emphasis has shifted subtly from the duties of the professional expert to an acknowledgement and recognition of the rights and expectations of the patient.

In the past, professional codes of ethics concerned themselves more with issues of professional self-interest and professional etiquette, such as restrictions on advertising, refraining from making disparaging remarks about colleagues, and provisions relating to referrals. In the last two decades, however, they have given greater stress to a patient-centred approach that places more weight on the autonomy of the patient and prioritizes the patients' interests above those of the practitioner. This has led to increased attention to matters such as patient consent, confidentiality and responding to complaints. Whereas codes of ethics previously regarded disparaging the work of one's colleagues as professional misconduct, modern codes stress that health practitioners will be acting unprofessionally if they fail to blow the whistle on unethical colleagues or alert the appropriate authorities to unethical practices occurring within their institution.

The shift from a paternalistic, beneficence-orientated model of health care professionalism to a model in which patient autonomy is highly valued may have had more to do with health professionals' fear of being sued than a genuine commitment to involving patients as active participants in their own healing. In highly litigious cultures, professional codes may be more inclined to stress legalistic and defensive requirements, such as the duty to obtain written informed consent and to keep detailed contemporaneous records of dealings with patients.

However, the conservatism and entrenched self-interest that characterizes the development of professions means that professional codes of ethics, which can only provide accepted generalized guidance, will be slow to respond to cultural shifts (Pellegrino and Relman 1999). A pertinent example here is that many bioethicists and health professionals now accept that an uncritical application of the principle of respect for autonomy may result in more harm than good (see, among others, Pellegrino and Thomasma 1988; Tobias and Souhami 1993; Pellegrino 1994). Notwithstanding current professional guidance to the contrary, a level of benevolent paternalism within health care relationships may persist because patients are comfortable with it and indeed expect it, and because alternative models are even less desirable. Professional codes of ethics, meanwhile, have only relatively recently moved away from a paternalistic stance towards a more patient-centred model, placing greater emphasis on the patient's autonomous choice. The mechanisms are therefore not necessarily in place to incorporate these subtle societal shifts, other than through a general requirement that practitioners should always act in the best interests of the patient.

The concept of self-regulation implies that standards within a profession can and should be set down by the profession, rather than being led by service users and other stakeholders. That right has been called into question if professions are thought to put members' interests before the public interest. Professions that cannot adequately police their own know that they may become subject to direct state regulation, or an independent standards authority. Although there has been an increase in complaints to the professional bodies of all major health professions in recent years, only a small proportion of cases proceed from an initial complaint to a full professional misconduct hearing, resulting in disciplinary action being taken. For example, in 1999–2000 only 164 out of the 1,213 cases reported to the Preliminary Proceedings Committee of the United Kingdom Central Council for Nursing, Midwifery and Health Visiting were referred to the Professional Conduct Committee (UKCC 2000).

Nonetheless, changes in ethical standards demanded by patients' rights groups and others may take some time to percolate through to professional bodies, especially those which lack sufficient lay representation at the various stages of their operation. It is a telling comment that most of the improvements to professional codes of ethics, and the reform of self-regulating bodies, have been prompted by external criticism, rather than self-generated attempts by professional bodies to bring themselves into line with current best practice. Having said this, Davies argues in this volume that the United Kingdom Central Council for Nursing, Midwifery and Health Visiting has taken a proactive approach in developing the lay role on the Council and being relatively transparent in its proceedings.

Can codes of ethics be anything other than tokenistic?

Since the content of professional codes is presumed to be self-evident, some would say that there is little point in professional bodies issuing codes of ethics. Arguably, registered health care practitioners ought to know how to behave 'correctly' without being told. If practitioners need to be reminded that they should not, for example, enter into sexual relationships with their patients, they ought not to be practising. This is, indeed, a compelling argument. Codes of ethics are unlikely to make someone behave ethically if they are minded to act unethically. However, if ethical codes are tied into disciplinary procedures, these may exert a deterrent effect. If this view is taken, then increasing numbers of cases resulting in professional disciplinary proceedings could indicate that practitioners do not take codes of ethics very seriously. Another explanation could be that the public in their role as regulators are demonstrating their opinion of how professional people ought to behave, in seeking redress where they feel ethical codes have been broken.

A common criticism of codes of ethics is that they are rarely contextualized and fail to take into account the complexities of modern health care delivery (Darvall 1993; Singer 2000). Accordingly, they contain aspirational sets of rules that fail to take account of how resource constraints, hierarchical power structures, gender imbalances, multiculturalism, and institutional racism – to name but a few issues – impinge on ethical practice. By placing unrealistic responsibilities on individual practitioners, professional bodies may fail to challenge structural and institutional problems in health care. As with a criminal prosecution, this may result in the scapegoating of individual practitioners, with little being done to prevent similar mistakes from happening again. Another criticism of codes of ethics is that they are worded in such vague, generalized terms as to be of little practical use. From an ethical perspective, however, the inevitability of moral disagreement is such that any guidance that goes beyond tokenistic, aspirational statements would be unworkable. Since any attempt to offer more prescriptive guidance would be unenforceable, there may be little pragmatic option other than to leave the provisions of a code of ethics deliberately wide.

The corollary of this position is that it is also worth asking whether, empirically, there is any correlation between what ethical codes say and how health professionals act. Although the teaching of ethics and law is thought to be important, health care practitioners may be more likely to learn how to practise ethically 'on the job', rather than through pre-registration training or professional guidance. Sadly, in the real world of health care delivery, as opposed to the idealized world envisioned by codes of ethics, this may amount more to learning how to do the minimum compatible with not being sued or being the subject of a formal complaint or claim. Professionals, though, are also influenced by many informal sources (Rosenthal 1995). Media discussion of ethical issues (however polarized) and storylines in television series such as 'ER' and 'Casualty' may do more to stimulate a practitioner's ethical thinking than numerous ethical codes. This is not to say that there is no point in maintaining ethical codes. Some possible benefits of codes of ethics are set out below:

- Codes represent an idealized, aspirational statement of professional values and attitudes.
- Codes of ethics give patients an idea of what sort of conduct they can reasonably expect and demand from practitioners.
- Codes of ethics proscribe certain specific forms of activity and, in doing so, provide disciplinary procedures with a starting point for determining whether a practitioner's conduct was or was not acceptable.
- Codes of ethics identify professional standards that are helpful to the courts in assessing the requisite legal standard of care.
- Codes give practitioners a broad moral framework within which to work. This not only promotes consistent, high standards, but can be particularly helpful for health professionals who work alone in private practice and do not have regular contact with other practitioners. They may also provide guidance for the vast majority of health care practitioners who do not take an active role or interest in the politics of their profession.

The ethical content of codes of ethics

As most professional codes of ethics are bland, a sceptical practitioner might also justifiably ask why any or all of the requirements of a code of ethics should be adhered to. While some training in ethics and law might begin to answer this question, even a thorough grounding in bioethics fails to account for why codes of ethics prioritize some requirements over others. Many of the rules outlined above are grounded in the principle of respect for autonomy – with the requirements related to justice largely being excluded from codes of ethics. This omission is becoming more unacceptable as ethics starts to take on a global perspective. However, one possible response as to why practitioners should pay any regard to these codes is that duty-based theory – that is, the profession's code of conduct – is itself a set of ethical rules that ought to be observed. One problem with this answer is that, as with other sources of duty, if the professional body decreed that practitioners should follow practices that were unethical, would practitioners still be duty bound to obey the rules uncritically?

The mere fact that there is such a large degree of similarity between codes of ethics suggests that they represent broadly accepted, if culturally biased, norms of how professionals are currently expected to behave. Without arguing in support of moral universalism, it might be possible to agree that within contemporary, democratic societies, there are certain expectations as to how health care professionals ought to conduct themselves and relate to their patients. Codes of ethics are unquestioned simply because they tend to go no further than stating what is commonly agreed and uncontroversial. In practice, though, codes of ethics tend to represent an attempt to combine a number of ethical theories widely used in the teaching of bioethics (Beauchamp and Childress 1994). None of these provides a complete account of how to live a moral life, but they all have some use in determining the scope of professional duties.

The ethical theories that might be thought to inform the bulk of ethical rules are consequentialism, deontology, rights-based theory and virtue theory. Consequentialism, or outcome-based theory, posits that an action is morally desirable to the extent that it maximizes good outcomes and minimizes bad ones. The form of consequentialism most commonly invoked in health care ethics is utilitarianism. This theory is often invoked in debates over allocation of scarce resources, where the correct choice of action is that which will bring about maximum benefit to as many people as possible while harming as few as possible. Utilitarianism is attractive to health care practitioners who are already used to basing their technical decisions on risk/benefit calculations. Its major shortfall as a moral theory is that it is rarely possible to predict what the outcome of any action will be, and different parties to a decision may profoundly disagree as to what constitutes a benefit and what constitutes a harm. A second problem is that in achieving the 'greater good', utilitarians may, on occasion, have to sacrifice the rights of the individual.

Deontology, or duty-based theory, proposes that an action is morally right if it complies with rules. Deontologists hold that if there is an obligation to act in a certain way in a given situation, then one should act in that way in every similar situation regardless of time, place or person. As an example, if there is a professional duty to maintain confidentiality, then confidentiality must always be maintained, in every situation, regardless of the outcome. A deontologist may consider an action to be the morally right or obligatory one even if it doesn't promote the greatest possible balance of good over harm. While professional regulation draws heavily on duty-based theory, there may be problems in determining which rules are appropriate and what to do when rules conflict. How far, for example, can a health professional maintain a patient's confidentiality when that patient's actions are putting others at risk? Rights-based theories are a form of deontology, drawing on the notion that if a patient has a particular right, a health professional has a corresponding duty. Rights talk may serve to increase patient expectations unrealistically. Whereas the rights not to be prevented from following a course of action may be possible, resources limit positive duties of assistance, making some 'rights' unattainable. The 'right to reproduce', for example, does not guarantee that every infertile couple has automatic access to infertility services.

Virtue theory proposes that morality is to be found in the development of good character traits, or virtues. Based largely on Aristotelian ethics, this agent-centred theory states that a person is good if he or she has virtues and lacks vices. The virtues that are commonly invoked include benevolence, truthfulness and justice. Virtue theory suggests that a person who possesses a virtuous character will be inclined towards virtuous action. Development of professional skills and attitudes in education and training for the health professions can be seen as part of a modern-day acceptance of this theory.

A synthesis of these theories has resulted in a version of bioethics known as the principle-based approach, which draws on the four principles of respect for autonomy, the duty of beneficence, the duty of non-maleficence and the principle of respect for justice. These principles form the bulk of the provisions contained in codes of ethics. Many bioethicists are acutely aware of the limitations of existing theories, and are looking for alternative theoretical bases to account for moral action, such as an ethics of care, revitalized approaches to virtue ethics, and narrative-based ethics (see Nelson 1997; Greenhalgh and Hurwitz 1998). While these may influence codes of ethics some years down the line, one suspects that professional bodies will stick to duty-based guidance for simplicity and to avoid the complexity of contemporary moral philosophy and its troubled application to health care practice. In so doing, professional bodies offer a narrow theoretical perspective that fails to consider both ethical and cultural pluralism.

Space does not permit a more detailed examination of the ethical theories that are represented in codes of ethics, all of which are well explored in the bioethics literature (see Beauchamp and Childress 1994; Gillon 1994). Besides, a reading of professional codes would indicate that professional bodies do not anticipate that practitioners have an *a priori* knowledge of ethical theory. This again suggests that the legitimacy of the rules is intended to be self-evident and that there is a requirement for professionals to follow them because they represent the rules of the profession by which a member implicitly agrees to be bound, in becoming registered.

The legal content of codes of ethics

The increase in litigation against health care practitioners is a clear manifestation that practitioners who fall short of the prescribed standard of care will be held to account. Students and practitioners of health care may claim not to care about theories of ethics, but they do care about the possibility of being sued. The legal content of codes of ethics varies significantly, although many codes now include some relevant statutory provisions and outline important case law. Few codes detail how practitioners can avoid being sued for negligence or trespass – although the literature from the defence societies offers guidance. Given that all health care practitioners owe their patients a legal, as well as an ethical, duty of care, this may seem like a curious omission. This information would be immensely useful to practitioners, but presumably it is excluded because the law of negligence only requires that a health care practitioner acts as a 'reasonable practitioner', using the 'Bolam test' discussed in detail by Montgomery (1997). In the United Kingdom, the law demands only standards of ordinary competence. In other words, practitioners will not be held liable for negligence unless they fail to act in accordance with a practice accepted as proper by a responsible body of professional opinion.

Although the standard of care is ultimately determined by the courts, in the past the Bolam test has meant that, if the threshold of care is substandard but widely shared, a practitioner may not be found liable for acting in accordance with those minimum standards. Another way of conceptualizing the Bolam standard is that a practitioner will only be negligent if he or she acts in a way that no reasonable practitioner would have acted in those circumstances. Ethical standards, by way of contrast, exhort practitioners to aspire to the highest standards of care and competence. Since the courts would reasonably expect that a professional body's guidance represents that particular profession's standards for best practice at any given time, any practitioner who is following the advice contained in their code of ethics, will, *prima facie*, be acting as a reasonable practitioner.

In any event, should the practitioner be involved in a legal dispute, this will be decided on the facts of the particular case. Once again, a generalized code of ethics could never predict every possible adverse outcome, which is a further possible explanation for why codes of ethics are written in deliberately vague terms, recommending that practitioners seek legal advice from their defence organization where necessary. Furthermore, just as bioethicists fail to agree on ethical theory, so lawyers will dispute the implications of case law for practice. As an example, many practitioners are aware of the Gillick standard for judging the competence of minors. This landmark House of Lords ruling held that parents' right to make decisions, including medical decisions, on behalf of their children yields as soon as the child has sufficient decision-making capacity to understand fully the nature of what is proposed. At this point health care practitioners can rely on the decision of the child whether to consent to treatment or not.[5] The thrust of this judgment was incorporated into the 1989 Children Act and most codes of ethics make provisions for respecting the decision-making capacity of mature minors. However, few health practitioners fully understand the ramifications of subsequent legal decisions that have limited the scope of 'Gillick competence'. Although competent minors are allowed to consent to treatment, if a parent, health professional or court thinks that treatment should be given, their authority to refuse treatment may be taken away. Once again, it is understandable that professional bodies have attempted to steer a neutral path through these murky legal waters and not get too embroiled in the detail of case law.

Why is the ethical and legal basis of codes of ethics not made explicit?

The most obvious explanation for why professional codes of ethics fail to make the ethical or legal basis of their guidance more explicit is that health care practitioners are not, and do not want to become, mini-ethicists or lawyers. Codes of ethics, therefore, attempt to synthesize agreed ethical standards and minimum legal requirements for the ease of their membership. A further, more pragmatic reason for continuing to provide guidance in its present form is that no single ethical theory provides an adequate account of what it means to act morally. If bioethicists cannot agree on what it means to act ethically, what hope is there for professional bodies? In any event, practitioners are rarely, if ever, asked to explain their actions in terms of ethical theories. Disciplinary bodies, when judging the ethical propriety of alleged professional misconduct, do so with reference to their own rules and not to ethical theory or legal rulings.

However well intentioned, this approach to codes of ethics is destined to result in overly generalized statements that are of little use in specific situations. As ethics and law are complex disciplines, health care practitioners should have prior training in ethics and law in order to apply the codes of ethics in a meaningful fashion. Although this knowledge is essential to safe and competent practice, this practice does not always occur.

Codes of ethics as part of a larger regulatory picture

While codes of ethics may have symbolic value, they will not influence behaviour unless other conditions exist. Professional bodies are no longer solely responsible for ensuring the ethical conduct of their members. Under the principles of clinical governance, it is intended that professional regulation will be tied into a wider quality framework (Department of Health 1997). Nonetheless, regulatory bodies play a central role in defining and maintaining standards, and as such have particular duties in relation to patient protection. Regulatory bodies for medicine, nursing, midwifery and health visiting and the professions supplementary to medicine have all been subject to recent extensive review. New regulatory bodies in complementary and alternative therapies are also now beginning to emerge (Saks 1998).

There are various ways in which professional bodies can take steps to increase ethical awareness among their membership. For codes of ethics to have meaning for newly qualified practitioners, it is essential that ethics, law and communication skills be incorporated into professional training. Ongoing exploration of these subjects should be included in continuing professional development programmes. For reasons already discussed, codes of ethics may be somewhat removed from the realities of clinical practice. They should be related to everyday experience. Such codes should be a living document, capable of reflecting professional and societal changes. In addition to professional journals, IT and other media resources, such as like newsletters and Internet groups, should be used by professional bodies to disseminate information. Trained staff should be available to deal with individual ethical inquiries and this source of information should be available to the public as well. Codes themselves should be available to patients. They should also be tied to grievance procedures and the outcome of such inquiries should be fed back into professional training. Taken together, these measures could improve the relevance of codes substantially.

Conclusion

The existence of a professional code of ethics is only one aspect of a larger strategy that professional bodies must adopt in order to foster high ethical standards. The existence of a code of ethics and an effective grievance procedure sends the message that the professional body takes its responsibilities to the public seriously and will deal with unethical practitioners effectively. In matters of professional self-regulation, however, actions speak louder than words. Codes must not only exist but also be adequately enforced. Aspirational statements are of little value to patients so long as professional bodies concentrate only on flagrant examples of abuse and fail to consider innovative ways in which ethics, law and communication skills can be enhanced and put into practice. As new patterns of health care delivery evolve, professional bodies must accept that they can no longer operate from their former positions of insularity and territoriality. Achieving consistent, high standards requires the forging of new partnerships between health care providers, managers, the government, health service users and pressure groups. Unless they are used as a benchmark against which to judge practice, the impact of codes of ethics will remain limited and fail to have a positive effect on day-to-day practice in the United Kingdom and elsewhere.

Notes

1 *Bolam v. Friern* HMC [1957] 2 All ER 118.

2 *Maynard v. West Midlands Regional Health Authority* [1985] 1 All ER 635 (diagnosis); *Whitehouse v. Jordan* [1981] 1 All ER 267 (treatment); *Sidaway v. Bethlem RHG* [1985] 1 All ER 643 (failure to disclose information).

3 For example, Allitt, a serial killer, was given 13 life sentences in 1991 after murdering four children and attacking nine others while working as an enrolled nurse at Grantham and Kesteven Hospital in Lincolnshire. An inquiry, chaired by Sir Cyril Clothier, introduced recommendations aimed at preventing a similar tragedy, including the screening of unsuitable nursing candidates and improved procedures for reporting untoward incidents. The more recent case of Shipman, a general practitioner and one of the most prolific serial killers in history, is discussed further by Allsop in this volume.

4 The effect of defensive medicine on caesarean rates has been particularly noticeable with the likelihood of defensive practice varying according to the socio-economic status of the mother (Dubay et al. 1999).

5 *Gillick v. Norfolk and Wisbech Area Health Authority* [1985] 3 All ER 402.

References

Allsop, J. and Mulcahy, L. (1996) *Regulating Medical Work: Formal and Informal Controls*. Buckingham: Open University Press.

Andersen, R. (1999) 'Billions for defense: the pervasive nature of defensive medicine', *Archives of Internal Medicine*, 159: 2399–402.

Beauchamp, T. and Childress, J. (1994) *An Introduction to Biomedical Ethics*. Oxford: Oxford University Press, 4th edn.

Coope, C. (1996) 'Does teaching by cases mislead us about morality?', *Journal of Medical Ethics*, 22: 46–52.

Darvall, L. (1993) *Medicine, Law and Social Change: The Impact of Bioethics, Feminism and Rights Movements on Medical Decision-Making*. Aldershot: Dartmouth.

Department of Health (1997) *The New NHS: Modern, Dependable*. London: HMSO.

Department of Health (2000) *The NHS Plan*. London: The Stationery Office.

Department of Health (2001) *Building a Safer NHS for Patients: Implementing an Organization with a Memory*. London: The Stationery Office.

Dubay, L., Kaestner, R. and Waidmann, T. (1999) 'The impact of malpractice fears on cesarean section rates', *Journal of Health Economics,* 18: 491–522.

Dyer, C. (1994) 'Inquiry into serial killer criticises hospital response', *British Medical Journal*, 30: 491.

Fenn, P., Diacon, S., Gray, A., Hodges, R. and Rickman, N. (2000) 'Current costs of medical negligence in NHS hospitals in NHS hospitals', *British Medical Journal*, 320: 1567–71.

Gillon, R. (1994) 'Medical ethics: Four principles plus attention to scope', *British Medical Journal*, 309: 184.

Greenhalgh, T. and Hurwitz, B. (1998) *Narrative-Based Medicine: Dialogue and Discourse in Clinical Practice*. London: BMJ Publishing.

Harris, N. (1989) *Professional Codes of Conduct in the United Kingdom: A Directory*. London: Mansell.

Macer, D. (1999) 'Bioethics in and from Asia', *Journal of Medical Ethics*, 25: 293–5.

Montgomery, J. (1997) *Health Care Law*. Oxford: Oxford University Press.

Mulcahy, L. (2000) *Mediating Medical Negligence Claims: An Option for the Future?* London: The Stationery Office.

National Audit Office (2001) *Handling Clinical Negligence Claims in England. Report by the Comptroller and Auditor General*. London: The Stationery Office.

Nelson, H. (1997) *Stories and their Limits: Narrative Approaches to Bioethics*. London: Routledge.

Pellegrino, E. (1994) 'Patient-physician autonomy: Conflicting rights and obligations in the practitioner–patient relationship', *Journal of Contemporary Health, Law and Policy*, 10: 47–68.

Pellegrino, E. and Relman, S. (1999) 'Professional medical association: ethical and practical guidelines', *Journal of the American Medical Association*, 282: 47–68.

Pellegrino, E. and Thomasma, D. (1988) *For the Patient's Good: The Restoration of Beneficence in Health Care*. Oxford: Oxford University Press.

President's Commission for the Study of Ethical Problems in Medicine and Biomedical and Behavioral Research (1983) *Making Health Care Decisions*. Washington, DC: US Government Printing Office.

Rosenthal, M. (1995) *The Incompetent Doctor: Behind Closed Doors*. Buckingham: Open University Press.

Saks, M. (1998) 'Professionalism and health care', in D. Field and S. Taylor (eds) *Sociological Perspectives on Health, Illness and Health Care*. Oxford: Blackwell Science.

Singer, P. (2000) 'Medical ethics', *British Medical Journal*, 321: 282–5.

Tobias, J. and Souhami, R. (1993) 'Fully informed consent can be needlessly cruel', *British Medical Journal*, 307: 1199–201.

UKCC (2000) *Annual Report*. London: United Kingdom Central Council for Nursing, Midwifery and Health Visiting.

PART TWO
PROFESSIONAL CASE STUDIES

5 Regulation and the Medical Profession

Judith Allsop

For the last decade, the medical profession has been at the centre of the debate on the utility of self-regulation in the contemporary context. This may be due to three main factors. First, medicine has dominated the division of labour in health care and particularly within the National Health Service has had a powerful position within decision-making structures. This has been seen as a factor inhibiting change. Second, the prototype for self-regulation is based on medicine. In the mid-nineteenth century, medical practitioners obtained the statutory right to regulate their own occupational practice. As Moran (1999) has said, this provided a form of private interest government. It gave the profession a large degree of autonomy in determining what the content of medical practice should be, how medical work should be carried out, and protection from both the market and the state. As a number of writers have pointed out (Freidson 1970; Larson 1977), the arrangement could be seen as a professionalizing strategy. It enabled medicine to negotiate favourable terms and conditions of service as the state became a funder and provider of health services. However, there are now questions as to whether the professions serve the public interest. Third, the current arrangements for regulating medicine have been challenged as they have been shown to be inadequate in protecting the public from incompetent doctors. Although, as other chapters in this volume indicate, most areas of health work have had their share of scandals, those within the medical field have kept the profession constantly under the spotlight.

The main focus of criticism has been the General Medical Council because it is the symbol of self-regulation. However, it will be argued here that the regulation of medical work is conducted by a variety of bodies and is a multi-layered activity, as institutions external to the profession, governments and other state agencies carry out a number of regulatory roles through formal and informal mechanisms. Various internal formal and informal controls also exist within the profession itself. The chapter shows how regulation both external and internal to the profession has shifted in recent years as a consequence of political and public pressure. The General Medical Council itself has introduced a raft of changes, some of which are still under negotiation. The current President of the General Medical Council, Sir Donald Irvine, claims: 'We are witnessing the fashioning of a new relationship between the medical profession and the public, and an approach to medical regulation to which all major stakeholders must contribute' (GMC 2000a: 3). The concluding discussion will assess these changes and the challenge they present in developing a more sophisticated version of traditional forms of self-regulation.

The formal structures of self-regulation: the profession and the state

The regulatory bargain and the long arm of history

The popular perception of self-regulation is that medicine is a closed shop. Doctors protect each other.[1] However, the ethos of both protectionism and public responsibility has been interwoven in the history of the profession. Formally, the General Medical Council regulates the profession on behalf of the state. It is empowered by Act of Parliament to carry out the functions of registration, certification and discipline – and those who are found to be below standard can be excluded from the register. These powers derive from the 1858 Medical Act that established what was then called the General Council of Medical Education and Registration. The Act gave the Council powers to maintain a register of qualified practitioners and to determine what those entry qualifications were. Entry on the register gave protection of title. Those who were registered as qualified could display their title and call themselves a 'medical practitioner'. The unqualified were thus excluded.

The obverse of this is that medical practitioners could also be removed from the register if, through a judicial process, they were found guilty of 'serious misconduct in a professional respect'.[2] In the nineteenth century, cases generally related to adultery or the disparagement of medical colleagues (Smith 1994). Through this arrangement, which in essence remains unchanged, a regulatory bargain was established. The General Medical Council would ensure that those who practised had been trained in a manner that met with the clinical and ethical standards of the day. Members of the public who needed medical care could also be assured that when they consulted a registered practitioner, that practitioner had completed a recognized course of training. In return, the profession was trusted to govern itself – this was symbolized by the introduction of the Hippocratic oath, which was an oath of allegiance to the brethren, not to the Crown or the state.

Politically, the Act was an achievement. It established a common entry standard and unified under one register medical men who practised in settings from general practice to public health and hospital medicine. Each of these groups had a long and diverse organizational history, marked by rivalry. In part as a result of this, since the beginning of the nineteenth century many bills had failed to reach the statute book. The Act established a mechanism for co-operation. However, it was only the beginning of a long consolidation process. It was not until 1886 that there was a unification of the registration qualification based on training in the three elements of clinical practice: medicine, surgery and obstetrics (Waddington 1984). Even then, qualifications continued to be awarded by a variety of bodies, an arrangement that still continues with a split between the General Medical Council, controlling undergraduate medical education, and the Royal Colleges, governing postgraduate training.

From the sixteenth century, a number of associations had provided credentials and represented the interests of those concerned with treating the sick. The Royal College of Physicians was incorporated in 1518. By the eighteenth century, it consisted of high-status, classically educated university graduates who practised 'physic'. In contrast, surgeons were a craft-based occupation. In 1540, surgeons had initially joined the Barbers Guild of London but separated from them in the mid-eighteenth century. The Royal College of Surgeons was incorporated in 1800. The apothecaries, or suppliers of medicines, were originally shopkeepers, but were granted a royal charter in 1617 (Stevens 1966). As noted by Moran in this volume, they were the first group to experience state intervention when, in 1815, a period of training was legally required as a condition of examination entry.

In the first decades of the nineteenth century, the hospitals in London, Edinburgh and Dublin became both the settings for more active treatment of the sick and teaching institutions that were the sites for the development of a more systematic, experimentally based medical knowledge. The study of anatomy was particularly significant, and research on cadavers gathered pace after the passage of the 1832 Anatomy Act allowed the dissection of corpses. During the latter half of the nineteenth century, the cognitive knowledge base of medicine developed and medical interventions became more effective. New scientific knowledge was incorporated in a sequence of training for safe practice. Sinclair (1997) considers this common knowledge base and the overlapping teaching and governance roles of the medical elites as contributing to occupational cohesion. Doubtless, too, the narrow class and gender base of recruitment also played a part.

The political organization of medicine, which included the establishment of the British Medical Association in the mid-nineteenth century, provided a number of channels for the profession to negotiate with the state, as the latter began to legislate for the public provision of personal health services. It did this first through the 1911 Insurance Act which provided access to medical care for working men, and then through the 1946 Act which introduced a tax-funded National Health Service (Allsop 1995). Since 1948, the medical profession has been incorporated in the politics of the National Health Service as a major structured interest. This has brought constraints through a web of state regulation. The Department of Health determines the funding levels and the supply of doctors to meet the requirements of the service. Terms and conditions are negotiated and state employment has, at least until recently, brought shelter from competition, access to facilities, considerable clinical autonomy, and a dominant position for doctors in the division of labour in health care.

Disciplinary mechanisms related to doctors exist in contracts of employment, the civil litigation system and other state mechanisms to provide for the redress of grievance. However, the General Medical Council remains at the apex in that it alone has the power to register a doctor as fit to practice and debar a person from earning a living through the work for which they have been trained. Although self-regulation has been conditional in theory, the rules and regulations that govern the profession are based on statute and can be altered by Parliament. Over the last 150 years, there have been relatively few Acts to alter the rules and regulations under which the Council operates although, as Price indicates in this volume, this has now changed and primary legislation is no longer necessary.[3] As recently as 1975, the Merrison Report (1975: 5) endorsed the principle of self-regulation on the grounds that 'the most effective safeguard of the public is the self-respect of the profession itself'. By allowing the regulatory task to be delegated to doctors themselves, it was felt that they would be encouraged to act more responsibly. As Moran (1999) suggests, the Council has been insulated from interference from the state despite the social and economic changes in society.

Formal regulation rests on the assumption that each and every doctor will engage in two further regulatory activities. First, they will have the capacity for self-reflection. Ideally, education and training provide not only the technical skills, but also develop an ethos of self-criticism and of placing the interests of the patient above self-interest. As many interactions between the doctor and patient take place in private, keeping up to date by reading journals, taking opportunities for training and seeing how their patients fare in comparison with those of other doctors are essential. Second, colleague controls through informal interaction and peer review are an intrinsic part of regulation. They reinforce norms and values and determine what is accepted as good clinical practice. Indeed, one of the claims for a profession is that it is both a moral and a knowledge community. It is work colleagues who are most likely to see poor practice first and the operation of informal colleague networks is the first line of defence. Only as a final resort should recourse be made to formal mechanisms for assessment and discipline.

In the final decades of the twentieth century, the efficacy and efficiency of both the informal and formal regulatory mechanisms have been questioned. The General Medical Council has been seen as the body responsible for improving both. In a contemporary version of the regulatory bargain, Sir Donald Irvine commented:

> registration gives doctors privileges and benefits, including the right to earn their own living as doctors ... the flipside of privileges and benefits is that there are duties and responsibilities that go with registration – and that is what is set out in our statement on good practice. We want doctors to realize that the GMC is the custodian of good standards and therefore protects the good name of our profession. (quoted in Smith 1995: 1515)

The role and structure of the General Medical Council from 1978 onwards

As a professional body, the General Medical Council has a dual and potentially conflicting role. It must protect the public, but is also accountable to its membership. Members fund the activities undertaken on their behalf through an annual retention fee.[4] Following the 1978 Medical Act, the General Medical Council was constituted with 97 members. In the early 1980s, the rank and file of doctors elected 50 members, and 47 were appointed by the Privy Council acting for the government of the day from elite groups within the profession, such as the Royal Colleges, the universities and the laity. There were 7 lay members. By 1997, the balance of the General Medical Council had changed so that there were now 25 lay members out of 104 members in all (GMC 1998). Thus, the Council has attempted to be more responsive both to its fee-paying membership and to the lay public.

As recent votes of 'no confidence' have shown, the political reality is that the leadership must retain the confidence of doctors on the register, as well as of the government and public. Members of the Council serve on its various sub-committees, the most important of which are described below. These carry out the more detailed work of the Council. Encouragingly, lay members now play a more important role on all committees including those concerned with complaints and professional discipline.

The regulatory tasks

Registration

Doctors can be put on the register as qualified after one satisfactory year in practice following undergraduate training. By 2000, there were 193,000 doctors on the medical register with a further 5,700 overseas qualified doctors with limited registration (GMC 2000a). Over recent decades, the profession has become more diverse, and therefore the registration task is more complex. Women now account for more than 50 per cent of doctors leaving medical school and represent an increasing proportion of doctors under the age of 40. Approximately 9,200 new graduates register each year. Of these, in 1997, 41 per cent qualified in United Kingdom medical schools; 20 per cent were nationals from countries within the European Union who are entitled to registration on the same basis as United Kingdom graduates; and 39 per cent were graduates from medical schools overseas (usually India, Pakistan and Bangladesh). The latter are required to go through different procedures, which include both a clinical and a language test.[5]

Certification

The General Medical Council has a general duty to oversee medical education so that it can determine the standard required of those wishing to register. It works with the universities to develop guidelines for the content of courses in terms of medical science and clinical practice. It has planned visits to institutions, monitors the delivery of the curriculum and inspects procedures for the final qualifying examinations. It also has the power to refuse course recognition. Since 1992, the Council has also overseen the training during the pre-registration year that forms the bridge between formal education and independent practice. It has made the teaching of medical ethics compulsory too. Specialist medical education is overseen by the Royal Colleges but, until recently, there was no specialist register to indicate postgraduate qualifications. In line with other European Union countries, the General Medical Council established a specialist register. From 1997, doctors appointed to consultant posts were expected to be on this register (GMC 2000a).

Maintaining professional standards

There are two aspects to promoting high professional standards – positively, through producing guidelines for good practice and, negatively, through identifying and dealing with poor performance. Examples of positive guidance have related to the implications of computer storage of confidential data on patients; providing contraceptive advice to under-age children; and the importance of giving patients good information and involving them in decision making. Since 1995, the General Medical Council has produced a booklet on *Good Medical Practice*. This is regularly revised and now includes requirements for undertaking professional development, audit and appraisal; telling patients when things go wrong; putting things right if possible; and reporting the poor practice of colleagues. In relation to poor performance, the General Medical Council has a duty to protect the public, and since the 1980s, in response to public concern, arrangements have become more extensive and elaborate.

The negative sanctions of the Council relate to investigating complaints from members of the public or through referral from within the health service or when the council is informed that a doctor has been convicted of a criminal offence. There are a number of ways of dealing with allegations against doctors: through health procedures introduced in 1980 and poor performance procedures established in 1997 (GMC 2000b). These aim to identify and support the practitioners involved, as appropriate. However, if necessary, there is the power to suspend or limit the practice of such doctors. Both medical and lay assessors evaluate performance against a set of criteria and can suggest a course of action such as counselling or retraining. If a doctor does not agree, disciplinary procedures can be invoked. Here, the General Medical Council acts as both investigator and adjudicator. The process is reactive and is long-winded as cases pass through a series of filters. The final stages are adversarial. The General Medical Council's lawyers take up the case against the doctor, who is normally also legally represented. The onus of proof is on the Council and procedures are designed to protect the doctor against unfair removal from the register, as their reputation and livelihood are at stake. The process is subject to judicial review. The number of cases dealt with under these procedures remains small. In 1997, there were 45 cases. In six of these, doctors were found not guilty. However, such cases attract considerable media attention. In view of these arrangements, why, then, has medical self-regulation come under challenge?

The challenge to medical self-regulation

Changes in medicine and changing public attitudes

Those who practise medicine always derive power from their position as mediators. As Goode (1994: 4) comments: 'Sickness, death and finitude are found in the human body and salvation or at least some representation of it, is present in the technical efficacy of medicine.' During the past 50 years medical practice has altered dramatically. Science and technology have given doctors powerful tools to extend and improve the quality of life. Not surprisingly, access to good quality medical care is a priority for citizens. Increasing knowledge among the public has led to rising expectations. Health consumer bodies that promote and represent the interests of health care users have also grown in number and influence (Allsop et al. 2001). A central tenet of these organizations is the importance of the patient experience. What patients want has been shown to differ in certain respects from the assumptions of doctors.

In the early 1980s there developed a general critique of medical dominance (see, for example, Kennedy 1983). Social changes had led to a concern for patients' rights to autonomy, choice, equality of access to services and, eventually, a call for a new partnership with doctors (Coulter 1999). There is now also a greater awareness of the risks and uncertainty of professional practice, leading to greater scepticism towards the claims of experts. This has been noted by a number of theorists, notably Giddens (1990) and Beck (1992), and has been referred to by O'Malley (1992) as a 'new prudentialism'. These concerns have been reflected in the media interest in the failures of medical practice, the steady rise in complaints about health care, and the focus of government policy on safety – particularly through identifying and learning from adverse events (Department of Health 2000a; Allsop and Mulcahy 2001; Vincent 2001). This has been summed up neatly in the recent General Medical Council report attributed to Professor Sir Cyril Chantler: 'Medicine used to be simple, ineffective and relatively safe. Now it is complex, effective and potentially dangerous. Potential benefit and potential risk go hand in hand' (GMC 2000b: 8).

By the 1990s, as a consequence of new techniques for surveillance of the content of medical work, the detail of day-to-day medical work has developed and become more transparent. Outputs and outcomes can be more easily accessed. In the 1980s, research led by economists and epidemiologists indicated wide variations in clinical practice and in clinical outcomes. Subsequently, evidence-based medicine founded on the principles of the randomized controlled trial meant that some treatments could be evaluated in terms of efficacy and this offered a basis for developing guidelines and protocols. Both the profession and government embraced this development as a method for establishing good practice (Harrison 1998).

Most recently, the importance of identifying and analyzing adverse events has been highlighted (Leape et al. 1991). A recent report has indicated that there may be 850,000 adverse health care events each year in the National Health Service (Department of Health 2000a). Ways of learning from adverse events – as well as complaints from members of the public – and preventing them from occurring in the future are being developed. These techniques not only provide ways of assessing the content of individual doctor–patient interactions, they also hold up a model of perfectibility. They have led to a questioning of the adequacy of existing forms of regulation; the relationship between state and professional regulation; and about what interests should be represented in the regulation process. Unsurprisingly, they have led to demands to improve the efficacy and efficiency of the systems for professional regulation.

The shortcomings of professional and state regulatory systems

It was suggested above that there are different levels of regulation. This can take place through formal structures or informal networks. By the 1990s it had been demonstrated that, although poor practice was widely known within informal colleague networks, it was often condoned or ignored. Protecting the good name of the profession was more important than the public interest (Stacey 1992). This could be, and often was, construed as turning a blind eye to poor practice, and supporting colleagues in the face of criticism. The interview-based study by Rosenthal (1995) of attitudes among senior doctors confirmed a conspiracy of silence and the failure of informal networks to reveal and deal with poor practice. Similarly, in their studies of doctors' response to complaints, Allsop and Mulcahy (1998) found defensive attitudes towards admitting mistakes. Furthermore, the notion of self-appraisal could also be said to be psychologically flawed. The people who are least likely to be capable of assessing their own performance are those who are below standard.

These weaknesses have been exacerbated by the dominance of medicine, to the exclusion of other professions, in decision making within the National Health Service (Harrison et al. 1992). From 1948 until the mid-1990s, doctors controlled the review and redress mechanisms designed to scrutinize their work (Donaldson 1994; Allsop and Mulcahy 1996). Senior doctors shaped the culture and work life of their juniors and were largely insulated from managerial control (Salter 1999; Harrison and Ahmed 2000). These factors created barriers to identifying and dealing with poor performance quickly within the National Health Service. Moreover, its systems did not interface with those of the General Medical Council. In sum, poor practice was not typically 'seen' by colleagues, let alone by managers and the general public, and was not therefore referred to the Council. A remarkably frank consultation paper, *Supporting Doctors, Protecting Patients* (Department of Health 2000c), recently attempted to assess the scale of the problem. The statistics make cautionary reading. It indicated, for example, that 6 per cent of the senior hospital workforce in any five-year period may have performance problems, and 21–50 per cent of doctors in all career grades have been reported as having high levels of psychological disturbance. Subsequently, a number of measures – discussed by Price in this volume – have been introduced in response to this situation (Department of Health 2001).

During the 1990s, the weaknesses in both the General Medical Council and National Health Service regulatory systems were revealed in a number of widely publicized cases. Many of these were dealt with serially by different statutory mechanisms, as individuals and government sought explanations and/or justice in the public interest. A number came before the General Medical Council's Professional Conduct Committee. A close reading of these cases indicates some common themes, such as: the lack of insight that poorly performing doctors have into their own behaviour; the failure of informal peer networks to report persistent poor practice; and a failure by both the National Health Service and the General Medical Council to act with sufficient speed to protect the public. For example, the first negligence claim against Mr Ingolby, a surgeon, dated from 1989. By

1997, 84 claims had been made yet his contract of employment with the National Health Service was not terminated until 2000. Following this, his case was reviewed by the General Medical Council (Dyer 2000a; Dyer 2000b). A gynae-cologist, Mr Ledward, also continued to practise despite accumulating evidence of a high level of post-operative problems in patients, which were known to colleagues and managers over a long period (GMC 2000a: 43).

The public inquiry set up to investigate the treatment of babies treated for heart conditions at the Bristol Royal Infirmary, where there was a very high mortality rate, recently reported (Bristol Inquiry 2001). The inquiry followed the erasure of two cardiac surgeons from the General Medical Council register and the suspen-sion of a third in 1998. It showed a range of system failures, both professional and managerial, as well as a culture that did not focus on openness, partnership and patient safety. In 2000, Dr Shipman, a general practitioner in the north of England, was found to have murdered a large number of his elderly patients by prescribing lethal doses of drugs. Investigations to date have shown gaps in pro-cedures for reviewing unusually high numbers of deaths; shortcomings in the review of death certification; the possibilities for stockpiling drugs despite systems to review prescribing patterns among general practitioners; and a failure by the General Medical Council to keep people who have been suspended in the past under review. In all the above instances, the public had patently not been protected from persistent poor performance.

Weaknesses in the General Medical Council's quality assessment of medical education have also been identified. Reviews of curricula and delivery were infrequent. Until recently, junior doctors had little structured education. Frequent job changes, long working hours, little supervision, poor teaching and a lack of support were common experiences among junior doctors. One study showed that they could be de-motivated and cynical as a consequence (Dowling and Barrett 1991). More worryingly, junior doctors sometimes carried out work that was beyond their competence, without supervision (Vincent et al. 1993). In addition, a recent related area of concern has been that of good practice in medical research. Cases where doctors have submitted false case reports for publication, forged consent forms and falsified medical records have come to light. As a result, work is being undertaken to develop guidance in this area. These guide-lines have a value not only in encouraging good practice, but also in providing a measure for making judgements about poor practice (Committee on Publication Ethics 2000; GMC 2000a).

In summary, the inadequacy of informal networks and the weaknesses of National Health Service mechanisms, together with a more critical public, have led to increasing pressure not only on the General Medical Council, but also on the Health Service Commissioner and the courts. In relation to the latter, as Stone comments in this volume, claims for medical negligence have been rising steadily. For some years, the Council has been described by critics as arcane, slow, cumbersome, overly judicial and unable to grasp the patient perspective (Robinson 1988; Stacey 1992). Doctors themselves complained that it was remote and unapproachable. The General Medical Council itself now accepts the case for change (GMC 2000a). However, by the mid-1990s, there was a body of informed opinion that self-regulation itself should go (see, for instance, National Consumer Council 1999).

Changes in the state regulation of medicine

In the context of mounting concern, both government and the profession have introduced a variety of new measures, as set out below. These will increase the surveillance of medical work at all levels and across different sectors, within the National Health Service and the private sector (Health Committee 1999a).

Measures introduced by government

Until very recently, the efforts of Labour administrations have focused on institutional and managerial change rather than increasing resources to improve the quality of health care. Price outlined the institutional changes in an earlier chapter, including the introduction of the National Institute for Clinical Excellence and the Commission for Health Improvement. Within health authorities and trusts, clinical governance has brought a new statutory duty for senior managers to account for the quality of all health care in their organizations, including clinical care. They are responsible for ensuring that systems for monitoring and improving the quality of services and holding staff to account are in place. Systems for introducing evidence-based practice through audit, appraisal and professional development are also now required – as are systems for adverse incident and complaints reporting. In practice, the concept of clinical governance will take time to develop. However, the aim is to 'reduce variance' in standards of clinical care by identifying clinicians who are performing poorly, and encouraging those who are mediocre to aspire to better practice. It is also to check the work of individual practitioners. Implicit in clinical governance is a system of hierarchy in medical management, in which the medical director and the chief executive are responsible for clinical standards. This is a concept alien to traditional medical practice. The procedures are designed to ensure that doctors are up to date, to formalize peer review and to link these to systems being developed within the General Medical Council (Department of Health 1998; Department of Health 2000b).

Changes in the General Medical Council

Over the past five years, the challenge for the General Medical Council has been to move towards a managed and flexible organization able to respond quickly to public concerns. This has meant changing from an elite, closed and inflexible organization towards a more transparent and accountable body representing a wider range of interests, as well as the medical community. In making changes to satisfy the public, government and Parliament, it has had to maintain the confidence of its own membership as well as to address new problems such as the implications for registration of the expansion of European membership (GMC 2000a).

A new scheme for the regular reaccreditation of all practising doctors has been a major development. All doctors, whether they work within or outside the National Health Service and are in training or in temporary employment, will have to show every five years that they are fit to practise. This scheme, agreed in 1998 will be in place by 2002 (GMC 2000b). The aim is to seek evidence that doctors are practising to a safe standard in both the clinical and managerial aspects of their work. The definition of competence will include an assessment of relationships with patients; of effective teamwork; participation in continuing development and performance; and competency in diagnosis, management and the practical skills of good clinical care. A portfolio containing evidence of competence and performance will form the basis of the review and may also include other forms of assessment, such as observation or surveying patients' views. The review will take place at a local level and will be undertaken by a team that includes lay members and senior doctors. Registration will then either be revalidated or kept under review with the possibility of referral to the General Medical Council for formal consideration (Southgate and Pringle 1999).

A second area of change has been in the General Medical Council's fitness-to-practise procedures, relating to the work of what the General Medical Council now terms 'dysfunctional doctors'. In 1997, a new Fitness to Practise Policy Committee was set up to deal with doctors who persistently and repeatedly fail to comply with accepted standards. This has meant the appointment of about 400 doctors as well as lay people who can be drawn upon to act as assessors at the local level. The regulations have been altered so that decisions can be made speedily (within seven days) if there is thought to be a risk to patients. Taken as a whole, the scope of surveillance in relation to practising doctors has been extended and lay people will have a greater role in assessing the work of medical professionals.

A third set of changes relates to the structure of the Council itself. In 2000, radical revisions were announced by the General Medical Council to strengthen strategic management capacity and to extend lay representation. Although it will continue to be led by a medically qualified President, a small executive board of 35 members, 40 per cent of whom will be lay people, will develop policy and take responsibility for meeting its statutory obligations on a day-to-day basis. The changes will require legislation and represent an attempt by the General Medical Council to win back support from the public and manage its business more effectively.

Discussion and conclusion

In this chapter, it has been suggested that the high value placed on medical work linked to public expectations of high-quality performance is changing the relations between the state and the profession and what is understood by 'self-regulation' within medicine. The process of change has also been affected by the development of techniques for surveillance through information technologies and bureaucratic processes. This is altering how medicine is governed and who is involved in the process. In relation to the former, there has been a shift in what Dean (1999) calls the 'analytics of government'. In an elaboration of Foucault's notion of governmentality, Dean sees four dimensions to the process of governing. The first is the way in which people 'see' and 'perceive' issues. The second is the particular ways of thinking and questioning that draw on particular vocabularies and methods for validating knowledge. The third relates to decisions to intervene that use specific mechanisms or techniques. The last is based on identities and roles and can be constructed in particular ways.

The changes in the ways which both the state and the General Medical Council propose to regulate medicine indicate shifts in all of these dimensions. Put in a very simplified way, the problems are now perceived as poorly performing doctors, an out-of-date General Medical Council and a National Health Service which was managed in a way that has allowed the medical mandate to prevail. Perceptions about how these issues should be tackled have altered. A new language summed up by the term 'dysfunctional doctor' has emerged. New institutions and new methodologies for surveillance have been developed, as well as new hierarchies and roles. More doctors are involved in managing service delivery and in assessing each other's performance through clinical audit, appraisal and reaccreditation. There is a greater degree of hierarchy within the profession and greater diversity in roles and tasks. A major cultural change has been that it is a professional duty to refer colleagues should a doctor believe that their performance is deficient. This has replaced the professional code that doctors should not disparage each other as this would bring the profession into disrepute.

With respect to who does the governing, major changes are underway. The monitoring, checking, governing and regulating are being carried out by much larger numbers of people with clearly defined tasks and roles. As a result, more people at a local and national level will hold more information on individual doctors. This applies within the three spheres referred to by Salter (1999): knowledge creation, research and its application to clinical practice; knowledge transmission; training and education and the performance of medical work. The representation of the lay interest is much stronger, as also is that of government – either directly, or indirectly through managers.

The term 'stakeholder regulation' has gained currency, indicating that professional governance is the task of other interest groups besides doctors (Davies 2000). Managers, other health professionals, particular areas of expertise and the lay interest are represented in the new National Health Service and professional structures. The process of governance will also need to shift towards a more open, democratic and accountable form – described by Dryzek (1990), Giddens (1994) and Hirst (1996) as an associative, or deliberative, participatory democracy. These terms acknowledge a variety of interests and perspectives and focus on problem identification and problem solving through a process of discussion with the interests involved.

The changes already introduced, and those proposed by governments in their modernization programmes and by the General Medical Council, have met with opposition. Smith (2000) suggests that the changes currently proposed might go further than British doctors will accept. Some commentators are concerned about the large number of people involved in the new General Medical Council procedures and the consequent threat to the doctor's privacy. They draw attention to the problems of maintaining the confidentiality and privacy of both doctors and patients. There is also an anxiety about the overlap between state and professional procedures and the possibilities of over-regulation, with a concern with process rather than outcomes – which may limit the attainment of higher standards. Other more practically based criticisms are the difficulty of training and recruiting assessors; arranging programmes of continuing professional education and, if necessary, retraining; and providing practice supervision.

One benefit of the changes relates to poor professional performance. There is movement away from a prosecutory/disciplinary model of regulation where a few bad doctors are identified and blamed and then punitive sanctions are applied. It is recognized that weaknesses relate to systems as well to as individuals, and the responsibility for identifying and dealing with poor performance lies with managers and other professionals within the workplace as well as with doctors themselves. Similarly, changes in the governance structure in ways that widen access to other groups of stakeholders spreads the responsibility for professional governance. The development of ways of involving the lay public in regulation and ensuring professional accountability will be a challenge. If they are not centrally involved, new forms of regulation may prove simply to be a more sophisticated version of regulation by the professionals themselves.

Notes

1 These are the sentiments expressed by a number of complainants and patients' groups acting for them. See the Minutes of Evidence from the inquiry into procedures related to adverse clinical incidents and outcomes in medical care (Health Committee 1999b).

2 For further details see Allsop and Mulcahy (1996) and Kennedy and Grubb (2000).

3 This has changed as a consequence of the 1999 Health Act which gives Parliament powers to alter some regulations by statutory instrument.

4 Until the 1970s, there was a single registration fee. The introduction of an annual fee caused a revolt among rank-and-file doctors that led to the setting up of the Merrison Commission (see Stacey 1992).

5 Of these, 27 per cent obtained limited registration which entitled them to work in hospitals in the United Kingdom under supervision for five years (GMC 1998: 13). As Stacey (1992) comments, the National Health Service has come to rely heavily on overseas doctors. In 1938 they represented one-twentieth of the names on the Register and at the end of 1997 this was well over one-third. The General Medical Council has long experience of checking and maintaining the quality of overseas graduates, as links were formed with medical schools in the colonial past.

References

Allsop, J. (1995) *Health Policy and the NHS*. London: Longman, 2nd edn.
Allsop, J. and Mulcahy, L. (1996) *Regulating Medical Work: Formal and Informal Controls*. Buckingham: Open University Press.

Allsop, J. and Mulcahy, L. (1998) 'Maintaining professional identity: Doctors' responses to complaints', *Sociology of Health and Illness*, 20: 812–34.

Allsop, J. and Mulcahy, L. (2001) 'Dealing with clinical complaints', in C. Vincent (ed.) *Clinical Risk Management*. London: British Medical Journal Books, 2nd edn.

Allsop, J., Baggott, R. and Jones, K. (2001) 'Health consumer groups and the national policy process', in S. Henderson and A. Petersen (eds) *Consuming Health: The Commodification of Health Care*. London: Routledge.

Beck, U. (1992) *The Risk Society*. London: Sage.

Bristol Inquiry (2001) *Learning from Bristol*, Public Inquiry into Children's Heart Surgery at the Bristol Royal Infirmary 1984–1995. London: The Stationery Office.

Committee on Publication Ethics (2000) *Committee on Publication Ethics*. London: BMA Publishing.

Coulter, A. (1999) 'Paternalism or partnership?', *British Medical Journal*, 319: 719.

Davies, C. (2000) *Stakeholder Regulation: A Discussion Paper*. London: Royal College of Nursing.

Dean, M. (1999) *Governmentality: Power and Rule in Modern Society*. London: Sage.

Department of Health (1998) *A First Class Service*. London: Department of Health.

Department of Health (2000a) *An Organization with a Memory*. London: The Stationery Office.

Department of Health (2000b) *The NHS Plan*. London: The Stationery Office.

Department of Health (2000c) *Supporting Doctors, Protecting Patients. A Consultation Paper on Preventing, Recognising, and Dealing with Poor Performance of Doctors in England*. London: Department of Health.

Department of Health (2001) *Building a Safer NHS for Patients: Implementing an Organization with a Memory*. London: Department of Health.

Donaldson, L. (1994) 'Doctors with problems in the NHS workforce', *British Medical Journal*, 308: 1277–82.

Dowling, S. and Barrett, S. (1991) *Doctors in the Making: The Experience of the Post-Registration Year*. Bristol: School of Advanced Urban Studies.

Dryzek, J. (1990) *Discursive Democracy: Politics, Policy and Political Science*. Cambridge: Cambridge University Press.

Dyer, C. (2000a) 'GMC mishandled father's complaint', *British Medical Journal*, 321: 11.

Dyer, C. (2000b) 'Surgeon sacked for "misconduct and misjudgement"', *British Medical Journal*, 321: 321.

Freidson, E. (1970) *Profession of Medicine: A Study in the Sociology of Applied Knowledge*. New York: Dodd, Mead & Co.

Giddens, A. (1990) *The Consequences of Modernity*. Cambridge: Polity Press.

Giddens, A. (1994) *Beyond Left and Right: The Future of Radical Politics*. Cambridge: Polity Press.

GMC (1998) *General Medical Council: Annual Review*. London: General Medical Council.

GMC (2000a) *Changing Times, Changing Culture: A Review of the GMC since 1995*. London: General Medical Council.

GMC (2000b) *Proposals for Revalidation: Ensuring Standards, Securing the Future*. London: General Medical Council.

Goode, B. (1994) *Medicine, Rationality and Experience: An Anthropological Perspective*. Cambridge: Cambridge University Press.

Harrison, S. (1998) 'The politics of evidence-based medicine', *Policy and Politics*, 26: 15–22.

Harrison, S. and Ahmed, W. (2000) 'Medical autonomy and the UK state 1975–2025', *Sociology*, 34: 129–46.

Harrison, S., Hunter, D., Marnoch, G. and Pollitt, C. (1992) *Just Managing: Power and Culture in the NHS*. London: Macmillan.

Health Committee (1999a) *The Regulation of Private and Other Independent Healthcare*. London: The Stationery Office.

Health Committee (1999b) *Procedures Related to Adverse Clinical Incidents and Outcomes in Medical Care: Minutes of Evidence 24 June*. House of Commons Session 1998–9, London: The Stationery Office.

Hirst, P. (1996) *Associative Democracy: New Forms of Economic and Social Governance*. Cambridge: Polity Press.

Kennedy, I. (1983) *The Unmasking of Medicine*. London: Granada Publishing.

Kennedy, I. and Grubb, A. (2000) *Medical Law*. London: Butterworths, 3rd edn.

Larson, M. (1977) *The Rise of Professionalism: A Sociological Analysis*. Berkeley: University of California Press.

Leape, L., Brennan, T., Laird, N., Lawthers, A., Localio, A. and Barnes, B. (1991) 'The incidence of adverse events and negligence in hospitalised patients', *New England Journal of Medicine*, 324: 377–94.

Merrison Report (1975) *Report of the Committee of Inquiry into the Regulation of the Medical Profession*. London: HMSO.

Moran, M. (1999) *Governing the Health Care State: A Comparative Study of the United Kingdom, United States and Germany*. Manchester: Manchester University Press.

National Consumer Council (1999) *Self-Regulation of Professionals in Health Care Consumer Issues*. London: National Consumer Council.

O'Malley, P. (1992) 'Risk, power and crime prevention', *Economy and Society*, 21: 252–75.

Robinson, J. (1988) *A Patient Voice at the GMC: A Lay Member's View of the GMC*. London: Health Rights.

Rosenthal, M. (1995) *The Incompetent Doctor: Behind Closed Doors*. Buckingham: Open University Press.

Salter, B. (1999) *Medical Regulation and Public Trust: An International Review*. London: King's Fund Publishing.

Sinclair, S. (1997) *Making Doctors: An Institutional Apprenticeship*. New York: Berg.

Smith, R. (1994) *Medical Discipline: The Professional Conduct of the GMC 1858–1990*. Oxford: Oxford University Press.

Smith, R. (1995) 'The future of the GMC: An interview with Donald Irvine, the new president', *British Medical Journal*, 310: 1515–18.

Smith R. (2000) 'Should the GMC leader be put to the sword?', *British Medical Journal*, 321: 61.

Southgate, L. and Pringle, M. (1999) 'Revalidation in the United Kingdom: General principles based on experience in general practice', *British Medical Journal*, 319: 1180.

Stacey, M. (1992) *Regulating British Medicine: The General Medical Council*. Chichester: John Wiley & Sons.

Stevens, R. (1966) *Medical Practice in Modern England*. New Haven: Yale University Press.

Vincent, C. (2001) (ed.) *Clinical Risk Management*. London: British Medical Journal Books, 2nd edn.

Vincent, C., Ennis, M. and Audley, R. (1993) *Medical Accidents*. Oxford: Oxford University Press.

Waddington, I. (1984) *The Medical Profession in the Industrial Revolution*. London: Gill & Macmillan.

6 Registering a Difference: Changes in the Regulation of Nursing[1]

Celia Davies

Nursing is, and has always been, by far the largest and most diverse of the statutorily regulated health professions. Legislation in 1979 disbanded separate arrangements for health visitors and district nurses, amalgamating these and the different regulatory traditions of nurses and midwives into a single registering body.[2] By 1998, the total number of persons on the register was in excess of 600,000, the names of many registrants appearing on several of the 15 parts into which the register was divided. The overwhelming majority, more than 90 per cent of registrants, are women, whose career breaks and name changes on marriage necessarily present challenges for the upkeep of a register on this massive scale. Educational achievement ranges from those with graduate or post-graduate qualifications to those who would have had very little in the way of formal educational qualifications at all, such as those entering enrolled nurse training in the 1950s and 1960s. Nursing is less the province of young women than in the past. Less than 15 per cent of registrants in 1998 were under 30. This, however, is more a function of National Health Service employers in the early 1990s deciding to take on fewer students than a deliberate decision to diversify recruitment (Buchan and Edwards 2000). Shortages are prompting special initiatives designed to attract part-time recruits, older recruits, male recruits and recruits from minority ethnic groups. The routine registration statistics of the United Kingdom Central Council for Nursing, Midwifery and Health Visiting cast no great light on these matters. Other sources, however, would seem to suggest that little dent has been made in the white female image of nursing in the National Health Service, still by far the largest employer of nurses (Beishon et al. 1995).

What does it mean to attempt to set regulatory standards for such a group? This chapter will argue that regulatory practices in nursing must be understood in terms of the triple historical subordination of nurses – as principally employed by the hospital authorities, as 'handmaidens' in relation to doctors, and as women in relation to men. In 1919, when statutory registration was first introduced in England, there was little option but to accept as a legitimate route for entry all the trainings provided by the variety of voluntary and poor law hospitals, both large and small. The day-to-day work of student nurses on the wards was already too tightly bound up with the survival of these institutions for matters to be otherwise. This meant that the skills that students acquired were highly variable. The gulf between those who had trained in a prestigious teaching hospital in London or the provinces and those who gained their experience elsewhere was wide. The distance between the majority, who had enjoyed a general training in an acute hospital, and the minorities, who had taken a route through the more specialized hospitals, was also great. It was underlined by the creation on the one hand of the general register and on the other of what were termed 'supplementary' registers for sick children's nurses, mental nurses and nurses of the mentally subnormal (Dingwall et al. 1988; Carpenter 1993).

In relation to the entanglement of nursing with medicine, its early twentieth-century knowledge base was an amalgam of information gleaned from lectures by medical staff and practical skills learned on the job. These were laced with a nineteenth-century emphasis on creating a kindly and caring manner and enhancing the 'womanliness' of the nurse. Obedient rule-following in a nursing hierarchy, readiness to be deployed as a 'pair of hands', and a willingness to act as helper and handmaiden to the doctor were key qualities that were instilled. Those who thought otherwise had a hard path to tread (Rafferty 1996). Nurses' subordination as women both fed these other forms of subordination, and in turn was fed by them. From the start, regulating a group diverse in its experience, enmeshed in, and subordinated by, its employment relations and by the division of labour with medicine – as well as by gender – was going to be a challenge of a different order from regulating doctors.

The roots of this chapter lie in a theorization that brings to the fore the gendered character of professions. It focuses on the way in which institutions reflect the social, economic and political inequalities, principally of gender, but also of 'race' and class (Carpenter 1993; Davies 1995; Davies 2001). My aim is to draw attention to the specificities of the experience of statutory regulation of nurses and begin to examine the way this is inflected by their triply subordinated position in the health care division of labour. In the context of what has always been skeleton legislation, the scope of a regulatory body to interpret regulation appears very wide indeed. In practice, the power afforded by statute is a function not only of the detailed terms of the legislation, but also of the position of a group in the division of labour and the status and respect that it can command.

Legacies of initial legislation

In his classic nursing history, Abel-Smith (1960) regards the Nurses Act of 1919 as a high-water mark of recognition for nursing. Government had put in the hands of nurses themselves the legal right to make a distinction between the qualified and unqualified, to establish and maintain a register of the qualified and to decide on the educational conditions that would merit entry to it. Nurses, in his words, 'came to power' at this point. The implication was that they were now, in terms of institutional structures and legal standing, on a par with doctors. Writing 30 years later and in a very different climate, Witz (1992) comes to a different conclusion. She reads a thread of dismissiveness and misogyny in Abel-Smith's concern with a background of 'rampant snobbery and militant feminism' and his emphasis on personalities and factions within nursing that surrounded the establishment of registration.[3] The key point, she argues, is that it was the Minister of Health's Bill that reached the statute book. Nurses were 'tightly constrained within a state–profession relation in which they were the weaker partner' (Witz 1992: 165). Their subordination to their hospital employers and to doctors remained.

The newer historiography of nursing has produced accounts, both of the events leading to registration and of its subsequent development, that bear out this revisionist view (White 1976; Bellaby and Oribabor 1980; Davies 1980; Davies 1982; Dingwall et al. 1988; Rafferty 1996). These analyses document how the state repeatedly intervened to prevent the new statutory body, the General Nursing Council, from gaining a legal underpinning for the actions it wished to take.[4] In its early years, for example, the Council was thwarted on the matter of the content of a training syllabus; on whether the syllabus should be more than merely advisory; and on the question of grouping hospitals to ensure that students might access a range of experience. It was overruled in instances where it wished to withdraw approval from institutions; and it found no support for its wish to appoint inspectors. Rafferty (1996), in a detailed documentation of these events, goes on to refer to the mounting 'cascade of criticism' the General Nursing Council faced in the 1930s when its aim of more selective recruitment fell victim to employers' fears of dwindling supply. She sees the legislation in 1943 and 1949, including the creation of a second grade of nurse, as reflecting a 'deep-seated scepticism about the GNC's capacity to effect reform' (Rafferty 1996: 176). The subsequent pattern of policy development is also viewed as consigning the Council to the role of a mere 'figurehead' in the newly established National Health Service.[5]

Nurses and nursing were demoralized and demeaned by this specific history of regulation in several ways. First, their ability to give leadership to the profession was in doubt. The Ministry of Health, before and again after the formation of the National Health Service, allied itself with the employers in concerns about budgets and staffing. It regarded the General Nursing Council as unrealistic and inflexible in the goals it pursued. Perhaps it also saw members as lacking the intelligence to think strategically in policy terms and to understand the implications of the reforms they sought (Davies and Beach 2000). Nursing's own professional associations and trade unions were often equally disparaging. Viewed from their angle, there was deep frustration that the Council appeared unable to break the deadlock that exploited students as pairs of hands and readily substituted unqualified for qualified staff. This contributed further to a sense that nursing lacked coherent leadership. Secondly, social divisions within nursing if anything grew wider. A new university-educated elite started to form alongside the middle-class cadre in the high-prestige teaching hospitals and began to create an independent nursing knowledge, threatening to others in the profession. The expansion of higher education in the 1960s and the power of the General Nursing Council under the 1943 Nurses Act to approve experimental schemes facilitated this.

Old tensions between male and female nurses took a new form as male nurses on the mental health and mental handicap supplementary registers began to take a second qualification to join the general register, and thence to take a hold on senior positions disproportionate to their numbers. Acute shortages of staff had forced the reluctant acceptance of a second grade of nurse. This laid the ground-work for inequalities of 'race' to become institutionalized as nurses from the Caribbean, Mauritius and elsewhere found themselves channelled into enrolled nursing and their route out of it blocked. Black staff were also concentrated disproportionately in unqualified and auxiliary grades in the National Health Service (Doyal et al. 1981). Shortages also meant that for the first time, in the 1950s, married women returned to nursing on a part-time basis, producing tensions with the mainly single women in senior positions who had dedicated their lives to their work.

The third factor in this demoralizing and demeaning cycle stemmed from the action of the General Nursing Council itself. Its strategy, in face of opposition in other areas, was to maintain standards by being as prescriptive as it could about what was to be covered in the curriculum. It had some successes with this (Bendall and Raybould 1969). However, when this came together with a nursing labour force in the hospitals comprised of a transient student population and a high proportion of unqualified staff, the result was double-edged. It helped sustain a hierarchical, militaristic, rule-oriented culture with a checklist mentality in education and a top-down allocation of tasks. Those who were qualified felt that they could ensure good quality care only through exercising close hierarchical control over juniors. The nurse thus had neither a satisfactory educational experience nor the opportunity to carry out independent practice on qualification. To get the latter, many moved out – into district nursing, health visiting or midwifery.

The position of the nurses contrasts sharply with that of the doctors. The medical profession had achieved regulatory legislation before the state sought to intervene in any major way in health provision (Brazier et al. 1993). As the state took more direct responsibility for services, doctors were able to protect clinical autonomy and negotiate conditions reflective of independent practitioner status (see Chapter 5 by Allsop in this volume). Nursing regulation, by contrast, coincided with the formation of the Ministry of Health and came into being at a time 'when the state was not only assuming even greater responsibility for health care but also cutting back on its costs' (Witz 1992: 163). Qualified nurses have always been predominantly a managed labour force – rarely able to act as independent practitioners. With strong medical trade unions and respect for the profession, medical regulation could remain a 'light touch' affair. The General Medical Council could operate almost as a gentlemen's club, reflecting the esteem in which its members were held and having no aspirations to intervene in the activities of the medical schools and Royal Colleges (Stacey 1992; Davies 2001). Nursing regulation, by contrast, was from the start used as a mechanism to try to assemble that respect and prestige. It was all too easy for everyone, including nurses, to blame the General Nursing Council for this state of affairs. But this was too easy a target. Regulation was enmeshed in, and itself reflected, the subordinated position of nurses that it sought to change. Gender imagery lent ready explanations for the inadequacies and unrealistic aspirations of a group dominated by women.

New dimensions of regulation

In 1979, new legislation came at the end of a long period of demoralization and delay. The Nurses, Midwives and Health Visitors Act swept away a long trail of amendments to previous legislation and began again. It laid the basis for a single professional register, introducing greater heterogeneity by bringing together groups who had previously operated quite separately and reconciling the arrangements that had prevailed in the different parts of the United Kingdom. Midwives, health visitors and district nurses, who regarded themselves as having escaped from the particular contradictions and restrictions of nursing regulation, were doubtful about being brought into the fold. This was a key factor in the delay between the Briggs Report (1972) and the legislation in 1979 (Dingwall et al. 1988; Davies and Beach 2000). It was going to be a major challenge to hold such diverse groups together.

The Act said remarkably little that was new, indeed remarkably little at all, about the rationale, purpose and justification of professional self-regulation. The duty to prepare and maintain a register was familiar stuff of statutory regulation of professions, as was the requirement to enact provisions through secondary legislation. There were certain important new powers: to make registration subject to renewal; to decide on standards of further training; to give advice on professional conduct and to remove from the register on grounds of ill-health. However, it was the statement in the Act that the principal functions of the new Central Council for Nursing, Midwifery and Health Visiting were 'to establish and improve standards' both of training and professional conduct that was galvanizing. Having a direct remit to improve standards gave regulators a fresh sense of confidence about possibility and purpose. Reform of pre-registration education to remove the use about students as 'pairs of hands' in the hospital wards was at the top of the agenda (see Davies 1995; Davies and Beach 2000). But regulators also began to turn their 'improving' gaze to those already on the register. A distinctive and significantly altered understanding of statutory regulation through registration was the result. This is the focus of the discussion in the following parts of this chapter.

Actively reshaping professional identity

The new regulatory bodies had to make arrangements for dealing with removal from the register on the grounds of misconduct and now also of poor health. The view was that the primary purpose of such hearings was the maintenance of standards within the profession, not punishment of the practitioner (Davies and Beach 2000). Developments were put in train to enable misconduct hearings to be a learning experience for the profession. Attendance at hearings and discussion with panel members after the event was encouraged. There were increasing efforts to review the pattern of cases and a full-length textbook was prepared that ran to several editions (Pyne 1981). More important, and potentially more powerful, was the preparation of a Code of Conduct. In conduct hearings, it could help to indicate why behaviour was deemed inappropriate. What it could also do was to set expectations for the practising nurse.

The first edition of the Code (UKCC 1983) was made widely available. It stressed that registered practitioners should be accountable for practice and able and willing to take responsibility for personal and professional development. They should also be confident enough to question levels of resourcing and the behaviours of others, where these might compromise patient care. By 1992, when the third revision of the Code was issued, the message had become stronger and more direct. Practice in a professional area, it was emphasized, was an exercise of judgement and skill. Here was acknowledgement that nurses were now being asked to undertake extended and expanded roles. In relation to these, the United Kingdom Central Council offered guiding principles and questions to ask – such as whether change was in the interests of the patient or client and whether the practitioner's own knowledge was sufficient for what was proposed. The message was that nurses could, and should, take up the opportunities being afforded by the changing National Health Service to develop their practice, and that they should do so in a framework where they took responsibility for their decisions. In practice, this was often more easily said than done, given the unequal power relations that nurses faced (Dowling et al. 1996; Doyal et al. 1998).

It was clear that the demands of the Code could put those on the register in a dilemma about the right course of action to take, and efforts were made to be responsive and to offer help where this was needed. A Professional Advisor was appointed to deal with the many telephone calls being received asking for guidance. This work was to evolve into a full-scale Professional Advisory Service that was given the responsibility both to respond to, and to analyse, emerging themes. The new Standards and Ethics Committee, set up in 1988, also responded to practitioner concerns. Confusions over the role of nurses in residential care and over the proper use of practice nurses were topics tackled in its early days. Dialogue with practitioners preceded the preparation of later guidelines. A 1996 document dealt with the issues that practitioners were grappling with – patient advocacy, complementary therapy, informed consent, research and audit (UKCC 1996b). The appointment of specialist officers in the fields of mental health, learning disability and paediatric nursing extended the focus to specific specialist areas.

Could nurses practise the autonomy the statutory body preached? Certainly there was government pressure now for nurses to extend the scope of their roles, taking over, for example, some of the work of junior doctors whose hours of work had been reduced. But there was a danger, despite all the advice, that nurses would end up feeling that they were in a position of responsibility without power (Carpenter 1993; Orr 1995). The United Kingdom Central Council for Nursing, Midwifery and Health Visiting, however, was not just exhorting nurses to change, it was in the process of making their professional development mandatory, through an altogether new approach to registration.

The idea of an 'effective' register

Control over a register gives to a profession the power to decide who is qualified and hence to control many aspects of the character and conditions of its work. It is this that gives rise to such sociological understandings of statutory regulation as the granting of significant power, privilege and protection. But a statutory register, by providing the means of verifying a specific qualification, also has the potential to protect the public. This has always been, implicitly at least, part of its rationale. The physical availability of the published medical register, to which the public can refer, gives some meaning to this. For nursing, the sheer numbers of nurses had always worked against the possibility of producing a published document. Furthermore, with no contact following registration, there had been no easy way to keep addresses up to date, or even to remove the entries for those who had died, and, in a profession overwhelmingly of women, no means of keeping track of change of names on marriage or divorce. General Nursing Council records were not reconciled with those kept by district nursing, health visiting or midwifery bodies, so tracking an individual was not feasible.

After 1979, there was a new capacity for creating a unified, computerized database that after 1990 was available on-line. This brought the idea of a usable register back within reach. Employers could therefore play their part by routinely confirming the registration status of employees, although this was not mandatory. But was this enough? A qualification achieved at one point in time was neither an effective assurance that a person had kept up to date with developments, nor an affirmation that the skills were still current. A register that was effective in protecting the public, it was now reasoned, should surely ensure that those registered were currently fit to practise. As early as 1982, the United Kingdom Central Council accepted both the idea of working towards return-to-practice courses for those who had been absent and the notion of regular updating or 'mandatory refreshment' for those in work. In this way, the register would be an 'effective' register and registration would mean much more in terms of standards than it had previously done. There was an important precedent for this in midwives' annual notification to practice.

Periodic renewal of registration was needed to make a reality of this vision and was in place by 1987. Nurses, in the main, were prepared to accept the idea of maintaining their eligibility to practise and also saw the value of financial independence it would give to the Council. There was nothing like the furore that had been provoked in the 1970s when the General Medical Council, in funding difficulties, had suggested that doctors should pay periodic re-registration fees (see, again, Chapter 5). However, the immediate energies of the United Kingdom Central Council were caught up in the project to reform pre-registration education and in the workload presented by professional conduct hearings. Attention returned to this topic in 1989. A specific objective was set to develop the register 'for the recording and interrogation of data … for the benefit of the public, health services and the professions' (Davies and Beach 2000: 49). An overt public interest discourse and a new orientation towards involving consumers dates from this point.

As work commenced, nurses' doubts emerged. If the development of a 'personal professional profile' were to be a condition for re-registration, who would oversee this? Would management support the funding of it, or would costs fall on nurses themselves? Would management perhaps seek to use it in a punitive fashion? Specific proposals were put on the table later that year. Completion of the profile would be helped by five days of statutory study leave every three years. Anyone who had been out of practice for more than five years was to complete a mandatory return-to-practice course. With a profession of over half a million, monitoring this would be a massive exercise. A little later came the decision that a system of self-verification with periodic audit should be introduced in 2001.

Developments were now slowed by two factors. First, professional updating was being pursued as part of the Post-Registration Education and Practice Project. This aimed not only to set criteria for remaining on the register but also to devise a new and more coherent system of specialisms after registration and educational pathways to support them. This was a highly ambitious and deeply controversial enterprise. It called into question both the historic areas of special-ist practice and the array of new titles and practices that were growing up in National Health Service trusts and in primary care. It also challenged a higher education sector that had been forced into a new entrepreneurial mode and was busy creating advanced courses of its own. There was confusion, disarray and delay in the face of repeated efforts to define specialist and advanced practice. Second, government intervened: it was not inclined to detach any one element from the total package, and wanted to carry out its own calculations of the cost of statutory study leave.

Standards for maintaining registration finally came into force in 1995. It was now necessary for those who wished to continue in practice to meet certain crite-ria every three years. These were: to complete a notification-of-practice form indicating the area of intended practice; to carry out at least the equivalent of five days' study activity; and to maintain a personal professional profile detailing pro-fessional development (UKCC 1997). This was a remarkable development. Nursing had been the first profession to set in place standards for remaining on the register and to see them in a framework of continuing professional develop-ment. Taken together with the work done on the Code of Conduct, this repre-sented a powerfully interventionist regulatory stance. It was a strategy with a dual message – be more autonomous, but also be more demonstrably accountable. The question was, could nurses actually be either? Many still worked in systems where the roles and career structures, an unfavourable skill mix and low levels of professional support gave them little individual decision-making power and left them running ever faster to make up for deficiencies of staffing and resources. Should the United Kingdom Central Council seek to intervene here?

Towards an independent voice for standards

The experience of professional conduct work steadily pushed the Council in the direction of seeing itself as an independent, and sometimes decidedly critical, voice for standards. It was in the interests of the public and practitioners, said the first Annual Report, that 'representations should be made to government and employers when inadequate staffing or insufficient resources put patients at risk'. Not every Council member agreed. Donald Irvine, later to become President of the General Medical Council, argued that the United Kingdom Central Council as a standard-setting body should keep at arm's length from service provision (Davies and Beach 2000). Later Annual Reports repeatedly rapped employers over the knuckles for misuse of enrolled nurses and also for forwarding cases that could have been dealt with as disciplinary matters at local level. Individual representations were made to health authorities and trusts as a result of practices coming to light in conduct cases. Concerns over employment practices in the rapidly growing nursing homes sector led the United Kingdom Central Council to call a meeting with proprietors in 1990. Responses to government and other consultative documents also appeared on the agenda and formal comments on proposed policy changes became a substantial part of the work.

Newly elected members in 1993, especially those with trade union experience, however, wanted more. With the demise of much nurse management and new and enlarged responsibilities in the front line, why was the Council not pressing for legislation to prevent health care assistants acting beyond their role? Why was it not insisting that employers provide mandatory clinical supervision to support registrants? Officers replied that the legislation did not allow for this (Davies and Beach 2000). The following years, however, saw strong criticism of employment practices in the mixed economy of care that was emerging as part of Conservative health policy.

The question of standards in nursing homes was revisited in 1994 with an examination of the pattern of conduct cases heard. An unprecedented and hard-hitting report contained recommendations for improvements in the administration of medicines, the management of patients' finances, staffing policies and quality assurance systems (UKCC 1994). This report attracted substantial media coverage in which the United Kingdom Central Council figured not as a protector of professional interests, but as a strong and independent voice on the side of the public. A document the following year suggested some of the standards that might be incorporated into contracts between health purchasers and providers (UKCC 1996a). The Council was edging towards action that might be thought to trespass on managerial prerogatives. It was prepared to stand up to government to criticize health policy in a way that would have been unthinkable in earlier days.

If an influx of new members had something to do with this, then so too did an increasing pattern of lay involvement in the work of the Council. The details of misconduct cases had generated a growing sense that nurses were implicated in fundamental ethical and resource allocation dilemmas where there needed to be not just a professional voice, but a consumer voice too. In setting up the new Standards and Ethics Committee in 1988, a direct approach was made to the Patients' Association and to the Association of Community Health Councils and its counterparts in the other parts of the United Kingdom, requesting a nominee.[6] Government also appointed two representatives to the Council later that year who might be expected to bring more of a consumer voice. These two events were to mark the start of a series of moves, led by the United Kingdom Central Council, in which new voices and new perspectives were brought step by step into the business of regulation. Key among these was the establishment of an Annual Standing Consumer Conference – an unprecedented step for a regulatory body – and the formation of a panel of consumers who could be called upon to sit on professional conduct cases. By 1996, the shaky start of the annual conferences had turned into more positive joint working. Two years later the Council appointed a professional officer with a view to develop further its strategies on lay involvement.[7] The change of approach was particularly visible in the way in which a new review of initial education was conducted. Whereas in 1984 the work had been carried out largely internally, this time there was an external chair, and explicit scope to hear voices of consumers and service providers. Viewed from the outside, however, matters were not at all positive.

Negative assessments again

Government's first commissioned review of the regulatory structures under the 1979 Act, found the United Kingdom Central Council to be cumbersome and bureaucratic in its consultation procedures and committee structures (Peat Marwick McClintock 1989). Its second review, while covering many of the developments outlined here and finding good practice, judged the Council overall to be unfocused and lacking in a clear sense of core business. What the members saw as an important and courageous series of moves towards confronting employers and seeking to regulate practice standards as well as entry and conduct standards, the reviewers saw as incoherent, piecemeal and confusing (JM Consulting 1998). Divisions and 'factions' were noted on both occasions. The nursing press reinforced and seemed at times almost to revel in such criticisms. It had often found the Council secretive about its decisions and agreed with the judgement that it was an organization in a time warp, too inward-looking and out of touch with practitioners.[8] The 'tendency to tribalism' within nursing was accepted rather than countered or put in a bigger picture (Davies and Beach 2000).

A negative image of the United Kingdom Central Council also stemmed both from its professional conduct work and particularly from the implementation of pre-registration educational reforms. Misconduct procedures were complex, legalistic and hard to understand. Controversies over cases had begun to emerge in the early 1990s, with a run of decisions that supported applications for restoration to the register of practitioners previously found guilty of misconduct. These brought negative media comment and challenges from the Department of Health (Davies and Beach 2000). The reform of nurse education too had come in for particularly strong criticism from the National Health Service. Many felt that the new nurses were being given too much theory and not enough practical skills (Davies 1995; Peach Report 1999). If 'rampant snobbery' was not exactly an issue any more, divisions and factions were, and accusations of unrealistic aspirations, inflexible thinking, and poor leadership also continued to reverberate around the regulatory structure. Assessments such as these added fuel to the anti-professional climate that had come to pervade government thinking in the 1980s and 1990s.

Recent policy in relation to the regulation of the professions has been framed in the context of frenzied media attention, as case after case of misconduct and of poor medical practice has come to light, and as the General Medical Council has been judged seriously wanting in its response. Galvanized by this, government set powers in place in the Health Act 1999 that paved the way for the complex and overlapping project of reconstituting the General Medical Council, the Council for Professions Supplementary to Medicine and the United Kingdom Central Council for Nursing, Midwifery and Health Visiting. These also established new agencies and mechanisms to monitor clinical work. With its misconduct cases splashed over the press, medicine was singled out for censure, and the belief that regulatory bodies as a whole will tend to put 'profession before public'[9] and will protect their own, grew in strength. The directions for change – more accountability and transparency in the context of stronger lay involvement in the work – have nowhere been spelled out fully. The timetable of reform with a reconstituted Nursing and Midwifery Council and a Health Professions Council in the lead, and the General Medical Council holding internal discussions about future organization, suggests that the weaker professions are being used as a test-bed for restructuring.

The government pre-empted the Commission on Education of the United Kingdom Central Council with decisions to move to pilot schemes for reformed pre-registration nursing and to provide a more active leadership role in the education area inside the Department of Health (Department of Health 1999). Frustrated with inflexible boundaries between professions, government has also set out a vision of a future to be realized through education that would blur the boundaries between the traditional health professions (Department of Health 2000). It is already moving fast to create common foundation training for all clinicians. All the health professions are being tarred with the same brush. There is little acknowledgement of the relevance of the issues discussed in this chapter to the further development of regulatory regimes.

Conclusion

Statutory registration, traditionally seen by sociologists as the pinnacle of achievement for a profession, has been something of a poisoned chalice for nursing. This chapter has drawn attention to demonstrations of this for the inter-war period by revisionist nursing historians. However, the regulatory history of nursing after 1979 – the creation of a Code of Conduct, the adoption of standards for remaining on the register, the increasingly critical stance towards government and employers and the greater involvement of lay people in regulation – needs more attention. There are elements in this history that anticipate the demands that have emerged in recent years for greater accountability of professionals. Equally, there are elements that can be construed as continuing an elitist and divisive quest for greater recognition and status. The burden of this chapter has been to point to the contradictory nature of regulatory practice in a subordinated group such as nursing, and the way in which official assessments, as well as those of members of the profession, have continued to deliver particularly harsh judgements. Even as they have engaged in innovation, nurses have been locked in contradiction that reflected back images of them as quarrelsome, inadequate for the task of policy making, and for setting and enforcing regulatory standards. In terms of lived experience, working with regulation has not enhanced the confidence of the profession.

The roots of this are to be found in the complexity of statutory regulation in the context of a managed occupation subordinated to employers, doctors and the state. This complexity has nowhere been fully acknowledged or directly explored for its relevance to the agenda of contemporary regulatory reform. Instead, regulation, like professionalism, continues to be seen, by policy makers and academics alike, largely through a medical gaze. Without some corrective as new regulatory structures are being put into place to establish the Nursing and Midwifery Council, the question of what regulation can and should seek to achieve – what the promise of professionalism should be for all the health professions in the twenty-first century – threatens to remain as elusive as ever.

Notes

1 Much of the source material for this chapter can be found in a recent history of the United Kingdom Central Council for Nursing, Midwifery and Health Visiting (Davies and Beach 2000). The author would like to express her gratitude to Abigail Beach, whose historical work helped to make the present analysis and interpretation possible.

2 The chapter focuses on the regulation of nurses and not directly on health visitors or midwives. The latter in particular have a different regulatory history, which has led to tensions in a profession dominated by a nursing majority (Davies and Beach 2000).

3 She suggests that a similar stance has been adopted by sociologists such as Parry and Parry (1976).

4 Regulatory statutes have tended to take a skeleton form, leaving matters of substance to be set out in secondary legislation in the form of statutory instruments. Nurses are required to seek approval from the Minister of Health on all key constitutional and financial matters.

5 This analysis refers to the General Nursing Council for England and Wales. Much less historical work is available on the equivalent bodies in other parts of the United Kingdom.

6 Jean Robinson was appointed. A former Chairperson of the Patients' Association, she had been a member of the General Medical Council since 1979 and was a strong critic of aspects of its regulatory practice.

7 Some of the key steps relating to increased lay involvement were as follows: objectives for Council explicitly refer to standard-setting in the public interest (1988), appointment of a consumer nominee to the Standards and Ethics Committee (1988), start of Annual Standing Conference of Consumer Organizations (1991), appointment of a panel of consumer members to serve on Professional Conduct Committees (1993, extended 1996), consumer members to be part of Preliminary Proceedings Committee (1998), Professional Officer for Consumer Affairs appointed (1998), and strategy for consumer involvement agreed and developed (2000).

8 A 1997 survey of registrants commissioned by the United Kingdom Central Council for Nursing, Midwifery and Health Visiting, however, showed that 60 per cent viewed the Council as helpful, while 45 per cent still felt it was a remote body and 37 per cent believed that it was bureaucratic (Davies and Beach 2000: 66).

9 This phrase belongs to Margaret Stacey whose discussion of these issues for medicine a decade ago remains remarkably relevant to the present day (Stacey 1992).

References

Abel-Smith, B. (1960) *A History of the Nursing Profession*. London: Heinemann.

Beishon, S., Virdee, S. and Hagell, A. (1995) *Nursing in a Multi-Ethnic NHS*. London: Policy Studies Institute.

Bellaby, P. and Oribabor, P. (1980) '"History of the present" – contradiction and struggle in nursing', in C. Davies (ed.) *Rewriting Nursing History*. London: Croom Helm.

Bendall, E. and Raybould, E. (1969) *A History of the General Nursing Council for England and Wales 1919–1969*. London: H.K. Lewis & Co. Ltd.

Brazier, M., Lovecy, J., Moran, M. and Potton, M. (1993) 'Falling from a tightrope: Doctors and lawyers between the market and the state', *Political Studies*, XLI: 197–213.

Briggs Report (1972) *Report of the Committee on Nursing*. London: HMSO.

Buchan, J. and Edwards, N. (2000) 'Nursing numbers in Britain: The argument for workforce planning', *British Medical Journal*, 320: 1067–70.

Carpenter, M. (1993) 'The subordination of nurses in health care: towards a social divisions approach', in E. Riska, and K. Wegar (eds) *Gender, Work and Medicine: Women and the Medical Division of Labour*. London: Sage.

Davies, C. (ed.) (1980) *Rewriting Nursing History*. London: Croom Helm.

Davies, C. (1982) 'The regulation of nursing work: An historical comparison of Britain and the USA', in J. Roth (ed.) *Research in the Sociology of Health Care. Changing Structure of Health Service Occupations* vol. 2. Greenwich, CT: JAI Press.

Davies, C. (1995) *Gender and the Professional Predicament in Nursing*. Buckingham: Open University Press.

Davies, C. (2002) 'What about the girl next door? Gender and the politics of professional self-regulation', in G. Bendelow, M. Carpenter, C. Vautier, and S. Williams (eds) *Gender, Health and Healing: Reflections on the Public/Private Divide*. London: Routledge.

Davies, C. and Beach, A. (2000) *Interpreting Professional Self-Regulation: A History of the United Kingdom Central Council for Nursing, Midwifery and Health Visiting*. London: Routledge.

Department of Health (1999) *Making a Difference*. London: Department of Health.

Department of Health (2000) *A Health Service of All the Talents: Developing the NHS Workforce*. London: Department of Health.

Dingwall, R., Rafferty, A. M. and Webster, C. (1988) *An Introduction to the Social History of Nursing*. London: Routledge.

Dowling, S., Martin, R., Skidmore, P., Doyal, L., Cameron, A. and Lloyd, S. (1996) 'Nurses taking on doctors' work: A confusion of accountability', *British Medical Journal*, 312: 1211–14.

Doyal, L., Dowling, S. and Cameron, A. (1998) *Challenging Practice: An Evaluation of Four Innovatory Nursing Posts in the South and West*. Bristol: Policy Press.

Doyal, L., Hunt, G. and Mellor, J. (1981) 'Your life in their hands: Migrant workers in the NHS', *Critical Social Policy*, 2: 54–71.

JM Consulting (1998) *The Regulation of Nurses, Midwives and Health Visitors. Report on a Review of the Nurses, Midwives and Health Visitors Act 1997*. Bristol: JM Consulting Ltd.

Orr, J. (1995) 'Nursing accountability', in G. Hunt (ed.) *Whistle-Blowing in the Health Service*. London: Edward Arnold.

Parry, N. and Parry, J. (1976) *The Rise of the Medical Profession*. London: Croom Helm.

Peach Report (1999) *Fitness for Practice: The UKCC Commission for Nursing and Midwifery Education*. London: United Kingdom Central Council for Nursing, Midwifery and Health Visiting.

Peat Marwick McClintock (1989) *Review of the UKCC and the Four National Boards for Nursing, Midwifery and Health Visiting*. London: Department of Health.

Pyne, R. (1981) *Professional Discipline in Nursing, Midwifery and Health Visiting*. Oxford: Blackwell.

Rafferty, A.M. (1996) *The Politics of Nursing Knowledge*. London: Routledge.

Stacey, M. (1992) *Regulating British Medicine: The General Medical Council.* Chichester: John Wiley & Sons.

UKCC (1983) *Code of Professional Conduct for Nurses, Midwives and Health Visitors.* London: United Kingdom Central Council for Nursing, Midwifery and Health Visiting.

UKCC (1994) *Professional Conduct: Occasional Report on Standards of Nursing in Nursing Homes.* London: United Kingdom Central Council for Nursing, Midwifery and Health Visiting.

UKCC (1996a) *The Council's Proposed Standards for Incorporation into Contracts for Hospitals and Community Health Care Services.* London: United Kingdom Central Council for Nursing, Midwifery and Health Visiting.

UKCC (1996b) *Guidelines for Professional Practice.* London: United Kingdom Central Council for Nursing, Midwifery and Health Visiting.

UKCC (1997) *PREP and You.* London: United Kingdom Central Council for Nursing, Midwifery and Health Visiting.

White, R. (1976) 'Some political influences surrounding the Nurses Registration Act 1919', *Journal of Advanced Nursing Studies*, 1: 209–17.

Witz, A. (1992) *Professions and Patriarchy.* London: Routledge.

7   Regulating Dentistry

Nicki Thorogood

The chapter begins by looking at the social history of dentistry, considering first the reputation of dentists as 'sadists' or 'charlatans' and the process by which 'dentistry' has subsequently acquired the attributes of a profession. This analysis sheds some light on why, and how, dentistry has remained distinct from the profession of medicine (Nettleton 1992). The chapter then goes on to consider how dentistry has been regulated since the inception of the National Health Service. The impact of the public/private divisions within dentistry is addressed, as well as the recent changes in both the gender and ethnic composition of the workforce and their possible effect. Finally, recent policy changes and their likely impact on these issues are explored in the light of the characteristics generally taken to define a profession.

It is suggested in this chapter that a Foucauldian account of the shift towards a disciplinary society that produced the conditions for the emergence of the regulation of dentistry may also be used to interpret current changes (Foucault 1979). This account indicates that the distinction between the professions, in this case dentistry, and the state is a false dichotomy as both are mutually dependent (Johnson 1995). The state exists as a regulator only in so far as the activities that constitute dentistry are deemed 'professional' and therefore in need of regulation. From this perspective, dentistry only exists as a discursive formation. No matter what changes are made to statutory service provision, the regulatory relationship between dentistry and the state will remain. In short, according to this view, there can be no profession of dentistry that exists outside of the state, as this relationship is both produced by, and produces, the policies and the practices that become dentistry. Thus, the discursive formation of dentistry will not only continue to be regulated, but also to be a 'regulator' as it exercises disciplinary technologies over populations.

The history of dentistry as a profession

For many centuries dentists in England and other parts of Europe were considered to be artisans and tradespeople at best, quacks and charlatans at worst, taking people's money on false pretences. Why should this be? A social history of dentistry offers some sort of explanation. Rotten teeth, for example, have a long symbolic history and were once seen as the external manifestation of sinfulness.

Toothache, in this era, was 'the fiery torture of the damned in hell; the toothworm consumed the body whole and alive, like the diabolical serpent. The toothache was caused by the devil' (from Ring 1985, quoted in Kunzle 1989: 30). Even today rotten teeth are seen as evidence of having indulged in too much of the sweet things of life. Certainly in Europe from at least the sixteenth century onwards, the pain and suffering of toothache were strongly linked to sin and evil, and 'tooth pullers' were tainted by association. To some extent this view still prevails. However, there has been a fundamental shift in the conceptual framework of dentistry, which may be understood as paralleling wider paradigm shifts.

In the pre-Enlightenment period the Gallenic theory of 'humours' was prevalent. In this period, tooth decay was thought to be caused by the caries worm and the build-up of calculus was seen as a serious threat to the internal workings of the body. Subsequently, theoretical perspectives in Western European began to change with the emergence of a 'rational' worldview. Alongside this, emerged different forms of political organization and, with these, shifts in the organization of dentistry. By the nineteenth century, dentistry had moved indoors and the pain and suffering had become private. By the end of that century, dentists no longer simply extracted rotten teeth but filled and restored teeth and urged their patients to self-monitor. It was around this time, and much later than in medicine, that dentistry was also shifting from being a trade to becoming a profession.

Dentistry is somewhat different from other professions, as it does not have its own specialist body of knowledge, but shares that of another profession, medicine. It is both a part of medicine in terms of training and in university faculty terms, and apart from it in terms of professional regulation. As with doctors, the moves to occupational closure were made in the mid-nineteenth century when the first dental schools opened in London, and dental practitioners began to form associations. Nevertheless, dentistry remained a largely unregulated apprenticeship until the 1920s, when legal restrictions were placed on the practice of dentistry, and education and a specialist qualification became mandatory. The licensing mechanism, the Dentists' Register, was formed in 1918. After the Dentists Act of 1921, regulation was administered by the Dental Board of the United Kingdom, which was then subject to the over-riding control of the General Medical Council. The independent professional regulatory body for dentists, the General Dental Council, was not created until the 1956 Dentists Act – in contrast to the General Medical Council which was formed following the 1858 Medical Act (Levitt et al. 1995).

By the 1920s, dentistry had more or less fulfilled three of the four main criteria commonly recognized as defining a profession: a specialized body of knowledge; a monopoly of practice; and clinical autonomy (Seale and Pattison 1994: 21). However, the dentists' ethical code did not have the same status as the oaths that were sworn by the two archetypal professions, medicine and law, and, until recently, also by veterinary surgeons. Dentists did not have to swear to abide by particular principles, but were, for example, at their graduation ceremony simply read the code produced by the General Dental Council on the duties of a dentist (GDC 1997).

It is interesting to note that in 1995 dentists were granted the right to use the courtesy title of 'doctor'. This is, of course, how most medical practitioners use it – the majority of whom do not hold a Ph.D., but are seen nevertheless as 'real' doctors. The claim by dentists is often viewed as referring to something to which they are not entitled, conjuring up the old image of charlatan. Indeed, prior to this ruling any dentists calling themselves 'doctor' would have been found by the General Dental Council to be guilty of serious misconduct. On the other hand, the dentists in favour of the title point out that they train at least as long and as hard as medical practitioners and the title of doctor indicates this equality – even if it is not always appreciated by the general public. The use of the title doctor is popular among some women dentists, as it is a gender-neutral title. According to the national press at the time, both the General Dental Council and the British Dental Association greeted the change with caution. Both were reported as saying that dentists must be careful not to use the title in a way that would be misleading to patients or the public. Again, the taint of 'quackery' hangs over the profession – and the regulatory and representative bodies of the profession must be seen to be ensuring that dentists know their place.

Explaining the different development of dentistry from medicine

The historical origins of dental work may explain its difference from medicine. Dentistry was associated with moral laxity and sin and was practised by itinerants who had no formal training. It was perceived as being undertaken for profit and not necessarily carried out in the patients' best interest. For the most part, dentists have had customers or clients and not patients – and were not therefore seen as bound by the same code of ethics as other healers. There was no guild of dentists as there were guilds for other occupational groups. Perhaps, as a consequence, moves to professionalize the practice of dentistry came later and took longer.

Another aspect to consider is the development of dentistry's knowledge base and its theoretical underpinnings. As noted above, in the pre-Enlightenment period, some concepts of health and illness were based on humoral theory. During the nineteenth century, another prevalent theory was that of miasma – in which disease was seen as a consequence of poor air quality, with 'bad air' emanating from soil heaps in overcrowded city streets. The advent of a more scientific approach allowed different explanations to be produced. Humoral theories were displaced by the doctrine of specific aetiology of pathological lesion, and miasmatic theories were displaced by the 'germ theory' of disease and its later versions, bacteria and viruses. The source of disease was located outside the body, firstly in the sanitary environment of drains and dustbins, then in the 'community', among people.

Explanations of the aetiology of dental disease had therefore shifted from seeing the rotten tooth as an effect of internal bodily functions, to emphasizing the actions of 'germs' produced by the mouth and, lastly, to seeing dental disease as a consequence of the chemical interaction between teeth and elements introduced from the external environment. By the 1890s, the last two theories were combined. These two approaches have produced the current health care model in which hospital medicine focuses on disease within the body and intervention. In parallel with this, public health focuses on the interface between the body and society, on prevention and the monitoring and observation of bodies in a variety of sites such as schools and clinics (Armstrong 1993). Most modern dental practice is located in the latter and is thus part of the discourse of public health (see Nettleton 1992). The mouth was not seen as a part of the anatomy to be removed to the hospital for treatment, but rather to be monitored within the community.

The dental instruments used and the settings in which dentistry takes place have changed with this shift in paradigm. Tooth-drawers had pliers; modern dentists have probes and drills. Pre-Enlightenment teeth just rotted from within. Modern teeth are regularly brushed and cleaned with specially produced products. Mediaeval dentistry took place in the public sphere; modern dentistry takes place in the privacy of the surgery or the bathroom. Rotten teeth were once the consequence of sinful actions; now dental disease is the consequence of the failure to regulate properly one's personal hygiene, that is, to self-monitor.

So, in summary, by the mid-nineteenth century dentists had moved from pulling rotten teeth to restoring and rehabilitating and that meant routine monitoring of a client's mouth. By the early 1900s, dentists were establishing themselves as a legally recognized profession with a specific set of practices that were focused on prevention and rehabilitation. This accords with the shift from sovereign to disciplinary forms of power. It was no longer enough to simply observe and record the teeth. Dentists wanted to monitor disease by carrying out check-ups and to train 'patients' in appropriate dental behaviour. To this end 'tooth-brushing drill' was introduced in schools. Thus modern dentistry is based on routine monitoring and surveillance whether disease is present or not. It is only through regular observations that treatment can be avoided. So dentistry is right at the heart of our daily routines and practices. It is a disciplinary technique. This is what makes dentistry different from medicine and what makes the mouth and teeth separate from the rest of the body (Nettleton 1992).

Thus, the emergence of dentistry as a profession might be accounted for as part of the general shift from sovereign to disciplinary power. Whilst dentistry now meets most of the generally agreed criteria for a profession, it nevertheless remains in a marginal position. Historically, it was regarded as a trade, rather than as knowledge-based, and was consequently not part of a craft guild. When it did lay claim to a specialist knowledge base, this was already the domain of medicine, which had already taken the dominant regulatory ground. The history of dentistry shows that there is no such thing as 'objective' disease; what we see is a consequence of what we are looking for. This changes in different periods as different explanatory paradigms are used to provide interpretative 'maps', or ways of seeing. 'Dentistry' and its history are socially constructed. What dentistry is, depends on which line of thinking is popular at a certain time. This in turn produces what dentists actually do in any given period (Nettleton 1992) and what, therefore, might be subject to regulation.

The relationship between dentistry and the state

Dental services were included as part of the National Health Service from its inception. There are three branches to the dental service which fall within the scope of state regulation. First, there is the general dental service. Here each general dental practitioner maintains a contract with the local health authority and is remunerated from the National Health Service via the Dental Practice Board. The second branch is the hospital dental service, which provides specialist treatment and has the same staffing structure as hospital medical services, including such medical personnel as consultants, registrars, and house officers. Third, the community dental service provides community-based services for groups who are deemed to have special dental needs or cannot access other dental services. It was also given responsibility for oral health promotion and provides a screening service for all school children. The latter two branches are salaried, with the community dental services being purchased by health authorities. Currently too there are several Department of Health pilot projects for personal dental services, which are experimenting with alternative forms of dental service delivery.

The majority of qualifying dentists undertake a year's compulsory vocational training in general dental practice, during which time they are salaried, and then start practice as an 'associate' general dental practitioner. A small proportion of dental graduates go on to work as salaried employees in the National Health Service in either the hospital service or the community dental service. The White Paper *Primary Care: The Future* (Department of Health 1996) outlined a new scenario for primary care and was a precursor to the primary care groups and trusts at present being established. It declared a commitment to teamwork in general practice with a dental team with different skill mixes. This followed the publication of the Nuffield Report (1993) on the education and training of personnel auxiliary to dentistry, which recommended extending the areas of work of dental hygienists and nurses and introducing new groups of operating personnel. Parallels can be drawn here with the shifts in the division of labour between hospital doctors and nurses. These changes may reflect a concern on the part of dentists to pursue ever more technologically complex procedures rather than necessarily increasing the status of ancillary personnel.

A very small proportion of dentists practise wholly outside the National Health Service, seeing only fee-paying private patients. Most general dental practitioners are part of the National Health Service. Indeed, in 1996, the British Dental Association estimated that only 500 out of 29,055 dentists were wholly in the private sector (Calnan et al. 2000). However, all general dental practices operate as small independent businesses and are able to choose how they practise. Some general dental practitioners do only National Health Service funded work, but most have a mix of private and National Health Service patients within their practice. An increasing focus on private practice has been evident since the introduction of a new contract in 1990 and changes in the fee structure in 1992. These altered the system for remunerating general dental practitioners and were perceived by dentists at the time as a threat (Calnan et al. 2000). Currently, children, adults on income support and expectant mothers or those with a child under one year are entitled to free dental care under the National Health Service, while all other adults are required to pay four-fifths of the cost of treatment.

At the time, the changes to funding were heralded in the press as the 'end of National Health Service dentistry'. Although there has been a significant impact on the level of National Health Service care available, this has been greater in some areas than in others. In England, for example, there has been a greater scarcity of dentists taking National Health Service patients in the south than the north (Calnan et al. 2000).

As Downer, Gelbier and Gibbons (1994) note, the new remuneration policy created a dilemma for the practitioner, for

> a dentist's level of commitment to providing NHS dental care can vary from treating an occasional patient to a full time service. Some dentists accept only certain categories of patient or carry out a limited range of treatment under the NHS, perhaps providing a mixture of NHS and private dentistry in the same practice. ... Dentists working in general practice are self employed (except for a few salaried practitioners) and hold in tension the responsibility of being caring health professionals on the one hand and small businessmen or women on the other. (Downer et al. 1994: 47–8)

Charges for National Health Service dental treatment were introduced in 1950, although until recently they were nominal – and not based on a fee-per-item system. One rationale for direct charges is partly that these deter trivial attendances, as they introduce an element of self-rationing into publicly provided health care. However, they may also have a wider deterrent effect and people in need of services may not get them. Now patients are required to make a proportionate contribution to the cost of each of the procedures undertaken, this has revealed the real costs of dental treatment and differences in the cost of various procedures.

Research by the Consumers' Association (1992) has shown that access to National Health Service dentistry decreased among certain groups, noticeably fee-paying adults, and this was reflected in a decline in the number of National Health Service registrations among those eligible to make a contribution to treatment costs. General dental practitioners became increasingly unwilling to take these people on to their lists as treatment costs are fixed centrally and may not reflect the reality of a practice's overheads. Thus, although a practice may take National Health Service patients, the numbers may be limited. These trends have continued, with evidence of a drop in dental registrations from 24.4 million in 1992 to 19.7 million in 1999 (Calnan et al. 2000). Charges have also had a deterrent effect on access to eye tests (Green and Thorogood 1998). Indeed, eye tests have shifted from being a statutory right to being an individual responsibility. This self-surveillance can be interpreted as an extension of disciplinary power.

The barriers to seeking dental treatment have been well documented, with the two biggest being cost and anxiety. Indeed, only approximately 50 per cent of the adult population regularly visits a dentist (Finch et al. 1988). Recently, it appears that 'cost' has been a particular deterrent. Moreover, there is widespread confusion amongst the general public about the level of dental charges. Such uncertainty may have an effect on the dentist–patient relationship. If the dentist thinks work needs to be done, the patient is in no position to question this professional judgement. The fear of potentially being in such an awkward position may act as a deterrent to seeking treatment in anything other than in an emergency. It has been recommended that dentists display their charges and this would go part way towards remedying these uncertainties. However, even with this improvement, the final cost of treatment would still remain unclear, as interventions cannot necessarily be accurately predicted (Finch et al. 1988).

People may also be uncertain about whether their dentist will continue to treat them on the National Health Service and surveys on the registered population may underestimate problems with access as they exclude the unregistered who are nevertheless seeking treatment. According to the Consumers' Association (1992), 17 per cent of the survey sample had put off their next appointment as the dentist would only see them privately. What, though, have been the trends associated with this increasing 'commercialism' in dentistry?

Commercialism and dentistry

Calnan, Silvester, Manley and Taylor-Gooby (2000) show on the basis of a national survey of dentists that, while the National Health Service remains dominant, private practice is expanding. More than half of their respondents said that they were doing more private work in 1997 than they had done ten years earlier. The British Dental Association found that between the 1970s and the early 1990s, dentists received between 5 and 8 per cent of their income from direct charges to patients. This had risen to 25 per cent by the period from 1996 to 1998 (Calnan et al. 2000). There has also been a recent move towards chains of dental surgeries with a 'brand identity'. Thus, the old dentist/patient relationship based on trust and local knowledge, may be replaced with a 'label' that represents certain standards and quality.

Such developments may alter attitudes to work. Many dentists are sensitive to the dilemmas they face and have found National Health Service work increasingly stressful (Calnan et al. 2000). As a number of contributions to this volume indicate, there is an increasing willingness of patients to complain about the services they receive and this also applies to dentistry (see Green and Thorogood 1998). The relevant health authority may set up a review panel for complaints against National Health Service practitioners if they are not satisfied with the response given by their dentist.

Complaints made regarding matters of professional (mis)conduct are heard by the General Dental Council. These have doubled since 1995, albeit from only 11 in 1995 to 23 in 2000. The bulk of the complaints that are referred to the General Dental Council come from patients seeing private dentists. The numbers of such complaints have increased from 441 in 1990 to 782 in 1999. This may be due to cultural shifts in the amount of trust the public has in experts, as well as a shift in identity from 'patient' to 'customer' and the higher level of charges. National Health Service patients may also be more reluctant to complain in case they are de-registered by their dentist and are then unable to find another willing to take them on within the National Health Service (Thorogood 1997).

Recent changes to the composition of the dental profession

Another key recent trend in dentistry in the United Kingdom is related to the composition of the dental profession. Overall, there are some 29,000 dentists on the register. One of the most notable changes over the last 30 years has been the increase in the numbers of women and minority ethnic dental students. Since the numbers of dental school places are fixed, there has been a decline in the numbers of white males studying dentistry. Similar changes have occurred in medicine (Lewin and Olesen 1985). The major difference between medicine and dentistry in this respect is that the numbers of female and ethnic minority applicants, students and graduates has increased more rapidly. Nevertheless, males still form the largest group of applicants (54 per cent between 1994 and 1997), although proportionately fewer of them are white (48 per cent in dentistry as compared to 60 per cent in medicine). Among minority ethnic applicants, the largest groups are Indian (25 per cent of males and 19 per cent of females) and Pakistani (11.6 per cent of males and 8 per cent of females). The current profile in dental schools also suggests that the number of male entrants is declining, while the proportion from ethnic minority groups is increasing (Bedi and Gilthorpe 2000).

At present, just over 50 per cent of dental students and 30 per cent of those on the Dental Register are female (Newton et al. 2000a). There are few published data on the ethnicity of those who graduate or of those currently on the Dental Register. However, the collated data from the annual British Dental Association Omnibus Survey conducted between February and May 2000 shows that 14 per cent of the current dental workforce are from a ethnic minority background, compared to 6 per cent of the general population. The breakdown between ethnic minority groups in this survey found that amongst students – just over half were from India, Pakistan and Bangladeshi backgrounds (in that order) and fewer than 1 per cent of African and Caribbean origin (Newton and Gibbons 2000). According to these trends, it seems likely that dentistry will increasingly become the province of women and men from ethnic minority backgrounds. The feminization of the profession may also make it less attractive to the highest status males and therefore more available to males from lower status ethnic groups in future.

The changing role of women in dentistry can be charted more easily as the gender of applicants, graduates and registered dentists can all be identified. From these data, it appears that most women, like men, are employed in general dental practice. However, both the numbers and the proportion of women dentists in General Practice have increased even more sharply in recent times (Newton et al. 2000a). Surveys also suggest that women are not following the same work patterns as men. Women are less likely to be practice owners – in fact the proportion of women owners has decreased. Women also work fewer hours per week than men, with an average of 30 hours for women as compared to 38 hours for men. Both men and women, though, work a similar number of weeks each year (Newton et al. 2000b). Nonetheless, McEwen and Seward (1988) found that, although women were more likely to work part-time, the number of hours worked in a week was increasing.

Women dentists are more likely to be employed in the community dental service and in hospital dentistry than men, albeit at lower grades. However, Seward and McEwen (1987) reported a decrease in the proportion of practising women dentists employed in the community dental service from 42 per cent in 1975 to 29 per cent in 1986. There are also differences in the distribution of men and women between specialties. Women are more likely to be in orthodontics and in paedodontics, while men are more likely than women to be in oral surgery. Women are also more likely than men to treat National Health Service patients, with 80 per cent of women and 70 per cent of men being so engaged (Newton et al. 2000b). Similar changes in workforce composition also appear to have occurred in medicine (see, for instance, Lewin and Olesen 1985).

Changes in the workforce structure towards more part-time workers and more salaried posts appear to be well suited to the proposals set out in the new strategy for the regulation of dentistry discussed below. It may be that we are witnessing a shift in the concept of 'profession' from one based on the duty of autonomous individuals to one based on bureaucratic responsibility. There is a debate about the gendered nature of the concept of bureaucracy (Bologh 1990), from which one might conclude that the categories of a rational or objective bureaucracy and the emotional or intuitive woman are mutually exclusive. However, Davies (1996) has argued that professionalism and bureaucracy both actually have many of the same attributes. They are both oriented towards control and mastery. They both use abstract decision-making processes and both create hierarchical relations to achieve this. Moreover, both are constructed as masculine, which relates to the difficulties experienced by predominantly female occupational groups such as nurses, midwives and social workers in claiming independent professional status. The future in dentistry, at least, appears to be both bureaucratic and female. It remains to be seen how this will impact on the concept of dentistry as a profession, although it seems likely that this will lead to a lowering of the status of dentistry.

Future plans for the regulation of dentistry

Until February 2001, the General Dental Council comprised 50 members, of whom the majority were dentists – with one dental auxiliary, and unspecified numbers of appointed lay members and doctors nominated by the General Medical Council to advise on educational issues. However, there was a move to reform during 2000. In 2001, elections took place to reconstitute the Council with a smaller, more strategic, elected Board. This will include one dental hygienist and one dental therapist elected from the Dental Auxiliaries Committee, although the constitution also requires that registered dentists should form an overall majority in the Council. The newly constituted Council will have a committee structure to support what it identifies as its main areas of activity: that is, registration; conduct and health; education; and dental auxiliaries. In addition, a separate fitness-to-practice panel will be appointed to deal with the increasing numbers of disciplinary cases. A programme of compulsory professional education has also now been introduced.

Following a promise of reform in 1998, major changes to the organization and delivery of National Health Service dental care were also announced in September 2000 by the Minister of Health, Alan Milburn (Department of Health 2000). The new strategy was intended to address major sources of inequalities in access to oral health care and to raise the profile of oral health as a priority. It is perhaps no political accident that this strategy was promoted in the immediate run-up to the General Election of June 2001. The new strategy proposed, amongst other things, new direct access centres to address the problems of those not registered with a National Health Service dentist. There are also to be incentives for dentists to practise National Health Service dentistry through 'bonus' payments for 'loyal and committed' dentists. The newly defined health authorities in England are to be required to assess local needs and to make contracts as appropriate with the new pilot schemes, the community dental services and the recently established primary care trusts. Clinical governance is to be introduced into dentistry along with clinical audit, continuing professional development and peer review. Overall, this can be seen as part of the drive to develop dental services as part of a new expanded primary health care service.

The professional response has been mixed. On the one hand, it is difficult to fault the plans to increase access and regulate quality and standards, particularly since the flaws in the old funding system of capitation and fee for item have been addressed. Funds have also been earmarked to support change. On the other hand, government proposals have never been welcomed unreservedly. In this case, the dental profession has pointed out that not all the money is newly identified and that it almost certainly will not be enough to implement the changes proposed.

There is, however, another aspect to the dentists' disquiet, and this relates to the potential future of an integrated general dental service. The changes proposed in the new strategy might well signal the end of this service, as all but hospital dentistry becomes incorporated into an integrated primary health care service. This would expand the amount of dentistry provided by a salaried service, which in turn would increase the extent of regulation by non-dental statutory bodies such as health authorities and trusts. Might this then signal a decline in the professional status of dentistry? This is deemed a matter of concern for dentists, as expressed by a recent leader comment in the *British Dental Journal* (Grace 2000: 348) which remarked on 'the fact that the traditional ways of providing National Health Service dentistry are no longer appropriate and that the Government will make the best use of resources to help people get more from NHS dentistry'. The consequence of this was perceived to be that: 'Our freedom of the past 50 years is under threat.'

Here the state is being constructed as 'the enemy of the dental profession'. It might however be more useful to see this as a rhetorical device, following the argument by Johnson (1995) that the state, rather than being an institution in opposition to professional bodies, is in fact inseparable from the production of professions. This can be understood at a discursive level (in the production of regulatory guidelines, including those of clinical governance) and at an empirical level (in the production of new roles for dental professionals). Here, of course, the traditional dental activities of drilling, filling and prosthetics are in decline as rates of decay and of edentulism decrease, leaving the future to more 'preventive' dentistry such as periodontology and specialisms such as paediatric, orthodontic or special care dentistry. Much of this can be located as part of primary health care.

Conclusion

The discussion above raises many questions. What does all this say about the regulation of the dental profession? Is the new strategy evidence of the increasing bureaucratization of dentistry? And does this matter? Male dentists of the old school cry 'loss of control', but these changes may simply be a shift from one sort of control to another – from individual autonomy in practice to becoming an integral part of multidisciplinary health care teams with potentially more influence over wider policy making. How does the future of dentistry look in relation to the main criteria that denote a profession? Will being a part of integrated primary care lead to the lessening of professional autonomy? Will doctors take the lead in primary health care and therefore render dentists subservient? Or will it conversely increase the sphere in which dentistry operates?

Within dentistry, the specialized body of knowledge remains unchallenged. The General Dental Council still has control of the undergraduate dental curriculum, as well as postgraduate training and education. The evidence, moreover, suggests that this will increase as dental practice becomes increasingly specialized. Will the incorporation of dental services into broader based primary health care lead to a fracturing of professional self-regulation, possibly even leading to the disappearance of the General Dental Council as a regulatory body? It is hard to make such predictions. However, while the General Dental Council still has control over registration, it will surely remain responsible for disciplinary procedures leading to the loss of registered dentist status.

In relation to professional training, there has been a dramatic rise in the attention given in the curriculum to the subjects of ethics and law, alongside a rise of ethical monitoring in all areas. This may be an indication of yet another shift, towards a more litigious society in which the monitoring of professional standards becomes subject to the law rather than to internal regulation. This too would fit with a more bureaucratic approach to the regulation of professional services in dentistry in the disciplinary functions that it carries out in the United Kingdom and may well lead to a shift in the meaning of the concept of 'professions' and 'professionalism'.

References

Armstrong, D. (1993) 'Public health spaces and the fabrication of identity', *Sociology*, 27: 393–410.
Bedi, R. and Gilthorpe, M.S. (2000) 'Ethnic and gender variations in university applicants to United Kingdom medical and dental schools', *British Dental Journal*, 189: 212–15.
Bologh, R.W. (1990) *Love or Greatness: Max Weber and Masculine Thinking – A Feminine Inquiry.* London: Unwin.

Calnan, M., Silvester, S., Manley, A. and Taylor-Gooby, P. (2000) 'Doing business in the NHS: Exploring dentists' decisions to practise in the public and private sectors', *Sociology of Health and Illness*, 22: 742–64.

Consumers' Association (1992) *Which? Way to Health*. London: Consumers' Association.

Davies, C. (1996) 'The sociology of professions and the profession of gender', *Sociology*, 30: 661–78.

Department of Health (1996) *Primary Care: The Future*. London: HMSO.

Department of Health (2000) *Modernising NHS Dentistry: Implementing the NHS Plan*. London: The Stationery Office.

Downer, M., Gelbier, S. and Gibbons, D.E. (1994) *Introduction to Dental Public Health*. London: FDI World Dental Press Ltd.

Finch, H., Keegan, J. and Ward, K. (1988) *Barriers to the Receipt of Dental Care: A Qualitative Study*. London: Social and Community Planning Research.

Foucault, M. (1979) *Discipline and Punish: The Birth of the Prison*. Harmondsworth: Penguin.

GDC (1997) *Maintaining Standards: Guidance to Dentists on Professional and Personal Conduct*. London: General Dental Council.

Grace, M. (2000) 'The dental strategy', *British Dental Journal*, 189: 347–8.

Green, J. and Thorogood, N. (1998) *Analysing Health Policy*. Harlow: Addison Wesley Longman.

Johnson, T. (1995) 'Governmentality and the institutionalization of expertise', in T. Johnson, G. Larkin and M. Saks (eds) *Health Professions and the State in Europe*. London: Routledge.

Kunzle, D. (1989) 'The art of pulling teeth in the seventeenth and nineteenth centuries: From public martyrdom to private nightmare and political struggle?', in M. Feher (ed.) *Fragments for a History of the Human Body*. New York: Urzone.

Levitt, R., Wall, A. and Appleby, J. (1995) *The Reorganized National Health Service*. London: Chapman & Hall, 5th edn.

Lewin, E. and Olesen, V. (1985) (eds) *Women, Health and Healing: Towards a New Perspective*. London: Tavistock.

McEwen, E. and Seward, M. (1988) 'Women dentists at work', *British Dental Journal*, 165: 380–2.

Nettleton, S. (1992) *Power, Pain and Dentistry*. Buckingham: Open University Press.

Newton, J. and Gibbons, D.E. (2000) 'The ethnicity of dental practitioners in the United Kingdom', *International Dental Journal*, 51: 49–51.

Newton, J.T., Thorogood, N. and Gibbons, D.E. (2000a) 'A survey of the career development of male and female dental practitioners', *British Dental Journal*, 188: 90–4.

Newton, J.T., Thorogood, N. and Gibbons, D.E. (2000b) 'The work patterns of male and female dental practitioners in the United Kingdom', *International Dental Journal*, 50: 61–8.

Nuffield Report (1993) *Education and Training of Personnel Auxiliary to Dentistry*. London: Nuffield Foundation.

Seale, C. and Pattison, S. (1994) *Medical Knowledge, Doubt and Certainty*. Buckingham: Open University Press.

Seward, M. and McEwen, E. (1987) *The Provision of Dental Care by Women Dentists in England and Wales in 1985: A Ten Year Review*. London: Department of Health.

Thorogood, N. (1997) 'Constructing ethnic identities through oral health behaviours: Findings from focus groups'. Paper given to the British Sociological Association Medical Sociology Conference, York.

8 The Regulation of the Professions Allied to Medicine

Gerry Larkin

Historical and contemporary perspectives

At the start of the twentieth century, only the medical profession held statutory powers of self-regulation, dating from the 1858 Medical Act and subsequent amendments. The ensuing decades saw a transformation in the knowledge base, practices and technologies of medicine, and then, more extensively after the turn of the century, a corresponding expansion of the health care division of labour. This broadly took two linked forms through, first, further developments of separate specialities within rather than between medicine and surgery, and, second, the growth of other health care occupations which intensified through the twentieth century. Midwifery, nursing and dentistry attained statutory recognition in the first decades of the century, but these were not new occupations. Rather, their campaigns for statutory recognition reached completion at a point of further specialization and occupational differentiation. This chapter is concerned with this latter dimension, and that complex cluster of groups that by the mid-twentieth century were termed professions supplementary to medicine. From an early point of very small numbers, when they were variously termed aides or auxiliaries to medicine, the group of professions allied to medicine has expanded today to some 120,000 state registered practitioners.

This total number covers 12 professions either recognized by, or subsequently brought within, the provisions of the 1960 Professions Supplementary to Medicine Act. These include arts therapy, chiropody, dietetics, medical laboratory sciences, occupational therapy, orthoptics, physiotherapy, radiography, prosthetics and orthotics, speech and language therapy, clinical sciences, and paramedics. Each profession has its own history and modern identity, and the group is remarkably diverse in range and character, albeit linked through a common regulatory framework. This exceptional diversity in the field of professional regulation cannot be explored in this chapter, which instead will focus upon common factors in historical and contemporary developments. Thus the chapter will broadly fall into two parts. It will first cover the emergence of the professions supplementary to medicine and the historical stages of their regulation. The present-day changes planned for professional governance in this broad group of occupations will then be addressed.

Taking first the earlier period which sets the scene for both later continuities and changes, it is important to note at the outset that the health care division of labour, however reflective of scientific and technological change, is finalized in its social forms and boundaries by political processes. That is to say, the emergent structures are given shape by occupational groups competing to enhance their identity, control, skills and interests within their evolving areas. The growth in the division of labour, however, has not been one of evolving equal competition between all participants. Instead, it has been shaped until recently into hierarchic outcomes, with the organized medical profession in particular playing a highly significant role. Authority, expertise, status and above all statutory recognition and regulation have been contested areas between the older and new professions across the century. Even the kudos of the title of 'profession' was an issue up to 1960, at which point, although granted, the term was still qualified by the term 'supplementary'. As Freidson (1970) has influentially argued, twentieth-century professionalism in medicine became a means of advancing not just the immediate position of doctors in their own field, but extending their influence and authority over the ever more complex division of labour in health care.

Professionalism became professional dominance, which in Britain and elsewhere in the English-speaking world (Willis 1983) broadly generated four major stratagems. The first of these was the integration of rival occupations, or their skills, into the core professional fold, thereby reducing external competition between separate professions. The second was obstructing where possible any competitive claims from other practitioners to resources, whether material or symbolic, controlled by the dominant profession. The third was accepting other types of practitioners provided that they operated strictly within areas of practice or body site not claimed by medical or surgical specialities. The final strategy was that of according other occupations some formal legitimacy within health care, provided that this was linked to an articulated subordinate status. The stratagems are not mutually exclusive and vary in application to the same areas across time. This is highlighted by Saks in Chapter 10 where he charts the history of alternative medicine in the United Kingdom, in a journey from exclusion to selective statutory recognition. The professions allied to medicine, however, have mainly been affected by the latter two stratagems – limitation and licensed subordination.

Before outlining how these stratagems have affected the regulation of the allied professions, the changing character of professional dominance across varying historical contexts has to be noted (Light 1995). It is influenced by ever changing conditions and developments within medicine, but also has to be seen through successive phases of interaction with the modern state. Using language drawn from the work of Foucault, Johnson (1995) argues that professions and the state indeed share in a project of 'governmentality'. Without entering the theoretical debate surrounding the application of this concept, professional dominance and state development are seen here as intimately linked in varying stages of their interactive history. Through these stages, and in response to them, the character and purposes of the governance of professions has changed, and these changes have underpinned and conditioned new types of statutory regulation.

Taking the stages in professional dominance first, the challenges of socially organizing medical work have profoundly changed across the twentieth century. Initially, there was a period when medicine was still mostly delivered by solo practitioners, with fewer and rather different hospitals. This then developed to a period of expanding hospital medicine, dominated by the medical profession but only made possible through a supportive, ever expanding division of labour. Finally, we reached the period now upon us of established, and no longer formative, new professions, where the legacies of previous restrictive practices, demarcations and status distinctions are seen to be obstructing the delivery of effective health care. Very broadly, these three periods correspond to the decades before the First World War, between the wars and after the Second World War, and those since the 1960s. Indeed the third period has been characterized as one of crisis for all the professions associated with health care, but in particular as one of increasing conflict between the erstwhile dominant profession of medicine and the state (Webster 2000).

Turning to the related stages of state formation, and especially those parts which impact on health care, there have been three broadly corresponding stages. The first was that of a minimal state, associated with the era of solo practice, with very little involvement and investment in health care by modern standards. The second was a period of growing direct and indirect state sponsorship, co-ordination and financing of health care, associated with hospital medicine dominated by the medical profession. The third stage of state development was through an ever greater cumulative expansion of its commitment in an era of increasing direct state management of service arrangements. The nature of the relationship, through evolution on both sides, passed from a period of professional domination within the minimal state, to the rise of a medico-bureaucratic alliance (Larkin 1995), to the end – or more cautiously expressed, the beginning of the end – of the alliance. In this last phase, the state no longer is the ally of one, but the regulator of all professions as it manages the now vast costs of health care. Within these conditions rather different politics of professional regulation emerge.

The emergence of the allied health professions

Through the various phases of interlocked professional dominance and state formation, the forms and purposes of professional regulation themselves changed. The 1858 Medical Act gave no particular authority for the medical profession to govern other health care occupations, but subsequent advances in medical science intensified the profession's influence and social authority over them. Newly emergent occupations without resources, status and influence on a comparable scale sought shelter and advance within this influence. Patron and client relationships were characteristic of the early decades of this century, and provided the only available regulatory framework acceptable to the dominant profession. In the early decades of the twentieth century, three types of 'supplementary' profession were seeking to regulate their affairs at a national level. The development of laboratory medicine led to the need for laboratory assistants, and the increasing use of X-rays stimulated a demand for radiographers. This scientific group can be distinguished from a second cluster made up of physiotherapists, occupational and speech therapists, who were also forging their early modern identities in this period. All, however, especially emphasized their loyalty and subordination to the organized medical profession in this phase of development.

Professional regulation took the form of voluntary membership of a national association usually strongly influenced by prominent medical patrons and sponsors. More independently minded new practitioners sometimes contested this, but in effect at this point any other organizational and regulatory routes were blocked (Larkin 1983). The perils of taking a different course were evident in the experience of a third type of proto-profession, ophthalmic opticians, who were intent on winning separate state registration from the beginning, rather than any subordinate accommodation with organized medicine. In 1906 a Parliamentary bill to that end attracted the vigorous opposition of the General Medical Council. The Council claimed that optical defects and medical diseases were so intertwined that there was no rationale for the bill or need for the new profession. Indeed, all successive attempts by opticians were similarly blocked until 1958, when they finally gained statutory powers of professional regulation. Government departments, prior to the establishment of the Ministry of Health in 1919, and to some degree afterwards, routinely deferred to General Medical Council advice on matters affecting the regulation of other health occupations.

The establishment of the new Ministry of Health reflected the growing involvement of the state in health and welfare policies, and this expansion offered nascent professions a chance of challenging patron–client modes of regulation. Chiropodists, for example, although to some degree autonomous practitioners like opticians, up to this point had emphasized their submission to medical authority. In 1928 a more challenging section of this occupational group promoted a chiropodist registration bill, as did the osteopaths some years later, but all such attempts in the inter-war years foundered (Larkin 1995). Doctors staffed the new Ministry at senior levels, and following the 1919 Nurses Act, they shared the sentiments of their professional colleagues that medicine was in danger of dilution, fragmentation and decline if any more such legislation was enacted. The position and integrity of the medical profession was thought to require both a halt to any further legal recognition, and the continuity of supervised subordination. The medical–Ministry alliance against statutory developments held through the inter-war decades, but it would be wrong simply to see this period as a stagnant one. Indeed, developments in regulation occurred which strongly influenced events for the remainder of the century.

The oppositional stance of the Ministry in fact progressively became more problematic as the professional associations grew in numbers and membership, and as their experience of voluntary self-regulation developed. The Midwives Act (1902), Nurses Act (1919) and Dentists Act (1921) after all provided precedents, and a purely negative stance became decreasingly plausible. Thus, in 1932 the British Medical Association started, with tacit Ministry support, its own Board of Registration of Medical Auxiliaries. The notion of 'umbrella' regulation was therefore born, using a generic concept of medical auxiliaries. At first the

Society of Radiographers and the Chartered Society of Physiotherapy encouraged their members to apply for registration. In subsequent years, dispensing opticians, dieticians, speech therapists and orthotists joined them. By 1939 chiropodists also joined, after complex debates were resolved concerning limitations to their scope of practice, the depth of surgical incisions in treatment and their use of drugs.

The Board was notable for its strong emphasis on medical dominance over all its members, but it was also notable for a feature, which in various guises continues up to the present day. This was the attempt to create a collective framework for the regulation of a diverse range of aspiring professions, albeit through the notion of their status as medical auxiliaries, with directly implied tones of subordination. These hierarchic assumptions were to diminish in time, but the collective approach has had a lasting influence, and indeed was later to be reactivated in the 1990s with possible longer-term consequences for other professions. Throughout the 1940s, the British Medical Association lobbied to incorporate the Board into the National Health Service at its inception in 1948. It also wanted the Board to be backed up in its operation by statutory powers. The medical–Ministry alliance, however, by this time was beginning to show signs of having run its course. The state, as direct employer and manager of the new arrangements, was slowly moving on from its previous unconditional support for medical authority over auxiliaries as the model for the future.

Allied health professions in the National Health Service

The tensions of the period were reflected in the outcomes of the Cope Report (1951) on medical auxiliaries. Commissioned by the Ministry of Health to examine and recommend proposals for the future statutory regulation of eight groups – radiographers, chiropodists, physiotherapists, laboratory technicians, dieticians, almoners, speech and occupational therapists – it could not secure a consensus for its conclusions. Divisions of view were linked to concerns that have continued up to the present day. The inter-war Board of Registration of Medical Auxiliaries system was rejected, alongside the practice of the professional associations themselves in validating their own qualifications and training programmes. All parties favoured statutory registration, but they differed over both its nature and terms of operation.

The main problem lay in the model of regulation proposed by the medical members and their allies. This consisted of two levels of operation. The first was a supervisory council that held the major responsibility for policy matters, upon which medical auxiliaries were to be in a numerical minority to medical professional and Ministry of Health nominees. The second level of operation was formed by eight further sub-committees, with majority auxiliary memberships, acting as the executive arms of Council decisions. In effect, in the view of Cope's dissenting members, the British Medical Association's system was being re-introduced under a new statutory guise. They had accepted the inter-war system, but as a transitional arrangement representing a stepping-stone to self-regulation as mature professions, rather than a permanent form of subordination defined in statutory law.

Increasingly, self-regulation with statutory authority had come to be the very cornerstone of professional identity. As one group of dissenting auxiliaries pointed out in their separate submission to the government of the day:

> the basis of our inability to agree with the proposals is that we are here dealing with professions. A profession is a calling having its own standard of training, principles of practice and its own professional ethic. Having been trained to professional competence, its members on qualification assume personal responsibility as guardians of the quality and integrity of work in the profession which they practise. We feel convinced that the proposals would, if implemented, undermine this sense of responsibility within the professions concerned and adversely affect the quality of the services offered. (Cope Report 1951: 125)

The preferred model was one in which each profession was to be the guardian of its own standards, supported by statutory authority. The extent of the opposition persuaded the Ministry of Health to reject Cope's proposals, despite continuing pressure from various medical lobbies for their implementation. In effect, the state was assuming a more direct responsibility for the management of the ever more complex health care division of labour.

In this area, the once dominant profession, while not to be unduly antagonized, at least was beginning to be marginalized. The rejection of a previously ascendant mode of medical dominance did not, however, imply acceding to the ambitions of its adversaries. The claim to parity of professional self-governance for all was also problematic, not least if that were to imply separate statutory provision for every profession. Claims that might imply a multiplication of registration acts now could be seen to dilute state authority as the ultimate employer, manager and paymaster of services. Thus, the recoil from medical dominance at the time arguably also marked a turning away from individual professional self-governance. This became evident cumulatively through the ensuing decades.

More immediately, the 1960 Professions Supplementary to Medicine Act attempted to balance the persisting tensions and competing professional stratagems of the era. The Act provided for the initial registration of seven professions – chiropodists, radiographers, physiotherapists, dieticians, occupational therapists, remedial gymnasts and medical laboratory scientists – and reversed the central and most contentious feature of Cope's proposals. The balance of power between the Council and profession-specific boards was altered in the latter's favour. These agencies approved the necessary standards of training and conduct required for statutory registration, technically through recommendation to the new Council. While practitioners from the professions mostly dominated the boards, the Council was to be composed of seven representatives of the medical profession, and seven auxiliary and seven Ministry nominees. In the event of any disagreement between the two levels, the Privy Council was empowered to adjudicate. The state in effect came forward as a referee, granting a measure of professional self-regulation, but through a collective framework predicated upon agreement with the new Council.

Thus, the 1960 Act can be seen to contain concessions, continuities and the additional element of a more formally explicit expression of state authority.

Continuity, for example, can be seen in the contrived terminology of the description 'professions supplementary to medicine'. The medical profession believed itself exclusively to be *the* profession, and still was successful in opposing any titular signals of professional equality with others. Its direct control over them, as opposed to continuing influence, however, was ended – albeit without granting unhampered powers of statutory self-regulation separately to every new profession. More fundamentally, the Act tacitly assumed that role boundaries between medicine and the various professions were not too disturbed, but rather if anything consolidated through the new zones of interlocked authority. In this sense, the Act and the ensuing 40-year history of the Council for Professions Supplementary to Medicine was profoundly influenced by the pre-existing patterns of occupational jurisdiction. Using regulation as a means of addressing changes impacting on health care was to form part of a later state agenda, as was an increasing critique of the value of professional boundaries.

Contemporary challenges

The 1960 Act may be seen as a postponed catching-up with the past, rather than a preparation for the future role of professions in health care in the second half of the twentieth century. Over the ensuing decades changes already in train gathered further force, posing challenges to professional identities, working arrangements and to the effectiveness of regulation. These changes may somewhat artificially be divided into developments within medicine and health care, and broader changes derived from social, economic, cultural and political contexts.

Within medicine, knowledge, technologies and treatment options continued to grow, which affected both existing scientific and therapeutic professions and further expanded the division of labour. For example, innovations in diagnostic technologies, whether in imaging science or in laboratory medicine, required trained specialists who were not 'supplementary' but essential to modern medicine. Similarly, the various therapeutic professions developed their own knowledge and skills in ways best described as complementary, rather than in some sense secondary to the role of doctors and surgeons. Physiotherapists, occupational therapists and speech therapists had come to work with, rather than for, their medical colleagues in terms of any detailed prescription and supervision by the latter group. Indeed, medical specialization increasingly made doctors familiar with only a part of the spectrum of knowledge and practice required across all medical roles. They could not therefore credibly claim to have any real grasp of the knowledge and skills required by the allied professions. This particular point in fact had been reached well before the 1960 Act, rendering its contrived title even then somewhat archaic with regard to everyday professional realities. Social conventions of the day for the time being supported a regulatory myth, but these also were to change.

In the broader social context at least four major trends may be identified as strongly affecting the ensuing structure of health care professionalization, and in time the nature and purposes of professional regulation. These trends are interactive and are not discussed here in any order of importance. The first is the spread of university-based training, so characteristic of medicine, to the other professions – a development that gathered particular force over the last two decades of the twentieth century. Previously medical practitioners were in the main the only graduate health professionals. However, these status differences based upon educational capital increasingly faced erosion as newer generations came into practice.

The second trend is based on the fact that many of the professions once deemed to be subordinate to medicine were also considered to be 'female' in social image, while medicine held a superior 'male' status. Thus, professional dominance for much of the century was based upon a system of gendered concepts and practices (Witz 1992). Social attitudes, however, have undergone change – as has the gender composition of professions that helped sustain such stereotypes. Thirdly, and perhaps even more radically, patients have become increasingly knowledgeable consumers, such that their expectations have intensified across, and within, profession–client relationships. Indeed, legally, health professionals are liable for their own conduct and practice, and cannot take refuge in medical responsibility.

The fourth key trend is that, as attitudes and responsibilities have changed, so too has the status of all professions been questioned, especially in the 1980s and 1990s. Expanding costs, rising public expectations and economic uncertainties have in general led to changed profession–state relationships (Webster 2000). The medical profession in particular has ceased to be seen as a partner in the delivery of all the benefits of modern health care, but rather become a perceived obstacle to financial regulation and cost containment. In recent decades, during the Conservative administrations in Britain, an overt hostility to all professions extended beyond health care – and this suspicion of producer interests in the public sector, while moderated, has not entirely disappeared. Rather, with regard to health professions, it has become transformed into calls for a redrawing of professional boundaries and identities as part of the project of modernizing health care (Department of Health 2000b).

The direction of change

Against the background of these overall trends, all health professions increasingly have been pressed to reform their systems of governance. Previously, their claims to pursue the public interest through state registration were received more trustingly. However, in the mid-1990s, alongside other reviews, the government commissioned a specific examination of the continuing relevance of the 1960 Professions Supplementary to Medicine Act by JM Consulting (1996). Since the 1960s, both the memberships and types of these professions had grown – which by the turn of the century formed the second largest professional grouping in health care after nurses, midwives and health visitors. At this time, the Council for Professions Supplementary to Medicine covered 11 boards, having added arts therapists, paramedics, speech therapists and clinical scientists to the original cluster at its inception.

The issues were not, however, just those of increasing scale. The JM Consulting Report was a significant milestone in the regulation of this group of professions, and its contents pointed to a radically different future. Its findings and recommendations have resulted in statutory changes. The National Health Service Act of 1999 was drafted to carry forward these changes, through orders in council – a Parliamentary procedural device which enables changes to state registration to be confirmed or rejected by vote, without the full debate that normally accompanies proposed new statutes. The JM Consulting Report was notable both for its novelty of approach and for aspects of its contents. The novelty lay in the commissioning of consultants to review a professional area and associated legislation. More typically in the past, professions themselves have petitioned the government of the day to either promote or obstruct change. This initiative, though, was part of a government-sponsored review of all professional regulation. The professions supplementary to medicine, and the nursing profession – which was also reviewed through a parallel JM Consulting exercise – were not so much the principal advocates for their legislative development as in the past, but rather now more clearly the managed subjects of change. The content of the Report reflected this approach through a review of professional principles and practices deemed to require improvement and reformulation. Whilst not directly stated, beneath the range of recommendations touching on protection of title, the conduct of disciplinary and sickness procedures, continuous professional development and flexible qualification routes, there was a clear critique. This was that professions had used statutory mechanisms of registration and regulation to pursue their own particular agendas, rather than to secure public benefits in health care.

It was argued that the Council for Professions Supplementary to Medicine as operating from the 1960s has been flawed in some important respects. In particular, its single-profession boards were said by the JM Consulting Report to be at the root of the problem, by virtue of their relative autonomy and domination by the professions involved. This, it was claimed, led to a weakening of the influence of the Council, which had not been able to establish strong and clear cross-professional developmental strategies, to the detriment of all the professions regulated. The solution proposed was to remove the boards and strengthen the authority of the Council, whilst reforming its membership by removing medical representatives and adding lay and employer members. Although a major emphasis was still placed on identifying properly qualified practitioners, a new stress was placed on public protection. Statutory recognition benefited the professions concerned, but fundamentally it was only justified by ensuring the reduction of risks from invasive procedures or any practices likely to damage patient health and welfare. The new agenda was therefore linked to safety, enhanced employer influence and ever greater collaboration between professions, although this latter dimension particularly challenged traditional professional identities.

Particular professions, the Report acknowledged, may see their area of practice as unique, but it was clear that ever more separate professional identities were now seen to be problematic. As the Report observed, 'We see great strength in the multiprofessional concept as long as the umbrella body is able to add value to the process. All professions will gain from the authority and credibility which results, as well as increased efficiency' (JM Consulting 1996: 5). The newly strengthened Council was to be both the policy-making and supervisory agency, charged with protection of the public by specifying and monitoring standards of education, safe practice, qualification and conduct for this group of health professions. Furthermore, the existing profession-specific boards were to be abolished, and transformed in turn into multi-professional advisory committees. These were to be four in number, covering preliminary proceedings in cases of unsatisfactory practice; a conduct committee to hear cases; a health committee to receive referrals; and an educational advisory committee to serve the Council on issues of initial training and continuous professional development.

It was made clear to the professions concerned that these proposals were out for further consultation and fine-tuning, but not for fundamental alteration or reversal (Department of Health 2000a). The Council continued to hold major authority as in the Cope proposals, but was to be called the Health Professions Council. Any explicit connotations of subordination to the medical profession were now finally abandoned, but not through any move towards greater profession-specific autonomy. Outdated status distinctions across health care were therefore to be abandoned (at least in titular forms), while multi-professional governance was to be strengthened. In common with parallel revisions to the General Medical Council and United Kingdom Central Council for Nursing, Midwifery and Health Visiting, lay membership was to be greatly enhanced on the governing Council. A total of 23 members, made up of 12 practitioners and 11 lay participants was proposed. Professional members were to be elected by registrants, and the lay members appointed by the Privy Council, as nominees of the Secretary of State, through the Department of Health. The key position, the President of the new Council, was in the first instance to be a government nominee. Thereafter, the President was to be elected from within the Council.

The overall intended direction was clear. Individual professional self-regulation was to be set aside, while promoting its generic multi-professional survival – subject to a number of checks and balances. The Council for Professions Supplementary to Medicine has not attracted the same adverse publicity in recent years as has the General Medical Council, as described by Allsop Chapter 5. Nonetheless, it has been subject to similar forces. One consequence of this is that the state, as the advocate of patient and employer interests, has increasingly been drawn further into both the day-to-day and long-term operation of statutory regulation. Both medicine and the allied health professions are now seeing a process of state-sponsored managerialism replacing the medical–Ministry alliance that dominated much of the twentieth century. However, it is argued here that the advance of this more direct state management is not being carried forward through a well-developed system of coherent national planning, as the language of reviews and legislative modernization might otherwise suggest.

Piecemeal or fundamental reform?

Earlier relationships between organized medicine and the state may have served their time, but the transition has yet to yield any coherent overall replacement for medical dominance as a governing factor in inter-professional relationships.

Rather its formal demise provides a legacy of tensions, contradictions and challenges that at present still condition the evolution of alternative ways of organizing and regulating professions. For example, government consultation on reforming the Council for Professions Supplementary to Medicine began with the assertion that recent events have dented public confidence in professional self-regulation and have led to an expectation that regulatory bodies should work in a more open, responsive and publicly accountable way (Department of Health 2000a). The public now expects them to deliver greater protection within a more transparent and user-friendly framework. Thus regulation now has to be enhanced and renewed through a partnership with government which engages the energy and creativity of the professions.

In this respect, the consultation document argued that regulation through this recast alliance

> has to address the whole spectrum of practice. At one end, recent well-publicized cases have demonstrated the need for more effective measures to deal with individuals whose continuing practice presents an unacceptable risk to the public. At the other, the complex demands of modern health care are no longer the preserve of any one profession. Leading-edge developments increasingly demand a readiness to cross traditional boundaries both in training and practice. On both counts the government is determined to put the needs of patients, clients and carers – explicitly and for the first time – at the heart of professional regulation. (Department of Health 2000a: 6)

However, have traditional boundaries in regulation really been boldly crossed in the present ongoing proposals for reform? The evidence so far is mixed. As noted above, the proposals to reform the Council for Professions Supplementary to Medicine involve dismantling single-profession regulation, within a framework broadly resembling the rejected Cope measures of the early 1950s. This time, though, medical dominance is to be removed, as no one profession holds precedence in addressing the complex demands of modern health care. But these developments beg a more fundamental policy question than those addressed so far – namely, why the case for reform is so limited both in its analysis and aspiration. After all, the logic for reform of the Council, by dissolving its allegedly unhelpful internal professional boundaries, is surely the logic for reforming boundaries not just within this particular cluster of professions, but across the whole apparatus of regulation that reinforces the separation between all the major health professions.

The consultation document acknowledges that this point should be addressed through a tantalizingly brief statement, that

> there needs to be formal co-ordination between the health regulatory bodies. For this reason, a United Kingdom Council for the Regulation of Healthcare Professionals will be established, including the successor body to the Council for Professions Supplementary to Medicine. In the first instance the new body will help co-ordinate and act as a forum in which common approaches across the professions are developed for dealing with matters such as complaints against practitioners. Were concerns to remain about the individual self-regulatory bodies its role could evolve. These modernized and more accountable professional regulatory arrangements will work alongside the NHS's

own quality assurance arrangements to offer better protection for patients. (Department of Health 2000a: 6)

Such change is therefore taking place through separately reformed but otherwise preserved traditional professional jurisdictions. At present the proposed overarching agency, the Council for the Regulation of Healthcare Professionals, in a further consultation paper and ensuing legislation (Department of Health 2001c), seems to be cast as a forum for promoting good practice through overseeing but still preserving separate statutory authorities. The reserve powers taken under the 1999 National Health Service Act cover only the reform of the latter, not their dissolution and replacement with something new. The 'evolution' mentioned above is essentially a default position, to be further developed if presently envisaged reforms fail. Such an outcome would require entirely new legislation to be brought forward. As professional identities underlie regulatory frameworks, these are not necessarily changed by administrative adjustments alone. The assumption that changes within separate frameworks will promote more flexible inter-professional identities is also is open to question. Professional identities have been forged across decades precisely through stratagems of demarcation and status differentiation, and it may prove difficult to address this issue through arrangements, however adjusted, which continue to give such stratagems institutional and legal expression (see, for instance, Saks 1999).

Government policy, now aimed at more actively managing, rather than as in the past enabling, professional regulation, is in fact caught in a dilemma. On the one hand, it is promoting a breakdown of professional barriers in training and everyday practice in the interests of safety and quality, while on the other, professional work is becoming more, not less, complex and specialized. Ever more professional specialization is continuing apace in health care, ensuring that government has both to reform existing professions and to address further issues posed by emerging new groups. More direct management by the state brings involvement in greater complexity, an awareness of which is linked to the growing emphasis on the need for an overarching regulatory council made answerable to Parliament for the overall management of all health professions.

The complexities of professional specialization are most recently evident in the government's first ever review of the collectively termed 'healthcare science' sector. This is made up of some 40,000 specialist health care workers spread across 35 professional groups, mostly not covered by existing provisions for statutory regulation (Department of Health 2001b). They broadly fall into two clusters. The physical science cluster includes such groups as medical physicists, and nuclear medicine and critical care technologists. The physiology group ranges from medical geneticists to clinical embryologists and neurophysiologists. As their titles suggest, these and other occupations in this sector carry major responsibilities for highly specialized, ethically charged and potentially harmful spheres of practice in the physical and biological sciences. At present no further statutory provision is envisaged in this area, and the government strategy paper has the flavour of a concerned first-stage review of a complex area also likely to require more active state management. The new Health Professions Council is empowered to extend its revised provisions to new professions outside its remit. The Council, however, will only be able to initiate proposals. These will be subject to full scrutiny by the government of the day and separate legislation (Department of Health 2001a).

The interface between the healthcare science group and the other major reformed statutory agencies, therefore, has yet to be specified. Having consigned hierarchy, professional protectionism and medical dominance rhetorically to a world of pre-modernized health care, the government has yet clearly to identify the principles and mechanisms of co-ordination and co-operation between all of the spheres involved in health professional regulation. This may be linked to its reliance upon the recent in vogue concept of clinical governance, which emphasizes that all staff irrespective of position and profession must share a responsibility collectively for the quality of health care. However, governance in this sense is a diffuse and all-embracing responsibility and, whatever its importance, does not provide any precise vision or management plan for the links between reformed statutory authorities, or the complex cluster of agencies involved in professional governance, ranging from the universities to numerous health authorities. All involved may have a 'duty of partnership', but what this means has yet to be seen.

There are some signs that confidence in recent reforms is not complete, in so far as the new Council for the Regulation of Healthcare Professionals will hold a responsibility for reviewing the performance of the revised statutory authorities within its remit. Regulatory reform may, therefore, herald more intervention, particularly when professional worlds are deemed to be unresponsive to wider concerns. Statutory authorities, for example, have done little in the past to develop equal opportunities stratagems for the professions within their remit and this may presage further government action. The strategy for health care science argues that the professional workforce needs to reflect the diversity of the community served, particularly in terms of gender balance and the numbers of black, ethnic minority and disabled staff in each profession (Department of Health 2001b). Although detailed workforce statistics have yet to be developed in these areas, nursing, the allied health professions and health care scientists are all expected to match the diversity of the population in their memberships.

Conclusion

The extent to which the state will rest content with the regulatory reforms of the health professions discussed in this chapter, or will become ever more interventionist, is an issue which can best be analysed with the benefit of hindsight. At present, beneath the rhetoric of flexibility, teamwork, accountability and transparency, it is difficult to detect any guiding vision that is deeper than an impatience with the legacy and ethos of current patterns of professional regulation. Nonetheless, falteringly a new type of professionalism – that is not based upon exclusion, control and special status – is being encouraged. Its progress will be judged within a further era of state–profession relationships. If professionals are to become more flexible and no one profession is to have a special importance, then more fundamental transformations of identity, training and reward will be required to overcome the obstacles that exist than those so far envisaged.

At present in the United Kingdom it is not possible realistically to envisage the prospect of there being only one health profession based upon co-equal branches, with necessary occupational specialities derived from a common identity. Although professional dominance in all its various guises increasingly is seen as antithetical to the demands of modern health care, moves towards its displacement are currently very slow. The articulation of more fundamental alternatives to the legacy of professional dominance remains one of the most important challenges for twenty-first-century health policy. Professions after all have thrived on their sense of separateness. Present regulatory proposals only soften the edges between such groups, rather than fundamentally challenging the core range of statutory schemes for separated identities. This applies as much to the allied health professions considered in this chapter as to the other health professions considered in this volume.

References

Cope Report (1951) *Report of the Committee on Medical Auxiliaries*. London: HMSO.

Department of Health (2000a) *Modernising Regulation*. London: The Stationery Office.

Department of Health (2000b) *The NHS Plan*. London: The Stationery Office.

Department of Health (2001a) *Establishing the New Health Professions Council*. London: Department of Health.

Department of Health (2001b) *Making the Change: A Strategy for the Professions in Healthcare Science*. London: The Stationery Office.

Department of Health (2001c) *Modernising Regulation in the Health Professions*. London: Department of Health.

Freidson, E. (1970) *Profession of Medicine: A Study in the Sociology of Applied Knowledge*. New York: Dodd, Mead & Co.

Johnson, T. (1995) 'Governmentality and the institutionalisation of expertise', in T. Johnson, G. Larkin and M. Saks (eds) *Health Professions and the State in Europe*. London: Routledge.

JM Consulting (1996) *The Regulation of Health Professions. Report of a Review of the Professions Supplementary to Medicine Act*. Bristol: JM Consulting Ltd.

Larkin, G. (1983) *Occupational Monopoly and Modern Medicine*. London: Tavistock.

Larkin, G. (1995) 'State control and the health professions in the United Kingdom: Historical Perspectives', in T. Johnson, G. Larkin and M. Saks (eds) *Health Professions and the State in Europe*. London: Routledge.

Light, D. (1995) 'Countervailing powers: A framework for professions in transition', in T. Johnson, G. Larkin and M. Saks (eds) *Health Professions and the State in Europe*. London: Routledge.

Saks, M. (1999) 'Towards integrated health care: Shifting professional interests and identities in Britain', in I. Hellberg, M. Saks and C. Benoit (eds) *Professional Identities in Transition: Cross-Cultural Dimensions*. Södertälje: Almqvist & Wiksell International.

Webster, C. (2000) 'Medicine and the welfare state 1930–1970', in R. Cooter and J. Pickstone (eds) *Medicine in the Twentieth Century*. Amsterdam: Harwood Academic Publishers.

Willis, E. (1983) *Medical Dominance*. Sydney: Allen & Unwin.

Witz, A. (1992) *Professions and Patriarchy*. London: Routledge.

9 The Emergence of Clinical Psychology as a Profession

David Pilgrim

This chapter provides a brief socio-historical overview of the development of the occupation of clinical psychology and associated regulatory processes in the United Kingdom. A book-length account of the development of clinical psychology up to 1990 can be found in Pilgrim and Treacher (1992). The analysis will focus on the framework of indeterminate knowledge put forward by Jamous and Peloille (1970). Thirty years on, this French sociological analysis still remains applicable to the critical understanding of British clinical psychology. In order to understand the recent state of the profession, its history and character will be outlined. The author was a participant observer in the process of change, a reflexive footnote is provided.[1]

The clinical psychology profession: an overview

There are around 5,000 clinical psychologists practising in the United Kingdom, the great majority of whom work in the National Health Service. Academic clinical psychologists who are university employees usually also provide a sessional input to their local health service. Although many practitioners work in psychiatric services, the profession is divided into several specialties that are defined by different patient groups, such as adults with mental health problems, but clinical psychologists also work with children, people with learning disabilities, older people and people with physical health problems. They may also work in functionally defined areas such as the forensic mental health services. This diversity is reflected in varied work settings so that the profession is widely spread geographically.

To be eligible to enter clinical psychology training, a person must hold a first degree recognized by the British Psychological Society. Demand for training places has well outstripped supply over the past 20 years, and it is therefore very rare for psychology graduates to enter clinical training immediately. Courses can be highly selective from a large pool of competing applicants. This has had a number of consequences. New trainees tend to be in their late twenties or early thirties and they have had to accumulate relevant experience to warrant consideration. This experience can be gained through research on a clinical population and/or client work as an assistant to a qualified clinician. Mental health nurses who also obtain good psychology degrees are in a favourable position for consideration.

The supply–demand dynamic has raised the level of the academic qualifications required by successful applicants. It is very rare for a graduate with less than an upper second or a first to be considered for training and it is not unusual for new trainees to hold a Ph.D. or other postgraduate qualification. Since 1994, the British training system has been 'Americanized' – a doctorate in clinical psychology (D.Clin.Psychol.) is now awarded after three years following a taught course plus clinical placements. A research thesis is produced in the final year of training.

Once qualified, clinical psychologists work with one of the patient groups described above, although a minority work across more than one. Within their work, clinical psychologists are generally free to develop their own preferred clinical emphasis. Many clinical psychologists work wholly as therapists and so they may be indistinguishable in their occupational roles from psychological therapists trained in a different discipline, such as medicine, nursing or social work. Others focus on consultancy, research and training.

Those successfully obtaining their doctorates in clinical psychology are eligible for entry to the register as chartered clinical psychologists. Since 1988, this register has been held by the British Psychological Society. There are various sub-systems. For example, there are sections for academic interest groups such as social, developmental and experimental psychology, as well as for history and philosophy. There are also divisions for professional applications and Special Interest Groups for areas such as learning disabilities and neuropsychology. Trained clinical psychologists are eligible for full membership of the Division of Clinical Psychology. Thus the academic discipline of psychology underpins, but does not ultimately define, the profession of clinical psychology.

Prior to 1950: the prefigurative phase of professional development

All of the major historical roots of clinical psychology can be traced to events surrounding the First and Second World Wars. Dominant forms of psychology, which emerged from the academy, such as psychoanalysis, differential psychology and learning theory, were shaped by the military context of the wars, and post-war conditions between 1914 and 1950. The problem of shellshock after 1914 was a central spur for the formulation of psychological treatment (Stone 1985). The men breaking down in the trenches were seen to be 'England's finest blood' and not the 'tainted gene pool' commonly assumed to inhabit the asylums and workhouses. The soldier-patients were officers and gentlemen or squaddie volunteers, with the first group breaking down at a higher rate than the second. In this context, the eugenic bio-determinism favoured by asylum doctors was perceived as a sort of treason. Consequently, it fell from favour in government circles, creating a political space for the growth of psychological approaches.

The Psychological Society was inaugurated at University College, London, in 1901, taking on the term 'British' in 1906. It remained a tiny club of philosophers and psychologically minded medical practitioners until the First World War. In 1919, the first section of the British Psychological Society to be formed was the Medical, now Psychotherapy, Section and it was dominated by the returning shellshock doctors. In the same year the British Psychoanalytical Society was established, with an overlapping membership. During the war, increasing interest had been taken in the psychosomatic aspects of fatigue as manifested in the overworked female employees in the munitions factories. The Health of Munitions Workers Committee (soon to be renamed the Industrial Fatigue Board) was set up by Lloyd George in 1915 and was subsumed within the Medical Research Council in 1929. This formed the focus for the early development of industrial psychology in Britain, with Cyril Burt and others beginning to apply psychological methods to the military-industrial complex.

The returning shellshock doctors enlarged the status and influence of what was to become one of two key training bases for clinical psychology, the Tavistock Clinic. During the 1930s with another war becoming inevitable, the Ministry of Defence recruited psychologists and psychotherapists to oversee selection procedures in an attempt to filter out psychologically vulnerable military applicants. A symbol of the status of the psychoanalytic tradition was the appointment of J.R. Rees as head of the army psychiatric services in 1939. Rees was a psychoanalyst and had been director of the Tavistock Clinic since 1934. The Tavistock tradition, based upon psychoanalysis, was to drive the therapeutic community movement in the post-war years.

The new hostilities with Germany saw the return of 'war neurosis'. Various hospital settings were utilized to treat what has now become known as 'post-traumatic stress disorder'. In 1942 at one of these, the Mill Hill Emergency Hospital, Hans Eysenck was appointed as a research psychologist. When Mill Hill was reconstituted at Camberwell after the war, it formed the basis of the new Institute of Psychiatry with several academic departments. These were linked to clinical services in the Maudsley Hospital. Eysenck was appointed as head of psychology at the Institute of Psychiatry, and was to propagate a different tradition, that of differential psychology, brought from University College, London, and dating back to Francis Galton. The first clinical psychology course at the Institute was limited to the psychometric assessment of patients and emphasized the role of psychologist, not as therapist, but as applied researcher. The tension between the healing role with its fluid subjectivity on one hand, and the 'disinterested' scientific stance of the psychological researcher on the other, still characterizes the profession to this day.

After 1950: the formalization of the profession without registration

Between 1950 and 1980, the profession developed through three phases: psychometrics, behaviour therapy and eclecticism. These reflected epistemological tensions. Until the late 1970s there were few signs of clinical psychologists seeking to advance their status through formal state recognition. Although psychologists disagreed with one another about their role and its content, they all accepted that their academic credentials were sufficient to justify their social legitimacy and employment status. Postgraduate training developed at three main places in Britain – the Tavistock Clinic and the Institute of Psychiatry in London, and the Crichton Royal Hospital in Scotland. These were the first three courses to be recognized within the National Health Service Whitley Council negotiating system in 1957. In the 1960s and the years thereafter, Eysenck's course was to become the dominant influence in the profession. New courses were set up throughout the country, usually, but not always, in the old universities with medical schools and were headed up by Institute of Psychiatry graduates.

By the late 1950s, the psychometric phase of the profession gave way to behaviour therapy. Eysenck and his colleagues, Monte Shapiro and Gwynne Jones, suddenly shifted their focus in order to wrest control over the therapeutic jurisdiction of neurosis from psychiatry. This bid was made very publicly in a paper Eysenck presented, with Jones, to the Royal Medico-Psychological Association – which became the Royal College of Psychiatrists in 1971 (Eysenck 1958). This was significant because Eysenck had previously argued forcibly that the experimental/ psychometric role was disinterested, whereas therapy was about pursuing value-laden outcomes with patients (Eysenck 1949). In the early days of the profession, psychometricians and experimentalists saw their role as providing scientific scrutiny of the patient's functioning. They did not aspire to the medical task of treatment. Consequently, the behaviour therapy bid was a notable ideological U-turn by Eysenck.

The third phase of the profession was one of eclecticism. This was the case because clinical psychology had failed to develop a firm consensus about its core role. Since the early 1950s, the psychologist-as-scientist-practitioner had been predominant officially in both the American Psychological Association and the British Psychological Society. However, it had failed to displace completely other theoretical strands, particularly variants of phenomenology and psychoanalysis (Shapiro 1951; Raimy 1953). By the 1970s, pluralism became commonplace in National Health Service departments. This was reinforced by the shift in academic psychology from behaviourism to cognitivism, which was mirrored increasingly by a theoretically contradictory orthodoxy of cognitive-behavioural methods of treatment. Hybrids of cognitivism with depth psychology were also to ensue, such as 'cognitive-analytical therapy'. For the past 20 years clinical psychology has retained this eclectic and pluralistic character.

After 1979: self-regulation and its problems

During the 1970s, there was a move towards registration by both psychotherapists and clinical psychologists with varying degrees of success. These groups were helped or hindered by the political context at the time. There had been no proactive interest from the Ministry of Health in the post-war years in converting clinical psychology into a registered profession, but a number of problems were emerging for government about what were known in the 1970s as 'mind-bending techniques'. In the early 1970s, the Church of Scientology had attempted to infiltrate and take over the largest British mental health charity, MIND. Scientology offered a form of psychotherapy called 'dianetics'. This crisis stimulated an official investigation by Foster (1971) into the role and impact of Scientology and dianetics. Foster recommended that there should be state registration of psychotherapists. Although this lay fallow for a few years, the private psychoanalytical organizations (not the British Psychological Society) lobbied the government to support some form of registration.

The Report by Seighart (1978) on the registration of psychotherapists supported Foster, but no action was taken by government. However, the Trethowan Report on the role of psychologists in the National Health Service (DHSS 1977) had given the green light for clinical psychology's formal separation from psychiatry. For several years, clinical psychologists had been working with patients directly referred by general practitioners and were no longer subordinate to the psychiatrist in their clinical pratice. The juxtaposition of Seighart and Trethowan marked a turning point and there were increasing efforts on the part of clinical psychologists to seek recognition of their independent role. However, in the years after 1979, the British government under Margaret Thatcher became more hostile to professionals. As mainly public employees, clinical psychologists were affected by the marketization of the welfare state.

In relation to psychotherapists, the debate begun by Foster and Seighart about registration continued. In 1993, after many years of internecine disputes and tentative alliances between therapists from a variety of training backgrounds, the United Kingdom Council for Psychotherapy was set up. Since then, the Council has pressed for the voluntary registration of its members. However, at the time of writing, there remains no legal framework for psychotherapists to be registered. In 1979, the Division of Clinical Psychologists had rejected the Seighart recommendation on psychotherapy registration, but immediately began work on developing a case for government for the registration of clinical psychologists. The possibility of state registration of psychotherapists, who were seen as a motley group of therapists developing a specialist form of applied psychological knowledge, was perceived as a threat. In order to ward off this competing bid related to applied psychological knowledge, the Division of Clinical Psychologists pushed for registration for its own practitioners on its own terms.

The profession pursued a strategy that was doubly advantageous. It sought to operationalize the mandate to practise as an applied psychologist and did so in terms that coincided with the pre-existing credentials of the members of the Division of Clinical Psychologists. This had the advantage of keeping out competitors who were not qualified in academic psychology. In addition, the Division did not actually have to define what psychology was, except in the circular sense of the existing curriculum being delivered to undergraduates studying psychology at the time. This was particularly important, given the contested nature of psychological knowledge. Some professions, such as medicine and dentistry, are able to define their knowledge base with some degree of certainty in particular contexts. However, this is not the case with psychology. Psychological knowledge has always been divided, with incommensurable epistemological strands in its midst. Indeed, this may be an inherent characteristic of the human sciences (Foucault 1973; Smart 1990). Phenomenology, experimentalism, differential psychology, behaviourism, psychoanalysis, cognitivism and, latterly, social constructionism have jostled for position, and, in undergraduate studies and postgraduate training, have ebbed and flowed in fashion. All have had their devotees and factionalism has been endemic.

In this context, it would have been well nigh impossible for the British Psychological Society to offer government a coherent definition, let alone a coherent body of knowledge, that covered the academic discipline of psychology – or indeed, the scope of work undertaken by members of the Division of Psychology. It could be argued that, as a result of the contested terrain of their discipline, psychology graduates possess a tolerance of uncertainty and a tendency to examine knowledge claims sceptically. However, these laudable intellectual virtues have not, as yet, been used in the claim for registration. Rather, in the 1980s, the profession embraced managerialism (Pilgrim 1990). Not only did the profession seek to establish formally the conditions of self-management, but it also adapted to the government's policy for 'general management' in running the National Health Service.

In the 1980s, the campaign for registration was driven initially by the Division of Clinical Psychologists, but very soon the British Psychological Society itself as the parent body took up the cause. Between 1984 and 1988, a full-time employee was appointed to advance the cause of registration and to assist the Division of Clinical Psychologists to adapt to the demands of general management in the National Health Service. Unlike medicine, which resisted general management, the smaller and less secure profession of clinical psychology offered cautious support. Some psychologists, like many nurses, secured posts as general managers. The profession's leadership also agreed to a review by the manpower advisory group within the Department of Health. This was a controversial move as it exposed the profession to outsiders. It was resisted by a vociferous minority leading to a vote of no confidence, which was lost.

The manpower review was helpful for professional advancement, but in a way that had not been predicted. It was published in 1988 with no immediate catastrophic effect, but with little clear indication about how its recommendations about the numbers or role of clinical psychologists might be applied within a rapidly fragmenting National Health Service structure. However, it provided a focus for the development of a professional identity. A leading clinical psychologist, Glenys Parry, and member of the manpower advisory group, made the point that:

> The 1980s has been about establishing who we are, what we can do and what is our core identity. If you like it has been about establishing a proper rhetoric of justification. The hostile climate for professionals has put pressure on us to clarify and justify what we are about. (cited in Pilgrim 1990)

Indeed, Derek Mowbray from the Management Advisory Service and the consultant employed by the National Health Service manpower advisory group, put forward a rationale for the uniqueness of clinical psychology. He argued that the broadly based education in psychological knowledge put clinical psychologists in a position to offer special skills to the National Health Service that other professions could not. Mowbray argued that psychological skills could be divided into three levels. Level one was about basic counselling skills. Level two skills were cookbook-based approaches to psychological treatment. Level three skills were about being able to offer unique psychological formulations and interventions in relation to particular people and in specific contexts.

Thus, by 1990, the profession had an official report arguing for the profession's unique skills. It had also secured the right to keep its own register of qualified practitioners. However, it had failed to secure an independent statutory register, such as that established by the United Kingdom Central Council for Nursing, Midwifery and Health Visiting, and it had not managed to ensure mandatory registration of its membership. A campaign to achieve the latter is still underway.

The 1990s: consolidation and dealing with controversy

In the 1990s the profession has consolidated its new legitimacy. In 1994 the training period for the profession was increased to a three-year doctoral programme. A form of mimicry of medicine had already begun in the 1980s, when most senior grade clinical psychologists adopted the new title of 'Consultant'. The adoption of the title of 'Dr' completed this process of enhancing credentials and ensuring parity with medically qualified psychiatrists. As medical practitioners generally do not hold a doctorate, which therefore represents an honorary prefix for most of them, psychologists and latterly pharmacists are now arguably 'out-doctoring' medicine. Although today the salary levels of clinical psychologists remain below those of medical practitioners, this is not by a great margin.

In many respects, clinical psychologists have aimed to emulate the profession to which they were previously subordinated and to which they were hostile. This fuels the hypothesis that, during the 1970s, clinical psychologists not only began a campaign of escape from medical domination, but also strove to enhance their status through undertaking a professionalizing project (Larson 1977; Clare 1979). Indeed, as will be argued below, in many respects clinical psychologists now enjoy more autonomy than their medical colleagues.

Since 1997, the Labour government has continued to be fairly hostile to the health professions. However, the political tactics deployed have differed from those of the previous Conservative government. The latter aimed to improve the quality of public sector services through quasi-marketization on the one hand and bureaucratic controls over practitioners via general management on the other. The Labour government has been even more interventionist, introducing various measures, as described earlier in this volume by Price. It has also aimed to attribute responsibility and blame to practitioners for the various scandals affecting the clinical professions. Most of the latter headline cases, outlined in more detail by Allsop in Chapter 5, were about medical malpractice. This cluster of shamed medical practitioners was joined by another high-profile case that attracted attention from government and the media, and involved the British Psychological Society – the Slade case.

In 1998, the investigatory committee of the British Psychological Society found Peter Slade, Professor of Clinical Psychology at the University of Liverpool, guilty of sexually abusing several young female patients. What made the judgement controversial was not that he was found guilty of serial abuse, but that he was not expelled from the Society. It has been established through anonymous surveys that between 4 and 7 per cent of psychological therapists from all disciplines admit to sexual contact with clients. Some of these admit to being serial offenders (Pilgrim and Guinan 1999). Surveys in the United States indicate that the willingness of therapists to report sexual contact with clients has reduced, as sanctions for those who are found out have increased in severity. This poses a major dilemma for the profession. There is an understandable demand from clients for the robust regulation of abusers. However, it is also important to have an accurate estimate of the scale of sexual malpractice (Strasburger et al. 1995). It may or may not be that the reduced reporting rates reflect a reduced incidence of abuse.

The decision of the disciplinary board of the British Psychological Society was that Slade should be allowed to remain a member of the Society, although he voluntarily removed himself from the register as a chartered clinical psychologist.[2] The weak disciplinary response to Slade's malpractice provoked heated debate inside the British Psychological Society. One group of Slade defenders had acted as character witnesses in his disciplinary hearing and publicly supported the idea of him being retained as a Society member. Another group argued forcibly for his immediate expulsion. He had given an undertaking not to have any more contact with patients. However, his professional honours, such as being a Fellow of the Society, were not removed and no proactive strategy was announced to police his conduct in the future. The official rationale given by the British Psychological Society to defend the decision that Slade should remain as a member of the Society was that this would assist in future monitoring of his conduct.

Critics within the British Psychological Society had argued that the profession's reputation was at stake as there was considerable public anxiety. The Slade case simply added to the increasing numbers of clinical staff, across various the disciplines, who had been found to have mistreated their patients. The decision by the British Psychological Society could also be seen as part of a pattern of lenient treatment meted out by professional bodies. By the late 1990s, there was increasing public and political disquiet about clinical incompetence and the abuse of professional power. In this context, the Slade case brought to the fore a number of weaknesses in how voluntary self-regulation was being discharged. This had implications for the ongoing attempts by the Society to shift from voluntary to compulsory membership.

The first challenge was in relation to the cogency of the argument for registration. Part of the rhetoric for compulsory registration was that practitioners would be properly disciplined if they acted unprofessionally. Slade was already on the voluntary register and yet was not expelled. Consequently, critics argued that

British Psychological Society registration *per se* was no guarantee of client protection. Thus, although professionalizers in the Society wanted to emphasize the pressing need for compulsory registration on the back of the Slade scandal, their logic was inherently flawed. A second problem was that a number of practitioners had been subject to the British Psychological Society's disciplinary process in the recent past. They were less prestigious than Slade, but had been expelled for similar, or lesser, misdemeanours. At best, this reflected an inconsistent standard in dealing with malpractice in the profession. At worst, it suggested that higher-status members of the profession were more likely to receive lenient treatment.

Another problem highlighted by the Slade case was the poor communication between the British Psychological Society as a professional body and Slade's employer, the University. The latter offered him an early retirement package to end his employment – but he was not dismissed. The investigatory processes in the profession and the University were separate and were conducted using different rules of investigation. Currently, there is a large element of discretion between institutions and indeed sectors in how they deal with particular cases. Moreover, the various systems lack transparency.

Under the British system, as with many others internationally, sexual misconduct by psychological practitioners is not criminalized, although in some countries this is not the case and it is treated as a criminal act (Strasburger et al. 1995). At present in Britain, people with psychological problems are offered no legal protection against abuse – they rely on the efficiency of the professional and employment mechanisms for redress. In the Slade case, these mechanisms failed. Overall, the case indicates that, at present, abusive psychological therapists are dealt with leniently at the expense of robust client protection (Pilgrim and Guinan 1999). This highlights the difficulties of regulating a profession effectively where privacy is commonplace and the politics of intimacy determine outcomes for the client, both good and bad. The outcome research about psychological therapies indicates that the best predictor of mental health gain is a trusting and respectful working relationship between therapist and client. Symptomatic deterioration during therapy often reflects its absence.

The relationship for the psychological therapist is equivalent to the surgeon's cutting and stitching skills or the physician's medication practices. When the relationship is abused, it is like a botched operation or an iatrogenic medicinal remedy. Thus, while other health professions may abuse their trust and sexually mistreat their patients, it has particular salience in the domain of psychological therapy. In psychological work, a benign and respectful working relationship is not only a civil right, it is also the central means of psychological change on offer to the client. If it fails, the client suffers a double insult and betrayal.

Discussion

British clinical psychology has been co-terminous temporally with the National Health Service. Consequently, since 1948, the profession has been shaped by its organizational dynamics and affected by shifts in National Health Service policy and politics more closely than professions established prior to its formation. At first, the profession's legitimacy rested only on its scientific credentials and not voluntary or mandatory registration. The legacy of this history and the tensions it created in the drive towards professional regulation can be explored via the concept of indeterminacy. Jamous and Peloille (1970) elaborated this in their seminal analysis of French health professionals. They argue that the ratio between indeterminate and technical knowledge determines the claim to professional status. Although it has been pointed out that these factors are interdependent rather than oppositional (Atkinson 1981; Macdonald 1995), the concept of indeterminacy has a particular heuristic relevance for the work of clinical psychologists.

The structural separation between the British Psychological Society and local National Health Service employers creates an ambiguous space. Communication between the two currently can be poor or non-existent. Both have systems of accountability to ensure standards and to deal with rule breaking or role failure, but these systems contain different styles of investigation. Moreover, the separation of local employment arrangements creates a further fracturing, which can undermine efficient regulation in particular cases. Currently, it is possible for a clinical psychologist dismissed for malpractice to move successfully from one part of the National Health Service to another.

Turning to the processes that reflect indeterminacy in the profession, a number of related factors interact in daily clinical practice. First, there is the lack of consensus about psychological theory and practice. As was noted earlier, this is endemic in the human sciences. Pluralism, eclecticism and factionalism inevitably ensue, and these factors lead to a norm of mutual, if sometimes grudging, tolerance between practitioners of different orientations in the profession. This 'live and let live' norm is one constituent part of indeterminate clinical practice.

A second related factor is the contradictory norm of 'scientific humanism' (Richards 1983). This has emerged as the collective response to the lack of a shared cognitive knowledge base. Some practitioners operate at the scientific end of the spectrum, others at the humanistic end. In practice, the former operate within a form of binary reasoning especially related to questions of 'scientific/non-scientific' and 'evidence-based/not evidence-based' approaches. The humanistically inclined are more relativistic, generating idiosyncratic accounts of their healing relationship with different clients. Many practitioners inhabit an ambiguous middle position that may fluctuate according to situated roles and the audience being addressed. What practitioners say privately to trusted colleagues, is not always what they say publicly to clients or professionals in other professions. This situated nature of private and public accounts of professional action feeds into the indeterminate and fluid daily practice.

Another example of the tension between science and humanism that reinforces indeterminacy is the question of evidence-based practice. On the one hand, clinical psychology trainees are encouraged to see the scientist-practitioner model as central to their professional identity. On the other, individual psychologists are free to use evidence selectively in their daily practice. Even early in their training, neophyte clinical psychologists begin to express doubts and even cynicism about the authenticity of the scientist-practitioner identity (Cheshire 2000).

A third aspect of indeterminacy is that the logical implication of evidence-based practice for all clinical staff is having clear practice guidelines. A strong (North American) advocate of protocols for clinical psychologists has commented:

> Up until recently guild forces have resisted practice guidelines foreseeing interference and restriction. Guilds have preferred to emphasize the certification of people over procedures, in part because this approach has been shown over the centuries to provide an extremely effective method of enhancing economic success and professional power of particular groups. The problem with certifying people is that it is an extremely ineffective way of ensuring quality. It is not by accident that although the first meaning of licence in the dictionary is 'lawful permission', the second is 'excessive liberty'. People with licence do sometimes take licence. When one's judgment is officially sanctioned, it is but a small step to disconnect judgment from careful and defensible reasoning and base it instead on mere personal preference. (Hayes 1998: 36)

Hayes goes on to develop the point that clinical psychologists, like medical practitioners who solemnly protect their 'clinical freedom', have been prone to evade protocols and favour guild credentialism. However, what makes psychologists peculiar is that scientific rationality has been a central rhetorical device in their professionalization strategy. It is part of the 'scientist-practitioner' identity. The discourse of medicine is also peppered with scientific rhetoric, but it emphasizes the profession as an art in terms of situated, personal judgements. While all psychological therapists claim some degree of technical rationality in their work, those from other disciplines tend not to play the scientific card as strongly as clinical psychologists. It may be that if clinical psychology does not deliver, or modify, its scientific rhetoric then more plausible competing therapists will erode its role.

A fourth factor that feeds into the indeterminacy of practice is the relative lack of legal constraints on clinical psychologists as compared to other clinicians. Although they are bound under common law to a 'duty of care', they have no responsibilities under mental health legislation nor do they have prescribing rights. Consequently, this relative absence of legal duty weakens their need for external accountability compared, for example, to psychiatrists, psychiatric nurses or pharmacists. However, this may be changing. The new mental health legislation replaces the notion of the 'responsible medical officer' with that of 'clinical supervisor'. This could be a psychologist or psychiatrist.

A fifth factor leading to indeterminacy, is the scarcity of clinical psychologists in terms of numbers in the field. Not only are they a relatively small group of clinical professionals, with under-training leading to a supply bottleneck and many unfilled posts in the National Health Service, but they have developed at least four separate role expectations for themselves – assessment, therapy, training and research. As they are not as numerous in service provision as other professionals, they are left with a wide discretion about when, and how, to deploy their resources. In the same locality, one psychologist might operate purely as a therapist, another may predominantly favour training or research. Managers and colleagues from other professions rarely interfere with this discretion because all four roles can usually be justified in the interest of the service. The element of discretion is amplified further by difficulties in recruitment. Interested candidates are often tempted by offers of individually determined job plans from employers.

The sixth and final factor to consider as contributing to indeterminacy is the strong norm of individual consultations. Not only do different practitioners work with different models in dealing with clients, they do so often under conditions of privacy. This ensures that clients are highly reliant upon the continuing personal integrity of practitioners. Privacy is a precondition of both abuse and effective confidential conversations.

These six factors provide a checklist of interacting factors that highlight the indeterminate character of clinical psychological practice. As with other clinical professions, although arguably in a more extreme form, this indeterminacy is both structurally inherent and a resource available for professionals to either evade external scrutiny, or pursue a legitimate commitment to client-centred goals.

Pressures against indeterminacy include: the profession's own rhetoric about evidence-based practice; failures of its code of practice and disciplinary procedures; task encroachment from nearby professions; and strategies of bureaucratic subordination from central government through general management and clinical governance. Factors that help maintain indeterminacy include: the strategic preference for self-defined credentialism and mandatory state registration rather than task protocols; the lack of specific legal responsibilities compared to other professions; numerical scarcity; and the contested nature of psychological knowledge. These competing factors do not lead to a stable 'zero sum game' but represent elements in an unstable set of political dynamics within the profession and between the profession and other parties such as government and other health workers.

To date, users of psychological services have not been a salient determinant of professional action. Clinical psychologists have faced far less consumer hostility than psychiatrists (Rogers and Pilgrim 1991). Indeed, disaffected users of psychiatric services have tended to idealize the status of psychological therapies. However, the Slade case and others have led to the emergence of user organizations in Britain, such as the Prevention of Professional Abuse Network, which reflect and reinforce the de-stabilized public confidence in talking treatments. Disaffected mental health service users have continued to subscribe to their anti-psychiatry stance and hostility to biomedical interventions. Indeed, latterly suspicion has been cast upon psychological treatments as well (Pilgrim and Rogers 1999). Arguably, most people with psychological problems want more, not less, talking treatments (Masson 1989; de Swaan 1990), but this consumer-driven mandate is by no means inviolable. At present, the most powerful regulatory constraint on the indeterminacy of clinical psychology practice comes neither from service users nor from the British Psychological Society. Instead, it can be located in the matrix of bureaucratic subordination imposed on all health professionals. This has accrued from general management principles and the concern to raise standards in the National Health Service.

Notes

1 The first part of the chapter draws on Pilgrim and Treacher (1992) and provides a sceptical account of the profession. It initially developed from a Master's dissertation in sociology, but also draws on my work as an academic clinical psychologist from 1986–96. The second part reflects a return to clinical practice in a senior management position within the National Health Service with responsibility for psychological input into a local mental health service. Although this provides a deep experiential knowledge of contemporary practice, the disadvantage is that it is both personal and parochial.

2 Membership of the Society and chartered status are currently not synonymous.

References

Atkinson, P. (1981) *The Clinical Experience: The Construction and Reconstruction of Medical Reality*. Farnborough: Gower.

Cheshire, K. (2000) *The Professional Socialisation of Clinical Psychologists: Trainee Accounts*. Unpublished Ph.D. thesis, University of Liverpool.

Clare, A. (1979) 'Review of psychiatry observed by G. Baruch and A. Treacher', *Psychological Medicine*, 9: 387–9.

de Swaan, A. (1990) *The Management of Normality*. London: Routledge.

DHSS (1977) *The Role of Psychologists in the Health Service*. London: HMSO.

Eysenck, H.J. (1949) 'Training in clinical psychology: An English point of view', *American Psychologist*, 4: 173–6.

Eysenck, H.J. (1958) 'The psychiatric treatment of neurosis'. Paper presented to the Royal Medico-Psychological Association, London.

Foster, J. (1971) *Enquiry into the Practice and Effects of Scientology*. London: HMSO.

Foucault, M. (1973) *The Order of Things: An Archaeology of the Human Sciences*. New York: Vintage Books.

Hayes, S.C. (1998) 'Scientific practice guidelines in a political, economic and professional context', in K.S Dobson, and K.D. Craig (eds), *Empirically Supported Therapies: Best Practice in Professional Psychology*. London: Sage.

Jamous, H. and Peloille, B. (1970) 'Professions or self-perpetuating systems? Changes in the French university hospital system', in J. Jackson (ed.) *Professions and Professionalisation*. London: Cambridge University Press.

Larson, M. (1977) *The Rise of Professionalism: A Sociological Analysis*. Berkeley: University of California Press.

Macdonald, K. (1995) *The Sociology of the Professions*. London: Sage.

Masson, J. (1989) *Against Therapy*. London: HarperCollins.

Pilgrim, D. (1990) 'Clinical Psychology in the 1980s: A Sociological Analysis'. Unpublished MSc thesis, Polytechnic of the South Bank, London.

Pilgrim, D. and Guinan, P. (1999) 'From mitigation to culpability: Rethinking the evidence about therapist sexual abuse', *European Journal of Psychotherapy, Counselling and Health*, 2: 153–68.

Pilgrim, D. and Rogers, A. (1999) *A Sociology of Mental Health and Illness*. Buckingham: Open University Press, 2nd edn.

Pilgrim, D. and Treacher, A. (1992) *Clinical Psychology Observed*. London: Routledge.

Raimy, V.C. (ed.) (1953) *Training in Clinical Psychology*. New York: Prentice-Hall.

Richards, B. (1983) *Clinical Psychology, the Individual and the State*. Unpublished Ph.D. thesis, Polytechnic of North East London.

Rogers, A. and Pilgrim, D. (1991) '"Pulling down churches": Accounting for the British mental health users' movement', *Sociology of Health and Illness*, 15: 612–31.

Seighart, P. (1978) *The Registration of Psychotherapists*. London: HMSO.

Shapiro, M. (1951) 'An experimental approach to diagnostic psychological testing', *Journal of Mental Science*, 97: 747–64.

Smart, B. (1990) 'On the disorder of things: Sociology and the end of the social', *Sociology*, 24: 397–416.

Stone, M. (1985) 'Shellshock and the psychologist', in W.F. Bynum, R. Porter and M. Shepherd, (eds) *The Anatomy of Madness*. London: Tavistock.

Strasburger, L.H., Jorgenson, L. and Randles, R. (1995) 'Criminalisation of psychotherapist–patient sex', in D.N. Bersoff, (ed.) *Ethical Conflicts in Psychology*. Washington, DC: American Psychological Association.

10   Professionalization, Regulation and Alternative Medicine

Mike Saks

The field of alternative medicine in the United Kingdom covers a wide variety of therapies. These range from herbalism and reflexology to aromatherapy and massage and have been defined in a number of ways in the literature – including as 'complementary', 'holistic', 'natural' and 'traditional' therapies. However, each of these definitions has its drawbacks as some therapies are underpinned by theories that conflict with orthodox medicine (for instance, homoeopathy); others can be very mechanistic (such as osteopathy); still others are certainly not natural (like acupuncture); and many are of modern origin (for example, biofeedback). The definition preferred here is that of 'alternative' medicine, which is based not so much on the substantive content of such therapies, as on their political marginality. While there is little unity otherwise, all the therapies share a marginal standing in relation to orthodox biomedicine, with its characteristic focus on drugs and surgery. In this regard, they are not taught as a central part of the medical curriculum, do not receive mainstream research funding and are not usually covered on a regular and positive basis in the major medical journals in this country (Saks 1992).

This chapter considers the regulation of alternative medicine, as so defined, from a neo-Weberian perspective. As such, it places the analysis of their regulatory development in a world of sectional occupational power and interests, mediated by the state – through which professions seek to regulate market conditions to their advantage against competitors (see, amongst others, Collins 1990). Using this framework, this chapter examines the position of alternative medicine in the historical and contemporary context. Historically, the rise of the medical profession and the burgeoning division of labour within orthodox medicine have been centrally important. Within the neo-Weberian perspective, the notion of a 'profession' is seen as being based on legally enshrined exclusionary 'social closure' that enhances the social and economic opportunities of the group concerned (Macdonald 1995). In this sense, alternative practitioners have for long been viewed as rivals and cast as 'outsiders'. However, this is now changing, as their relationship with medical orthodoxy in the United Kingdom has shifted – not least because alternative therapists have themselves increasingly taken steps to professionalize, including by subscribing to ethical codes and extending their education to match that of more established health professions (Saks 1998).

Earlier chapters in this part of the volume have dealt predominantly with occupations that have already professionalized. Some of these have done so in the distant past (as classically exemplified by medicine in the mid-nineteenth century) and others more recently (as in the case of the professions supplementary to medicine in the latter half of the twentienth century). In contrast, most practitioners of alternative medicine have not obtained statutory regulation, the touchstone of state recognition. The two exceptions to this are the osteopaths and the chiropractors, who gained their professional standing in the first half of the 1990s, albeit on less robust terms than other health professions. Some groups of alternative practitioners – but by no means all – have put in place systems of voluntary regulation, following in the footsteps of the clinical psychologists, whose development was described in the previous chapter. This makes alternative medicine an interesting case study to include in this book, as it is currently a field in which professionalization is in process in the United Kingdom.

Alternative medicine is also an important area as it is far larger in scope than often supposed. Alternative practices cover a broad spectrum of therapies from acupuncture, centred on the insertion of needles into the body for therapeutic purposes, to homoeopathy, based on a belief in the potency of infinitesimal dilutions of specific remedies (Ernst 2001). Their scale of application is indicated by the extensive self-help use of alternative medicine by the public, including the widespread purchase of over-the-counter preparations (Bakx 1991). There are also now some 60,000 alternative therapists in the United Kingdom. Although many of these practise part-time, most are members of occupational associations (Mills and Budd 2000). While they do not yet numerically rival the nurses, their numbers exceed those of general practitioners in the United Kingdom. And while they do not typically share the privileged, state-sanctioned position of orthodox health professions, they are allowed to practise under the Common Law (Saks 1994). To understand more fully the regulatory framework under which they operate, though, it is necessary first to trace the historical background to the emergence and subsequent development of alternative medicine.

The historical background

The field of alternative medicine was not formally created until the 1858 Medical Act, which for the first time gave doctors as a unified group state-underwritten protection of title on a national basis, with self-governing powers through the General Medical Council (Stacey 1992). Before this, there had been a comparatively open field – notwithstanding the limited monopolies gained from the sixteenth century onwards through the establishment of bodies such as the Royal College of Physicians, the Royal College of Surgeons and the Society of Apothecaries (Porter 1995). By the eighteenth and early nineteenth centuries, there was intense competition in an ever more entrepreneurial environment between practitioners affiliated to these organizations and groups, such as bonesetters, herbalists, healers and purveyors of various forms of proprietary medicine.

They were very difficult to separate in terms of both their education and the content of their practice (Porter 1989). However, the more or less level playing field on which they operated was transcended following intense lobbying for professional standing by the Provincial Medical and Surgical Association (later to become the British Medical Association) from the 1830s onwards. This lobby included attacks on rival practitioners through the medical journals and other channels (Saks 1996).

The effect of the 1858 Act was to marginalize competitors, as well as to increase the income, status and power of doctors as a group through the *de facto* monopoly that was established. At this time, according to official figures, medically unqualified rivals outnumbered members of the newly formed medical profession by some three to one (Levitt et al. 1995). While practitioners such as hydropaths and homoeopaths were not formally prevented from practising under the Common Law, they lost legitimacy as a result of the Act, in addition to being prevented from engaging in state-funded employment. They also had to endure continuing opposition from the leaders of the medical profession, who branded them as unscrupulous money-grabbing 'quacks' in an effort to drive them out of business. Such attacks were made too on those who engaged in deviant therapeutic practices within the profession. This had the effect of increasing the unity of the medical profession around the developing platform of 'scientific' biomedical knowledge – which was to become a significant political resource in the interest-based turf war with its occupational rivals (Saks 1996).

Alternative practitioners were also further marginalized as state involvement in health care increased. Particularly significant in this respect were the 1911 Insurance Act and the 1946 National Health Service Act. By financially supporting doctors and the growing range of other professionally qualified health workers – from midwives and nurses to occupational therapists and physiotherapists – the disadvantaged market position of alternative therapists was further accentuated (Saks 1998). In addition, the close medical–Ministry alliance that developed in the inter-war years led to the rejection of the claims of alternative practitioners who sought to gain professional recognition – such as the osteopaths in the 1920s and 1930s (Larkin 1992). The marginality of alternative medicine was confirmed by the passing of the 1939 Cancer Act that prevented the medically unregistered from claiming to treat cancer, and the 1941 Pharmacy and Medicines Act that restricted non-medical practitioners from treating conditions such as cataracts, diabetes, epilepsy and tuberculosis (Larkin 1995). It is not surprising that by the 1950s the regulatory controls imposed by the profession over the previous century had led to the decline of the numbers of alternative practitioners, almost to the point of extinction (Saks 1995).

The contemporary development of alternative medicine

Nonetheless, from the 1960s onwards the fortunes of alternative medicine in the United Kingdom began to change for the better. This was particularly associated with rising public demand – such that around one in seven people are now said to visit alternative practitioners each year (Sharma 1995). This is related to factors such as the growing recognition that orthodox medicine can have counter-productive effects and the desire of patients for greater involvement and control over their own health care (Bakx 1991). The strong medical counter-culture, which emerged between the mid-1960s and mid-1970s, seems to have had a substantial impact (Saks 2000a). Under its impetus, the numbers of alternative practitioners rose to some 30,000 in the early 1980s (Fulder 1996) and to 45,000 by the mid-1990s (Mills and Peacock 1997), before reaching their current heights – with the most popular therapies including acupuncture, homoeopathy, healing and osteopathy. Grassroots health professionals like doctors and nurses also increasingly used acupuncture and other alternative therapies in settings such as pain clinics and hospices, as well as in general practice (see, for example, Trevelyan and Booth 1994; Lewith et al. 1996). Medical practitioners employed homoeopathy too in the handful of homoeopathic hospitals that came into the National Health Service at the outset as a result of royal patronage (Nicholls 1988).

However, alternative therapies faced strong initial resistance from some quarters, particularly when used by non-medically qualified practitioners. This came in part from medical practitioners who were using alternative therapies themselves and wished to limit competition from their lay exponents, especially in private practice. This is exemplified by members of the Faculty of Homoeopathy and the British Medical Acupuncture Society who claimed that the therapies employed by their members should be restricted to doctors alone, not least because of the dangers involved (Cant and Sharma 1995b; Saks 1995). Powerful players at higher levels in the medical game also obstructed the formal acceptance of alternative medicine. These included bodies like multinational surgical and pharmaceutical companies which perceived alternative therapies as a threat to their commercial interests and were therefore not always enthusiastic about sponsoring their development (Walker 1994). The leaders of the medical profession too took a negative stance towards alternative medicine. This is highlighted by the British Medical Association (1986) report on alternative therapy that condemned it as based on mediaeval superstition rather than science. This was part of a wider attack on alternative practitioners in the medical journals that was paralleled in some cases by ostracism and career blockages for doctors engaged in such practices within the profession (Saks 1996).

From a professional self-interest perspective, this medical resistance could be seen as an attempt to counter the growing external challenge to professional knowledge posed by alternative therapies based on their conflicting philosophies and limited educational underpinning. This climate of rejection by the guardians of medical orthodoxy has recently been increasingly displaced in the United Kingdom in face of rising political pressure. In addition to fast expanding and now widespread popular support for alternative medicine, the Parliamentary Group for Alternative and Complementary Medicine, composed of all-party Members of Parliament, has been an important lobby (Saks 1992). Amongst many well-known supporters of such therapies, Prince Charles has perhaps been the key advocate. It was he indeed who instigated the British Medical Association inquiry into this area in the 1980s, in his term of office as its President. It was he too who subsequently sponsored the production of the influential report on *Integrated Healthcare* through the Foundation for Integrated Medicine (1997). Drawing on high-level national medical and other expertise, this document charted a positive course forward for the field that included establishing appropriate professional regulatory systems for alternative medicine.

With pressure both from within its own ranks and from outsiders, limited incorporation rather than outright rejection became the best strategic option for the leaders of the medical profession to control the threat from alternative medicine. The first indication of this at a macro-level was when the General Medical Council dropped its longstanding prohibition on collaboration between doctors and alternative practitioners in the mid-1970s that had previously led to doctors being subjected to disciplinary proceedings (Fulder and Monro 1981). While a pioneering step, this was not as challenging to professional self-interests as it may at first appear. Given the professional accountability and potential liability involved in any delegation or referral arrangements, such a move was never likely to open up the floodgates to the increasing numbers of alternative practitioners, particularly in view of prevailing uncertainties about their qualifications and competence (Stone and Mathews 1996). At the same time, it importantly indicated that the profession was not unresponsive to public opinion. Although the British Medical Association took many years to follow suit in its advice to members – and indeed to soften its stance on alternative therapies more generally – the action by the General Medical Council set the tone for the years that lay ahead.

This was underlined when the British Medical Association (1993) produced a new report on what had then become defined as 'complementary' rather than 'alternative' medicine. This report took a more conciliatory stance in relation to non-medical practitioners of such therapies, urging enhanced communication with doctors, as well as recognizing the need to place on a firmer footing the education and training of doctors who wish to practise non-conventional therapies. It also highlighted the need for considered judgments as to whether voluntary or statutory regulation was required, depending mainly on the degree of invasiveness of the therapies concerned. Although the report superficially represents a professional retreat, its primary focus actually seems to have been on ensuring that unorthodox therapies are regulated in a manner designed to preserve professional dominance. This is very evident in its recommendations that medical referral should only be permitted where such therapies have been granted statutory self-regulation; that medical authority for patients should be maintained when delegation occurs; that the ethical, educational and disciplinary regulatory template for medicine should be applied to unorthodox therapies; and that the core curriculum for alternative practitioners should be centred on basic medical subjects like anatomy and physiology, while student doctors should simply be given an appreciation of non-conventional therapies.

As a recent report on acupuncture by the British Medical Association (2000) attests, it continues to hold a similar general policy line. This publication also indicates that bodies like the Royal College of Physicians now accept that they can no longer afford to ignore alternative therapies. The position taken by the British Medical Association clearly has the advantage of enabling the profession to respond to internal and external pressures by engaging with unorthodox medicine, while controlling it to protect its strategic interests and create new market opportunities for members of the profession. A key part of this strategy now involves doctors in not only adopting such therapies, but also sub-delegating them to other health personnel in the orthodox division of labour (Vincent and Furnham 1997). How, though, have alternative practitioners themselves responded to the regulatory challenge in the United Kingdom – particularly in terms of professionalization?

The professionalization of alternative medicine

In this respect, the professionalization of alternative medicine carries a certain irony, as the parallel process in relation to orthodox medicine some 150 years ago had such a crucial effect in marginalizing such therapies. It is not therefore surprising that some alternative practitioners have distanced themselves from the drive to professionalize for ideological reasons (Cant and Sharma 1995a). The factors that have motivated the majority of alternative therapists to embrace professionalization include the desire to enhance their organizational coherence, as well as to give a firmer educational foundation to their work. This contrasts with the more individualistic motif of the past based on the apprenticeship model and idiosyncratic training arrangements (Fulder 1996). The appeal of professionalization is underlined by the threat to the longstanding Common Law right of alternative therapists to practise in the United Kingdom posed by membership of the European Union. This brings with it the prospect of more restrictive legislation based on harmonization and mutual recognition policies, given the less than inclusive stance taken by most member states towards the non-medical practice of unorthodox medicine (Huggon and Trench 1992). In these circumstances, it has clearly been in the interests of most alternative practitioners to develop a more substantial professional framework for their operation.

.This said, the extent to which particular alternative therapies have become professionalized in the United Kingdom has been very variable. The least progress has typically been made with therapies that have the strongest self-help usage and a more limited knowledge base. This is well exemplified by crystal therapy. Other more accepted and widely used therapies such as aromatherapy and reflexology also have further scope for development in this respect. Although both of these therapies are practised by many thousands of exponents, the training involved usually lasts for no more than weeks or months rather than years, with many dozens of training schools and a diverse range of associations representing practitioners (Cant and Sharma 1995a). While this is changing as attempts are made to bring the training schools and associations together to agree on common standards and codes of ethics, there is still some distance to travel (Saks 1999). However, other groups of alternative practitioners such as acupuncturists and homoeopaths have gone further down the road of setting up effective mechanisms for voluntary self-regulation.

In the case of acupuncture, a number of non-medically qualified acupuncturists founded the Council for Acupuncture in 1980 based on a common code of discipline, education and ethics. This brought together the previously divided British Acupuncture Association and Register, the Chung San Acupuncture Society, the International Register of Oriental Medicine, the Register of Traditional Chinese Medicine and the Traditional Acupuncture Society. The union was developed further in the late 1980s with the establishment of the British Acupuncture Accreditation Board, which prescribes minimum educational standards, and the British Acupuncture Council, which serves as the registering body (Saks 1995). This process has similarities with developments in homoeopathy, where the Society of Homoeopaths has been the main focal point for non-medically qualified practitioners. Since the Society was formed in 1981, it has also established a register and code of ethics. Although this area of alternative medicine is not yet as unified as acupuncture, many homoeopathic colleges have had their training formally accredited by the Society of Homoeopaths. This has helped to provide a more systematic body of expertise, based on the standard European Union model of three years of full-time education (Cant and Sharma 1996). The state, though, has not as yet formally sanctioned a position of exclusionary closure in either of these areas.

However, the state has now statutorily recognized osteopathy and chiropractic. Like many other alternative therapies, significant internal divisions have beset these fields (Fulder 1996). In view of its widely acknowledged educational strengths, though, sufficient agreement was possible to allow the Osteopaths Act to be passed in 1993, on the basis of a private member's Bill. The result was protection of title, a register, self-regulation, and legally underwritten ethical and educational standards – policed by the newly formed General Osteopathic Council (Standen 1993). This was swiftly followed by the Chiropractic Act in 1994 that set up a parallel form of state regulation for chiropractors, based on the creation of a General Chiropractic Council (Cant and Sharma 1995a). As a consequence of state regulation, the legitimacy and market position of both therapies in the United Kingdom has been enhanced. However, whilst the regulatory model is heavily based on medicine, it does not enable direct financial support to be given to such therapies within the National Health Service – in contrast to other orthodox health care professions (Saks 1999). While the state-supported professionalization of osteopathy and chiropractic has therefore given them a foot in the door of mainstream health care, they remain 'alternative' in relation to funding.

Alternative medicine and the state

This sense of continuing social exclusion bolstered by state policy is reflected in other ways. Writers interested in the gendered aspects of professionalization in patriarchal societies (for example, Witz 1992), might do well to reflect on this hitherto neglected area. Whilst alternative medicine is largely practised by females, osteopathy and chiropractic – the first alternative therapy groups to gain statutory regulation – are male-dominated occupations (Cant and Sharma 1999). There are therefore potential parallels with the state-underwritten ascendance of the male medical profession in the mid-nineteenth century. A number of more popular alternative therapies also have strong ethnic minority roots and widely serve such communities in the United Kingdom. This is true, for instance, of Traditional Chinese Medicine and Ayurvedic Medicine that have particular, but not exclusive appeal, to indigenous Oriental and Asian populations (Fulder 1996). Their persisting marginality may again be a comment on the relative lack of progress made by the state in combating social exclusion in health care. Much the same might be said about the limited extent to which opportunities for access to alternative medicine have been opened up, given the current patchy geographical spread of such therapies both inside and outside the National Health Service. The position here is not helped by the fact that they are mainly available in the private sector, which also provides potential cost barriers for consumers (Cant and Sharma 1999).

Leaving on one side these important questions about the hitherto restricted role of the state in reducing inequalities in this area, the comparative success of the osteopaths and chiropractors shows that it has a critical part to play in the professionalization of alternative medicine. In this regard, the legal sanction obtained in the first half of the 1990s by osteopathy and chiropractic contrasts with the 1960s and 1970s when their applications to become professions supplementary to medicine were turned down (Fulder and Monro 1981). This shift arguably reflects a change in the relationship between the medical profession, alternative medicine and the state in the United Kingdom. Whereas in the past state policy was heavily determined by the advice given by the British Medical Association and the Royal Colleges, the linkage between established professions and the state has now become less straightforward – even in the classic case of medicine (Larkin 1995). With the transcendence of the hegemonic relationship of medicine to the Ministry of Health in the inter-war period, the independent role of the state in health care decision making is now crucial. This also applies to the way in which it conceives the framework of regulatory arrangements that are necessary in relation to alternative medicine.

This was underlined in the 1980s when the Conservative government sought a united approach from the various alternative therapies under one umbrella as a prelude to enacting further regulatory legislation (Sharma 1995). However, such expectations were doomed to failure, given the rifts at this time both within and across alternative therapies – largely as a result of different practice styles and philosophies (Fulder 1996). Attempts were nonetheless made to facilitate unity through a number of existing and newly created bodies in the field, such as the Institute for Complementary Medicine, the Council for Complementary and Alternative Medicine, and the British Complementary Medical Association. These were predictably not able to bring together the diverse elements making up alternative medicine at this stage and in the early 1990s the state decided that each specific form of unorthodox medicine should determine its own place in the health care system (Saks 1994). Together with increased collaboration within the sector, this meant that individual therapies could henceforth present a case for professional standing in their own right with greater prospects of success (Cant and Sharma 1999). It was also helpful in the search for professional recognition by groups of unorthodox therapists that a health minister was given a brief for alternative medicine by successive Conservative administrations (Saks 1991).

Indeed, in 1991 Stephen Dorrell, the then Parliamentary Secretary of State for Health, announced for the first time that doctors in the National Health Service could sub-contract to alternative practitioners, providing that they remained clinically accountable for patients (Stone and Mathews 1996). This formally opened up state health practice to non-medically qualified alternative therapists, albeit in a subordinated and limited manner. Over the past decade, the growing emphasis of state policy on the safety of the public has had significant implications for the regulation of alternative medicine. This strand has been reflected in debates by professional bodies such as the United Kingdom Central Council for Nursing, Midwifery and Health Visiting over the part that they should play in relation to the regulation of health support workers (Davies and Beach 2000). These debates have of necessity covered those practising alternative medicine in support roles. There is also a link to the reform of the Council for Professions Supplementary to Medicine under the Labour government that recently led to the creation of the Health Professions Council (Department of Health 2001b). Osteopaths and chiropractors are to form part of this body, alongside longer established professions allied to medicine. The new Council may be able to expand to incorporate further groups of alternative practitioners in a manner precluded by the rules governing its predecessor. Where, therefore, is alternative medicine going in future?

The future of alternative medicine

The House of Lords Select Committee on Science and Technology (2000) on complementary and alternative medicine is very significant in assessing the likelihood of further professionalization. This report puts forward a number of recommendations to government, which have generally been well received (Department of Health 2001a). Many of these derive from the threefold distinction it makes between complementary and alternative therapies. More specifically, the Committee differentiates a first group composed of the principal disciplines of osteopathy, chiropractic, acupuncture, herbal medicine and homoeopathy. These are held to have an individual diagnostic approach; to encompass the most organized groups of practitioners; and to possess the most credible evidence base in the field. A second group of therapies exemplified by aromatherapy, massage, counselling, hypnotherapy and reflexology is also identified. Unlike the first group, these are seen as largely being used to complement conventional medicine and not requiring diagnostic skills. Therapies in the third group provide diagnosis and treatment, but are viewed as being based on very different philosophical principles from conventional medicine – including those associated with long-established systems such as Ayurvedic Medicine and Traditional Chinese Medicine, as well as therapies like crystal therapy, iridology and radionics. It is felt that the weakest research evidence currently underpins this group.

From the viewpoint of regulation, the Committee argues that there should be a coherent professional structure for complementary and alternative medicine, albeit with a specific body for each therapy. The report particularly singles out acupuncture and herbal medicine as ripe for statutory regulation because of the risks to patients in the hands of the unqualified; the existence of well-organized voluntary systems for regulation; the level of consensus amongst practitioners about the desirability of the move towards a statutory framework; and the extent to which they have developed a credible evidence base. It believes that the remaining therapies should put voluntary self-regulatory structures in place, including guidelines on competency and training. The following measures are also favoured: the establishment of independent accreditation boards; more stan- dardization of courses in specific disciplines; greater liaison with higher educa- tion; and continuing professional development. The report only recommends that training in subjects like anatomy and physiology is incorporated into educational programmes where alternative practitioners are acting as more than adjunct ther- apists. It is, however, felt that all complementary and alternative therapists should be trained in research and statistical methods and receive clear instruction on the circumstances in which medical referral is necessary. Reciprocally, it is argued that students in medical and other orthodox health professions should be famil- iarized with the use of such therapies.

In this latter regard, the aim is to increase the integration between conventional and non-conventional medicine, with all National Health Service provision being accessed through referral by orthodox practitioners. The Committee also believes that, where a critical mass of evidence exists for specific types of complementary and alternative medicine, the National Health Service and the medical profession should ensure that the public has access to the therapies concerned. It notes that new research will be needed to examine the efficacy of such therapies as com- pared to placebos and other forms of orthodox medicine, as well as their safety and relative cost-effectiveness. It is felt that this should draw on randomized con- trolled trials, as well as other research designs – supported by the establishment of a number of university-based centres of excellence, with co-ordination and pump-priming funding provided by the Department of Health. The report also comments that more information on complementary and alternative medicine should be provided to the public through such vehicles as NHS Direct, including that on the evaluation of different therapies.

The above recommendations are similar in some respects to those contained in the earlier report of the British Medical Association (1993). They could also be seen to bolster the interests of the medical profession against those of alternative practitioners. This is illustrated by the central responsibility that the House of Lords report says should be assumed by doctors in referral relationships and the extent to which biomedicine is felt to be needed in the core training of comple- mentary and alternative therapists. However, the report goes beyond that of the British Medical Association too, not least by arguing for government funding support for developing an evidence base for complementary and alternative med- icine. This recommendation could help alternative therapists escape from the financial double bind in research in which they have for so long been trapped in comparison to their far more substantially funded orthodox medical counterparts. It also introduces major questions about the relative efficacy, safety and cost- effectiveness of such therapies, which are central to public protection. These are fundamental to developing the regulatory structure most appropriate to specific alternative therapies and in mapping their future role within the National Health Service.

The report rightly suggests, therefore, that the regulation of alternative medicine should be examined primarily from a public interest perspective. This has been discussed by Saks (1994) who notes that – despite revolutionary developments in such areas of modern medicine as hip replacements and life-saving surgery to repair faulty heart valves – controlled trial evidence indicates that some types of alternative medicine may be more efficacious than conventional medical treatment. This can be illustrated by the use of chiropractic for back pain, instead of hospital outpatient treatment. Equally, the occurrence of collapsed lungs as a result of acupuncture treatment and adverse reactions to herbal remedies should not mask the apparent relative safety of many alternative therapies as compared to orthodox medicine. This is underlined by the fact that orthodox medicine carries its own hazards – as the victims of thalidomide and Opren can testify. Moreover, despite the additional costs of the generally more time-consuming and labour-intensive process of administering alternative medicine, there are large potential savings to be made through its use, especially when orthodox treatment might otherwise involve the application of expensive high-technology equipment and drugs.

The upshot of this analysis is that some types of alternative medicine may have value and be worth regulating to gain greater public benefit, not least through professional self-regulation. However, this is a contentious area. As Saks (1994) also notes, the evidence for alternative medicine remains limited. There are major disputes too over whether the same methodologies can be employed for evaluating more individualized alternative therapies based on holistic principles as for standardized biomedical interventions. This is particularly apparent in relation to randomized controlled trials that are generally treated as the 'gold standard' in orthodox medical circles. In this respect, alternative therapists often claim that the placebo effect should be positively employed in the healing encounter, rather than being eliminated in the interests of scientific rigour (Pietroni 1991). Alternative medicine also continues to have entrenched medical detractors – including members of the Campaign Against Health Fraud – who have lobbied against it on the basis of their perception of the hazards involved (Cant and Sharma 1999).

Conclusion

Whatever view that is taken about the therapeutic potential of alternative medicine, the public interest debate seems to take the reader into territory beyond the classic neo-Weberian analysis of this area, based on conflicts between self-interested occupational groups. As pointed out in the Introduction to this volume, though, such interests may coalesce with, as well as diverge from, the public interest (Saks 1995). Whether professional self-interests and the public interest come together in the current trend towards the medical incorporation and control of alternative therapies is a moot point. Nonetheless, the discussion clearly suggests that popular support for alternative medicine is likely to increase still further. This means that political pressures are liable to grow for such therapies to become more professionalized – through either voluntary self-regulation or more developed, legally underwritten, patterns of exclusionary closure.

Debates are bound to continue about the most appropriate form of regulation for particular alternative therapies (Stone and Mathews 1996). However, from the viewpoint of the report of the House of Lords Select Committee on Science and Technology (2000), the introduction of professional forms of regulation is particularly needed for group one and two therapies to protect the public. There is a precedent for such developments in the United States where the professionalization of alternative medicine has generally moved further and faster than in the United Kingdom (Saks 2000b). If past history is a guide, future forms of professionalization in this field may also well bear the imprint of the interests of sections of the medical profession in perpetuating and extending their privileged position in terms of income, status and power. In this situation, it should not be forgotten that alternative therapists themselves have self-interests in ensuring their professional ascendancy in the division of labour, whether or not there is a discernible public benefit. The scenario that emerges will doubtless be based on negotiation and compromise – although it may be weighted against alternative therapists because of the pre-existing structures of power and dominance associated with orthodox medicine (Saks 2001).

References

Bakx, K. (1991) 'The "eclipse" of folk medicine in Western society', *Sociology of Health and Illness*, 13: 20–38.

BMA (1986) *Report of the Board of Science and Education on Alternative Therapy.* London: British Medical Association.

BMA (1993) *Complementary Medicine: New Approaches to Good Practice.* London: British Medical Association.

BMA (2000) *Acupuncture: Efficacy, Safety and Practice.* Amsterdam: Harwood Academic Publishers.

Cant, S. and Sharma, U. (1995a) *Professionalization in Complementary Medicine.* Report on a research project funded by the Economic and Social Research Council.

Cant, S. and Sharma, U. (1995b) 'The reluctant profession: Homoeopathy and the search for legitimacy', *Work, Employment and Society*, 9: 743–62.

Cant, S. and Sharma, U. (1996) 'Demarcation and transformation within homoeopathic knowledge: A strategy of professionalization', *Social Science and Medicine*, 42: 579–88.

Cant, S. and Sharma, U. (1999) *A New Medical Pluralism? Alternative Medicine, Doctors, Patients and the State.* London: UCL Press.

Collins, R. (1990) 'Market closure and the conflict theory of the professions', in M. Burrage and R. Torstendahl (ed.) *Professions in Theory and History: Rethinking the Study of the Professions.* London: Sage.

Davies, C. and Beach, A. (2000) *Interpreting Professional Self-Regulation: A History of the United Kingdom Central Council for Nursing, Midwifery and Health Visiting.* London: Routledge.

Department of Health (2001a) *Government Response to the House of Lords Select Committee on Science and Technology's Report on Complementary and Alternative Medicine.* London: The Stationery Office.

Department of Health (2001b) *Modernising Regulation: The New Health Professions Council*. London: Department of Health.

Ernst, E. (2001) *The Desktop Guide to Complementary and Alternative Medicine: An Evidence-Based Approach*. London: Mosby.

Foundation for Integrated Medicine (1997) *Integrated Healthcare*. London: FIM.

Fulder, S. (1996) *The Handbook of Alternative and Complementary Medicine*. Oxford: Oxford University Press, 3rd edn.

Fulder, S. and Monro, R. (1981) *The Status of Complementary Medicine in the UK*. London: Threshold Foundation.

House of Lords Select Committee on Science and Technology (2000) *Report on Complementary and Alternative Medicine*. London: The Stationery Office.

Huggon, T. and Trench, A. (1992) 'Brussels post-1992: Protector or persecutor', in M. Saks (ed.) *Alternative Medicine in Britain*. Oxford: Clarendon Press.

Larkin, G. (1992) 'Orthodox and osteopathic medicine in the inter-war years', in M. Saks (ed.) *Alternative Medicine in Britain*. Oxford: Clarendon Press.

Larkin, G. (1995) 'State control and the health professions in the United Kingdom: Historical perspectives', in T. Johnson, G. Larkin and M. Saks (eds) *Health Professions and the State in Europe*. London: Routledge.

Levitt, R., Wall, A. and Appleby, J. (1995) *The Reorganized National Health Service*. London: Chapman & Hall, 5th edn.

Lewith, G., Kenyon, J. and Lewis, P. (eds) (1996) *Complementary Medicine: An Integrated Approach*. Oxford: Oxford University Press.

Macdonald, K. (1995) *The Sociology of the Professions*. London: Sage.

Mills, S. and Budd, S. (2000) *Professional Organisation of Complementary and Alternative Medicine in the United Kingdom. A Second Report to the Department of Health*. Exeter: University of Exeter.

Mills, S. and Peacock, W. (1997) *Professional Organisation of Complementary and Alternative Medicine in the United Kingdom. Report to the Department of Health*. Exeter: University of Exeter.

Nicholls, P. (1988) *Homoeopathy and the Medical Profession*. London: Croom Helm.

Pietroni, P. (1991) *The Greening of Medicine*. London: Gollancz.

Porter, R. (1989) *Health for Sale: Quackery in England 1660–1850*. Manchester: Manchester University Press.

Porter, R. (1995) *Disease, Medicine and Society 1550–1860*. Cambridge: Cambridge University Press, 2nd edn.

Saks, M. (1991) 'Power, politics and alternative medicine', *Talking Politics*, 3: 68–72.

Saks, M. (1992) 'Introduction', in M. Saks (ed.) *Alternative Medicine in Britain*. Oxford: Clarendon Press.

Saks, M. (1994) 'The alternatives to medicine', in J. Gabe, D. Kelleher and G. Williams (eds) *Challenging Medicine*. London: Routledge.

Saks, M. (1995) *Professions and the Public Interest: Medical Power, Altruism and Alternative Medicine*. London: Routledge.

Saks, M. (1996) 'From quackery to complementary medicine: The shifting boundaries between orthodox and unorthodox medical knowledge', in S. Cant and U. Sharma (eds) *Complementary and Alternative Medicines: Knowledge in Practice*. London: Free Association Books.

Saks, M. (1998) 'Professionalism and health care', in D. Field and S. Taylor (eds) *Sociological Perspectives on Health, Illness and Health Care*. Oxford: Blackwell Science.

Saks, M. (1999) 'The wheel turns? Professionalization and alternative medicine in Britain', *Journal of Interprofessional Care*, 13: 129–38.

Saks, M. (2000a) 'Medicine and the counter culture', in R. Cooter and J. Pickstone (eds) *Medicine in the Twentieth Century*. Amsterdam: Harwood Academic Publishers.

Saks, M. (2000b) 'Professionalization, politics and CAM', in M. Kelner, B. Wellman, B. Pescosolido and M. Saks (eds) *Complementary and Alternative Medicine: Challenge and Change*. Amsterdam: Harwood Academic Publishers.

Saks, M. (2001) 'Alternative medicine and the health care division of labour: Present trends and future prospects', *Current Sociology*, 49: 119–34.

Sharma, U. (1995) *Complementary Medicine Today: Practitioners and Patients*. London: Routledge, revised edition.

Stacey, M. (1992) *Regulating British Medicine: The General Medical Council*. Chichester: John Wiley & Sons.

Standen, C.S. (1993) 'The implications of the Osteopaths Act', *Complementary Therapies in Medicine*, 1: 208–10.

Stone, J. and Mathews, J. (1996) *Complementary Medicine and the Law*. Oxford: Oxford University Press.

Trevelyan, J. and Booth, B. (1994) *Complementary Medicine for Nurses, Midwives and Health Visitors*. London: Macmillan.

Vincent, C. and Furnham, A. (1997) *Complementary Medicine: A Research Perspective*. Chichester: John Wiley & Sons.

Walker, M. (1994) *Dirty Medicine: Science, Big Business and the Assault on Natural Health Care*. London: Slingshot Publications.

Witz, A. (1992) *Professions and Patriarchy*. London: Routledge.

Index